Journalism's Martyrs

Journalism's Martyrs

*Profiles of Reporters and Others
Murdered in the Line of Duty*

ANDREW WEEKS

McFarland & Company, Inc., Publishers
Jefferson, North Carolina

ISBN (print) 978-1-4766-8664-6
ISBN (ebook) 978-1-4766-4614-5

LIBRARY OF CONGRESS AND BRITISH LIBRARY
CATALOGUING DATA ARE AVAILABLE

Library of Congress Control Number 2022003534

Front cover image: © 2022 Shutterstock

Printed in the United States of America

*McFarland & Company, Inc., Publishers
Box 611, Jefferson, North Carolina 28640
www.mcfarlandpub.com*

For journalists, no matter the time or place,
who have given their everything in defense of truth.
You are not forgotten.

Truth writ in the heart and mind
has no uncertainty or doubt;
but only aims to seek and find
one's life work and to make it count.

From the author's unpublished *Book of Poems.*

Table of Contents

Acknowledgments

Writing this book—a rather lonely project during the first year of the coronavirus pandemic—involved many hours of research and writing over several months, made no less hectic by also working for a substantive business publication. In my solitude I had the chance to read about and ponder upon the journalists mentioned within these pages. Sometimes such ponderings have brought tears to my eyes and prayers to my lips.

I also have reflected on my own career as a journalist and the many experiences that moved me to join this league of professionals and the reasons I have, at least to this point in my life, remained a journalist. It hasn't been an easy path to tread, but at the end of the day it has, for the most part, been rewarding. If it were not for my beautiful and talented wife, Heidi, I might have pursued other career paths, but she knows me perhaps better than I know myself and has reminded me time and again that I probably would not be happy if I weren't doing the work of journalism. "If anyone truly bleeds ink," she has told me more than once, "it is you." It is a sentiment that similarly has been expressed, at one time or another, by our son, Brayden. Heidi has told me many times over the course of my research and writing that this was an important book for me to complete. She truly has been one of the main backbones of this project. I also appreciate her help with the notes and bibliography and for her always being willing to be the reviewer of my work. Thank you, Heidi, for your encouragement and faith in this book and, with deeper sentiments, for your faith in me.

Brayden and his sweet wife, Ashlyn, also have been supportive and encouraging. I appreciate them checking in with me from time to time to ask how the writing was coming along. It has been fun for me to watch Brayden dive into the world of modern media with his excellent photography skills and keen eye for detail. I cannot wait to see what successes he will continue to achieve in the mediums of photography and film. He also is becoming quite the writer and I love reading his work. As for Ashlyn, an exceptional potter and artist in other ways too, I couldn't have asked for a better, more talented daughter-in-law. I am happier and more excited than words can express about my grandchildren.

Others to whom I owe a hearty thanks include David Alff, my first editor at McFarland, and Layla Milholen, my second editor when David retired, as well as others at this expert and progressive publishing house. Editorial Assistant Sophia Lyons helped streamline the publishing process, copy editor Judith Ludwig put her keen eyes on the manuscript, and Marketing Coordinator Kristal Hamby helped with promotional materials. I thank them all for recognizing the value and importance of a book about slain journalists and the attacks on the free press. I also appreciate the extended deadline they gave me when personal matters dictated that more time was needed to complete the manuscript. Executive Editor Lisa Camp was most gracious, allowing me extra time when it was needed during a difficult period. I thank the folks at McFarland, one and all, for kindness, professionalism and expertise and for allowing me to be listed among your expert authors.

I would be remiss if I also did not give a nod to journalist colleagues, past and present, who have taught me something valuable about life and hard work and about being a journalist in the Land of the Free and Home of the Brave. Though I mention only one by name, others—reporters, photographers, editors and publishers—have influenced my career in some way.

Whether he knows it or not, I learned a great deal from Korrie Wenzel, publisher of the *Grand Forks Herald* and *Prairie Business* magazine in Grand Forks, North Dakota. Korrie is an exceptional journalist, a fantastic editor, and one of the best publishers in the business—a sentiment I have no doubt is echoed by others. Among other things he has taught me is that in my role as editor of a multistate business publication, it was my obligation to teach readers something they may not have known. While visiting with him in his office soon after I joined his team, he dramatized the effect by taking a blank piece of paper and, with a ballpoint pen, scrawling the word TEACH. I still have that piece of paper hanging above my desk as a reminder of my obligation to teach readers but also as a token remembrance of Korrie and the time and interest he took to invest in me.

Not least of all, I express my affinity for those who have died while doing the work of journalism and for those who honorably do the work of journalism today. It is true that journalism seems to be an ever-increasingly thankless profession in this deepening reckless and divided world, but there are those who understand and value what you are doing. Keep it up. You are as soldiers on the front lines of democracy.

Ultimately, what is written herein is my own doing, with my perspective and insight from more than two decades of being a journalist and working in newsrooms in several states. If there are errors, they are mine, and I apologize in advance for any that may be found within these pages. But please know that I have tried diligently to record, to the best of my understanding, the events depicted in these pages and have sought to honor those who have given their lives for truth's sake.

I hope you gain something of value from reading this book. Though it was not an easy topic for me to write and ponder, especially when much of the drama contained within these pages was happening in real time as I was preparing the manuscript (journalists arrested during the summer of 2020, for instance, and assaulted during the capital invasion in early 2021), it has been a rewarding experience in that I have wanted for several years to write something that honored slain journalists, those who have been assaulted or attacked, and those who remain at risk. This book, then, is the culmination of that idea that fermented in my mind for a few years before I got serious about writing it. With all that was happening in 2020, it seemed like the perfect time to complete the project.

Lastly, I want to thank you, the reader, whether you are a journalist or not, for taking the interest and time to pursue this book. There are millions of books to choose from, and having you choose mine to spend some time with means more to me than you'll ever know. I hope what follows will give you food for thought, that perhaps you will find what is written herein to be of some value and good use to you. I hope it is received in the same spirit in which it was written: as a tribute to journalism and those who have and continue to sacrifice for its cause. It is my hope that in writing about a few journalists, all slain journalists are thereby honored. They are not forgotten … not by me.

Preface

A number of books have been written about the falsities, misdeeds, and weaknesses of the American press. This book is not one of them. It instead takes a higher aim, honoring what is right with journalism and why it is still important and much needed today. It also discusses some of the attacks made on members of the press, and it seeks to honor some of the many journalists who have lost their lives while trying to bring the public information. Being correctly informed helps us all become better citizens, allowing us to make more informed decisions about issues and topics that affect our lives. When journalism is assaulted, so is the public's right to know. That means *your* right to know.

I cannot put a date on exactly when I started thinking about a book that, at least in part, would include profiles of slain journalists, but I know that it was in 2015 that I first started putting words to paper that would turn into this book. By that point I already had wanted to write a book about journalism for some time, but I wasn't sure what angle I wanted to take. I had always admired journalists long before I became one and pursued my career path in the newspaper world because I believed that, even with changing and evolving technology, journalism would continue to play an important role in the continuing American drama. I was educated in the field on the cusp of the digital age and missed the heyday of newspapering—a sad time for me because I have always loved the printed word—but I knew that even if I did not remain with newspapers, I would remain a member of the press, or as it more frequently is called these days, the news media, because of its multitude of platforms. I learned about journalists who went to foreign lands to cover conflict, and I was heartbroken when I learned that some of them did not return home to their loved ones. I started learning about other journalists who died while investigating crime or in other ways uncovering facts and reporting news. I wanted to do something to honor them. My book angle started to form, and I began putting words to paper. But the words, amounting to only three or four partially written, rough chapters a few years later, sat on my computer waiting for the time that I'd get serious about the project. Over the next five years while the idea sat in the back of my mind, fermenting, it crept ever closer to the front during the administration of President Donald J. Trump.

The conflict between him and the national press gave me much fodder that I could use in a book about the importance of journalism in the age of shifting values and ever-widening partisan politics. But I never did much with this plethora of information because, frankly, I was busy enough with my own daily journalism and other life pursuits and responsibilities. Not much has changed in that regard now; life seems to have become even more busy these days. But when I saw three broadcast journalists arrested in the spring of 2020 in Minneapolis, I knew it was time for me to write my book—the book you are now holding in your hands, be that in hard copy or digital format.

It is not the same book I originally imagined, and whether it is better or worse I do not know. I only know that I have spent countless hours after work and on weekends working on this project that I hope honors journalists who have died, as well as those who have not, including those who continue to work in this crazy, often thankless profession that is safeguarded by the United States Constitution. I hope it also honors that Constitution, principally the First Amendment. There is a reason freedom of the press is listed as one of the country's first freedoms. As I write elsewhere in this book—probably more than once, and so please forgive me if it is repeated—I believe that having a free and independent press is one of the surest ways we can protect the other liberties named in the Bill of Rights. Journalism must be protected so it can fulfill its obligation of protecting all of our rights.

As for the slain journalists mentioned within these pages, obviously a work such as this is limited with the number of journalists it can profile, and so I had to be selective about whom I included. My solution was to profile some of those reporters—not all—who were killed in about a 50-year period, since 1970. A whole book, or multiple volumes, could be written solely about slain journalists. But I wanted my book to be different than that, and so this is what it evolved into—a book that profiles American journalists who died while investigating or reporting the news, whether in conflict or outside of it, but also discussing some other topics important to the profession, journalists, and news consumers alike, the latter of which journalists also are a part.

This book was written during the first year of the coronavirus pandemic, and so some of the contemporary examples are dated to reflect this time period. For instance, the year 2020 was a year unlike any other in recent history—from the coronavirus pandemic to heightened issues of racism to the contested presidential election. The year 2021 didn't start off any better. On January 6 the world witnessed American democracy on the fringe when domestic anarchists stormed the nation's capital in support of a sitting president who lost the election. Each of these topics is discussed in a context focused on the news media and journalists.

This is only one book in a library of probably thousands that in some form or fashion discusses the perks and pitfalls of the free press. As has been said, it has its own perspective, its own mission, which is to honor fallen journalists and defend the liberties we all hold dear. The Irish statesman Edmund Burke purportedly once said that all that is necessary for the triumph of evil is that good men do nothing. I hope I am counted among the world's group of good men; likewise, I hope my book is one deemed worthy in freedom's defense. It is hoped that it does some kind of good in the world for those who read it. These are idealistic notions, perhaps, but journalism and its values have always been idealistic to me.

Of course, there have been changes in journalism. The press, derived from the printing press but which refers to the many-platformed news media, today encompasses much more than newspapers and magazines. It includes broadcasters and digital journalists, staff reporters and freelancers, scribblers with notepads and photojournalists who see the world through the lens of a camera. Not only are there beat reporters but podcasters and videographers and strictly online writers. Though I worked for a time in radio and have friends in both that medium and television news, my passion has remained where my career first began—with the printed word. If at times this book feels like it leans heavily from that perspective, that is why. Print has not only been my passion, as well as my livelihood, but it is where I gained most of my media experience and perspective. Nonetheless, I have tried to share insight and understanding not only from the perspective of a print journalist (over the past many years even a print journalist is now a digital journalist, too) but a media workhorse, one who has reported in various mediums of the news business and has covered a number of topics and beats.

Besides the ambitions for this book previously mentioned, it also has personal meaning for me in another way. During the Donald Trump administration, journalists were under attack by an almost constant barrage of belittling and name-calling by the president. It is true the press was tough on Trump—sometimes I wondered early on if they really gave him a chance at all—but the 45th president of the United States was unforgiving and vehement in his attack on journalists and the news media. As such, and by his very example, he stirred his fan base to do the same. In so doing, and in a sort of vicious cycle, perhaps he also stirred the ire of the press. Was the reason there was so much news coverage about Trump because everything he said and did was truly newsworthy, or did the press deliberately find ways to attack him? Or, did Trump deliberately say and do things that he knew the press would jump on? Whatever the reason, perhaps all of the above, the press also was unnecessarily attacked. Trump and his fan base mostly verbally assaulted the "mainstream media," but such hate trickled down to community reporters and their news organizations in cities and towns across America. Some of the people closest to me, family and friends alike, verbally expressed disdain for my profession. Because I was a journalist—and thus a member of the opposition press, according to their own expressions—I was at one time or another and by various people laughed at, mocked, and basically called names. My profession was spoken of derogatorily and lifelong relationships were tested.

These were hurtful episodes in my life. Other presidents in my lifetime—and indeed throughout the whole of American history—had contentious relationships with the press during their administrations but perhaps nothing like the volatile relationship that existed between President Trump and the press. During other presidencies, journalists, myself included, were not threatened or assaulted the way we were during the Trump administration, nor did some family and friends call me names and attack my profession. That all started under Trump, a one-term president whom many feared was turning the United States into an autocracy.

Parts of this book discuss Trump and his attacks on the free press, but this is not done to take political sides. It is done because the controversy became such a theme over the past several years and because such episodes have had a deep impact on the topic of American journalism today and because they played such a heavy topic during the year this book was being written. As I write elsewhere in these pages, Trump is not the *cause* of the public's distrust of the news media—that trust has been dwindling for a long time—but he certainly added fuel to the flames and accelerated the problem. He is not the cause of the mistrust, but perhaps he has been the instigator to the volatility we have seen in recent years after he took office. A leader's example does matter and has an impact.

The attacks on journalists during his administration demonstrate this better than any book written about the problem. Simply put, I believe his rhetoric incited violence against journalists. This is one reason why some people, those who view things differently, may not like parts of my book. If that is the reason, then that is OK with me. I would rather stand with my journalist colleagues and in defense of the First Amendment than be found outside of that fence. As mentioned previously, this book was written during the first year of the pandemic, a time when, for many months of that period, Trump was in office; as such, the book's topics are written in light of an era of Trumpism.

Journalism, despite its faults and weaknesses, is one of the surest ways we can defend and make sure our liberties stay intact. That's why press freedom is so important. If it goes away, so do other freedoms. And then what happens? What has the United States become then? It would herald the collapse of the greatest country on planet Earth, a vision too disturbing to even try to grasp. It is often by small and simple means that great things are brought to pass; by small and simple efforts are great measures held aloft. The strings that hold the Constitution intact are fragile and can be severed if not constantly and cautiously protected. The free press is not the only thread upholding our constitutional values, but it is one of the main fabrics.

This book is a small and simple effort, written by a simple man, to defend that noble document and the principles it espouses. The book, especially those parts in which I offer suggestions for newsroom improvements, is not an attempt to admit expertise on any subject. I admit just the opposite. I am still learning, every day, how to be a better journalist myself. That is one of the things I like about this crazy profession—the opportunity it gives me to continually learn and grow both as a writer and reporter but also as a person. If this book were written a year from now, for instance, perhaps it would be a different book with new and sharper perspectives. Nonetheless, the perspectives and suggestions within these pages are my own, gleaned over more than two decades in the news business to this point in my life and career. I am the first to admit there are better journalists than me, but I'd be hard-pressed to find anyone who loves this field of study and career more than I do. Thus, this book is a small effort to honor that which I love.

Introduction

Journalism can never be silent: that is its greatest virtue and its greatest fault. —HENRY ANATOLE GRUNWALD

It was another balmy day in the Grand Canyon State when a car with no spectacular features, belonging to an unassuming man, exploded in the parking lot of a hotel in midtown Phoenix. Emergency crews and reporters swarmed to the scene, but what these field journalists soon found out was that one of their own had been targeted.

Don Bolles, a 47-year-old man who worked for *The Arizona Republic*, was now clinging to life after a bomb that was planted under his car went off, blowing a gaping hole in the vehicle's floorboard and critically injuring the journalist on the morning of June 2, 1976. He died 11 days later at a hospital in the same city.

Eventually three men were convicted for Bolles's death. Their reason for killing the journalist was because of his investigations into their elaborate business conspiracy. Bolles was not the first reporter to die for doing his job, nor would he be the last. Before the bomb blew up his world on that fateful day in mid–1970s' America, other journalists in the United States and elsewhere had been targeted for assassination because of their reporting. Over the next five decades dozens of other journalists, both men and women, would die for investigating crimes, uncovering scandals, or being targeted by militant-minded persons or groups who took revenge with deathly blows. Others, caught in the crosshairs of conflict or who were kidnapped and brought to an executioner's quarters, died while trying to tell the world the happenings of war. It has always been the case when nosy newshounds went afield to investigate and report. Sadly, it is likely there will be more reporters targeted and killed for the same causes—uncovering truth by looking where the average person does not dare to look.

It is sad whenever any life is snuffed out before its time, no matter where or when it happens. But the killing of a journalist raises the consternation of a free society that, at its very foundation, relies upon the checks and balances of the Fourth Estate. "The Bolles incident underscores the fact that journalism, especially investigative reporting, is a profession laden with risks, and one in which grudges are not quickly forgotten," wrote the editors of *The Michigan Daily* in a column published June 16, 1976. "Don Bolles was killed solely because he sought to uncover and print what the public has a right to know—the truth."[1]

I was young when Bolles was killed, but learning of his death years later when I became a professional journalist myself, and learning of other journalists who had lost their lives in the course of their work, including correspondents covering wartime battles, struck me with the tender feelings that perhaps only a colleague can understand, no matter the separation of time and space. Many journalists had died doing their jobs long before Bolles became a target, of course, but this book focuses on some of those tragedies that happened over just five decades, from the 1970s when Ruben Salazar and Don Bolles were killed to 2018 when five newspaper colleagues were gunned down in their own newsroom by a vengeful reader. Also, many foreign journalists have died in their own lands reporting news. This book does not downplay their sacrifices, but besides the brief last chapter on Jamal Khashoggi, I have chosen to write mainly about some of the issues confronting America's free press and its newsrooms and journalists. Only recently has the United States been added to the list of the top five countries most dangerous for journalists.[2] Even with its American theme, however, this book is for all journalists, everywhere.

It also discusses the assaults and arrests of journalists in 2020 and early 2021.

All of a sudden, the past didn't seem so distant. We witnessed firsthand a defunct society, where anger and emotion boiled over, and little respect was shown to our country's First Amendment. Journalists who were doing their jobs legally and professionally and with press credentials in hand were arrested by police, shot at with rubber bullets, pushed, shoved and physically harmed by those who took an oath to protect. Some protesters also assaulted journalists or damaged their equipment or vehicles. American citizens committing crimes in broad daylight at the nation's capital in January 2021 also assaulted and berated journalists and vandalized their equipment.

When journalists cover volatile events, whether it be war or riots, they know they are potentially putting themselves in harm's way; they know that just by being at the scene as eyewitnesses, where emotions run high, they stand the risk of experiencing the fallout. But reporters never go to a protest expecting to be assaulted by their country's own lawmen. That, more likely, is something seen in a dictatorial regime, not the United States of America, the world's bastion of freedom.

Or so we thought.

"While the United States has traditionally served as a beacon for press freedom, it is with troubling regularity that news media professionals face many dangers today, putting your right to know at risk," wrote Bruce D. Brown in a special to the McClatchy group on November 7, 2019. "Reporters are verbally harassed both on- and offline simply for doing their jobs."[3] There also are legal threats and denials of public records requests, all meant to suppress and silence the news. As Brown said, if a reporter cannot do her or his job dutifully, the results are damaging not only to "the story" but the public.

The Founding Fathers valued a free press and understood its importance to the unfolding American drama but also what it would mean for the country as it progressed into a world power. "Our liberty depends on the freedom of the press," said Thomas Jefferson, "and that cannot be limited without being lost."

Benjamin Franklin said: "Whoever would overthrow the liberty of a nation must begin by subduing the freeness of speech."

"The freedom of the press," John Quincy Adams said, "should be inviolate."

More recently, former U.S. Senator Christopher Dodd (1981–2011) said, "When the public's right to know is threatened, and when the rights of free speech and free press are at risk, all of the other liberties we hold dear are endangered."[4]

Does this mean the press is perfect? Of course not. The advent of blogs and social media has blurred the line between real reporting and "hearsay reporting," and opinion has been misinterpreted for those who do not know how to discern the difference between editorializing and news reporting. Also, as newsrooms continue to shrink and more responsibilities are added to journalists' portfolios, there is more likelihood of errors in reporting, which should quickly be addressed and corrected by the news organizations themselves.

Like consumers, journalists can experience news fatigue. But I believe and know firsthand from working in newsrooms in several states that the majority of journalists honor their profession and do their due diligence as reporters. I am not aware of one journalist I have worked with who has fabricated facts or twisted a story to meet his or her own agenda. There is such a thing as "fake news," but it is not always what a president or those who may have jumped onto his rhetorical bandwagon say it is.

While a portion of this book does discuss some of the weaknesses of the news media, it is not done in a way that belittles the newsroom or points fingers. Instead, it relates some transgressions so it can offer advice about how to correct and regret the errors. As journalists learn early on, there are two sides to every story. That means the story of journalism, too. One side attack it as being an imperfect narrative of events with an unfair agenda. This book is my attempt to tell the other side of the argument, namely the positives that come from journalism. Journalism is not by any means a perfect craft, but I believe it is our best hope of defending democracy.

One complaint we hear often is that the news media is too biased. I cannot argue with that; some news is slanted. In my personal career, I have always tried to be fair and balanced in my reporting and let the facts fall where they may. This book is different. This is a personal endeavor, and, as such, it may come across as demonstrating bias. For the first time in my career, I am OK with that. I *am* biased toward the press. It is my profession—an often thankless profession anymore, but one that has a long history tied to our very freedoms.

Some people will appreciate this book; others likely will not because of their contrary views. As one who is privileged to be counted among the ever-shrinking band of American journalists, this is one of my efforts to honor and defend the profession that I adore and the nation's documents that guarantee a reporter's right to publish and broadcast. This does not mean that I do not recognize where we, as journalists and newsrooms, may improve, but it does mean I will always defend the ideals of a free and independent press. That is my constitutional duty, and it is yours.

This book is divided into ten chapters, each separated by a profile of one of America's martyred journalists. The chapters offer insight into the role of the American press, its responsibility as the Fourth Estate, the public's right to know, and how the Founding Fathers viewed the free press and its importance for democracy. Within the book's pages are discussed the heightened attacks, both verbal and physical, on the news media and why such attacks are a threat to our other first freedoms. Chapters also offer suggestions for news reporters and news consumers alike and their obligation to defend the First Amendment, whether they agree with one political party or another. It also takes a look at the problems facing the country's newsrooms and what brought us to the point we're at today. The problems stem from many sources over a broad expanse of time, but the public's distrust of news organizations has increased as technology has expanded. This book attempts to address some of the hot-button issues facing today's newsrooms, as well as offer suggestions for news practitioners to regain the trust of the American public. It also warns that if assaults on journalists and legitimate news organizations are allowed to perpetuate, we all stand at risk of losing our first freedoms.

I fully realize many other topics could have been covered in a book like this one, but I purposefully stayed with specific items that I personally have witnessed or experienced as a new professional. Thus, this book is not a comprehensive nor exhaustive study, but it is one that the author hopes will open the door wider for readers to a study of the free press and those who have made it their life's work.

I have considered writing a second book about journalism, one that would include the personal voices and experiences of my colleagues across the country. As such, it would be a different book than what this one is you are now holding in your hands. The two-volume set, if the second book were to come about, then would become a duo of profiles—this one of slain journalists and the second of living journalists.

Time will tell.

A martyr, as Webster explains, is "a person who voluntarily suffers death as the penalty of witnessing to and refusing to renounce a religion." However, the word has another meaning that fits the slain journalist: "a person who sacrifices something of great value and especially life itself for the sake of principle." I view slain journalists as martyrs.

While slain journalists would rather be alive, enjoying time with family and friends rather than having died for doing their jobs, I have no doubt they also would believe that what they died for was for more than just covering an assignment. Much like the soldier on the battlefield, they died defending and heralding American liberties.

There is a certain egotistical trait that all reporters likely share: that of seeing their names in print; being recognized by their readers, listeners or viewers as local quasi-celebrities; and, in some instances, even taking the ire of their audiences. But no reporter has a death wish, even though sadly for some their sources had wished them dead and made it so. Many journalists in both the nineteenth and twentieth centuries, and many in the twenty-first, have died a martyr's death for uncovering scandal and crime or telling the stories of war.

This has been an interesting project to research and write but also a disheartening one. I have deep feelings about this crazy and demanding profession called journalism. I respect its practitioners, namely the reporters and editors and photographers who honor and respect their callings, which, in a very real sense, watch upon the tower of truth. Not all journalists have taken those obligations seriously, but I salute the countless many who have and continue to do so. And I honor the many journalists who put their lives in danger for causes that (in some respects but not always) are greater than themselves.

To all of them, whether they have found a place in these pages or not, this book is respectfully dedicated.

1

The Hard Knocks of Journalism

Freedom of the Press, if it means anything at all, means the
freedom to criticize and oppose. —GEORGE ORWELL

"Journalism will kill you," famed newspaper editor and publisher Horace Greeley intoned in his day, "but it will keep you alive while you're at it."[1] We can infer a couple of meanings from Greeley's comment. He may have been speaking of the constant high-stress demands of reporters and editors and the sometimes meager paychecks that follow, but his words have been proven all too true in another very literal way for a number of press professionals who have died while uncovering corruption or scandal, writing about war, terrorist activity or social issues or for investigating crime in high places and in low. Some journalists have been targeted for simply being members of the press.

Greeley, founder of the *New-York Tribune*, was an outspoken proponent of the free press who understood and defended its importance in the American drama—a democratic society in which a free press helps facilitate an open dialogue and transparent government. People on the other side of the aisle from Greeley, however, have expressed contrary sentiments about journalism and its practitioners.

"Kill the reporters," President Richard Nixon is purported to have said in 1971 during the Vietnam War and noted a few days later to the joint chiefs, "The press is your enemy." "In his wistful way," Thomas Peele wrote in a guest column for *The [Cleveland] Plain Dealer*, "Nixon made one of the greatest acknowledgements of the free press's role in the nation's history. Get rid of the journalists, the commander in chief was saying, and we can do whatever the hell we want."[2]

It may not come as a surprise that Nixon would intone such sentiments about reporters, but time and a viable Constitution have done little to erase the feelings that some people and institutions harbor against journalists. The same disdain that Nixon expressed for the American press has been shared by other political figures, more recently and perhaps most vehemently by President Donald J. Trump, who has called a number of legitimate news organizations, including the *New York Times, Washington Post* and CNN, "fake news" and "the enemy of the people." The Republican president at times also blasted Fox News, a traditionally conservative outlet, when it aired broadcasts he didn't like, such as when it was the first news outlet to call Arizona for Joe Biden during the 2020 presidential election. Trump made it a point of his administration to be antagonistic to the press in ways that no president has ever been, Nixon notwithstanding. During his presidency and with social media as his pulpit—something Nixon never had—Trump took to Twitter almost daily to denounce legitimate news organizations and their reporters. Booing and ridiculing the press had become a trademark of his administration, with constant name-calling taunts including the worst, echoing Nixon's sentiments by calling journalists "the enemy of the American people."[3] That a president, someone who has taken the oath of office to defend the Constitution, would attack the free press in such expressions is dumbfounding. Trump was not the first president to verbally attack journalists and news organizations, nor will he likely be the last. He was, however, at least up to that time, the most threatening president to the American press.

There is indeed such a thing as "fake news," but it is not always what Trump and his followers labeled it. He denounced the press for stories either broadcast or published that were unfavorable to his administration, shaming reporters during press conferences and often targeting his ire on a particular journalist, calling her or him "rude," "not a good reporter," "a terrible person" or "fake news," among other names. The ramifications of such drivel, especially when spouted by a sitting president, weighs heavy on the Constitution. Even though he came under constant scrutiny by the press, President Trump chose to fight back like an angry teenager instead of taking it in stride as the country's leader. Many people who seemed to agree with Trump's political platform shared his rhetoric on social media and elsewhere, labeling any news report they didn't agree with as "fake news." Such tactics are simply the easiest way for them to try to discredit what they don't agree with. More troubling, some of that rhetoric spilled over into actions against journalists. Reporters during the Trump presidency were called names, shoved, and threatened at the president's political rallies. Here are some examples:

- A crowd of Trump supporters gathered against the news media on July 31, 2018, in Tampa, Florida, shouting and gesturing obscenities at reporters who were there to cover the event. Jim Acosta, White House correspondent for CNN, shared a video of the scene on social media and captioned it with these sobering words: "Just a sample of the sad scene we faced at the Trump rally in Tampa. I'm very worried that the hostility whipped up by Trump and some in conservative media will result in somebody getting hurt. We should not treat our fellow Americans this way. The press is not the enemy."[4]

- A week after five journalists were killed by a gunman who stormed their newsroom in Annapolis, Maryland, at the end of June 2018, Trump again riled an audience during a rally on July 6 in Montana. In part, the president said: "I see it. I see the way they write. They're so damn dishonest. I don't mean all of them. ... But 75 percent of those people are downright dishonest. Downright dishonest."[5]

- On February 11, 2019, a BBC cameraman was shoved and verbally assaulted by a man wearing a "Make America Great Again" hat at a Trump rally in El Paso, Texas, where the president had complained about the news media being "fake."[6]

- On September 22, 2020, President Trump glorified and made fun of an attack by police of a CNN reporter covering protests in Minneapolis. "They grabbed 'em. They were grabbing 'em left and right," Trump said over the microphone at his rally. "Sometimes they grabbed, they grabbed one guy, 'I'm a reporter! I'm a reporter!'—Get out of here! They threw him aside like a bag of popcorn. But honestly, when you watch the crap we've all had to take so long ... when you see it, it's actually a beautiful sight."[7]

- On October 1, 2020, a WCCO-TV photojournalist was attacked by a Trump supporter outside a rally in Duluth, Minnesota, punching a cellphone out of the journalist's hands and telling him, "You are not authorized to take my picture."[8]

- On October 28, 2020, CNN's Jim Acosta once again shared on social media a large crowd at a Trump rally shouting repeatedly for the cameras, "CNN sucks! CNN sucks!" Acosta said, "This happens at just about every Trump rally. I've covered five presential campaigns, long enough to know this isn't normal." The crowd continued to chant its drivel as Acosta broadcast his report. "Sometimes I'll scan the crowd," he continued, "not for the folks who are chanting but for the people who look back at me silently, letting me know they know it's wrong."

- CNN, one of the president's direct targets of his venomous speeches against the news media, received much of the hate, with Acosta posting again that while covering a rally in Phoenix he was told by a Trump supporter to "get the hell out of our country." On social, Acosta lamented: "Tell that to my grandfather who is buried at Arlington and my dad who fled to the US as a refugee from Cuba."[9]

Attacks on journalists stretched even further into the political aisle when Greg Gianforte, a GOP representative, physically assaulted a reporter with *The Guardian* newspaper in May 2017 in Bozeman, Montana. A year and a half later and on another rant about the news media, President Trump made light of the incident while at a rally in Missoula, Montana, telling an enthusiastic audience, "Any guy that can do a body slam, he's my kind of— he's my guy." What did the audience do? Cheered and laughed.[10] All of this cheering happened while a *Washington Post* columnist, Jamal Khashoggi, was reported missing and presumed dead at the hands of conspiratorial thugs for reporting about the Saudi government.[11]

The writing was on the wall even before Trump took the oath of office. He belittled national news media, got into verbal arguments with reporters, and even made fun of a disabled reporter during one of his pre-election rallies in Myrtle Beach, South Carolina.[12] Not much changed after he lost the 2020 election to Joe Biden, nor did he alter course once he left the White House—only by that time he didn't have social media as his bully pulpit. Twitter and Facebook banned Trump from their platforms because of the inciteful messaging he posted—including his taunts that the election had been fraudulent and rigged—when the nation's capital was invaded by flag-waving Trump supporters he had riled up over a long period, telling them even in 2016 that if he lost to Hillary Clinton, it would only be because it was rigged. It prepared his supporters for the battle he knew would come in 2020. Now that he had lost, he used that unfounded and long-planned-for claim as the framework in his battle to contest the election results. And in the process, it caused an insurrection at the People's House.

He had for a long time grown angry and distrustful of legitimate news organizations and journalists, trying to delegitimatize the truth. In some ways he has succeeded. His supporters seem to believe only what Donald Trump says, regardless of the discernable facts elsewhere. The coronavirus pandemic is a prime example, when not only the news media was knocked by the president but so were medical professionals and scientists. It didn't matter what field; experts, if they contradicted Trump, were labeled as "fake" or given other names by the president.

It wasn't only Trump supporters who jumped on the bandwagon and assaulted press professionals during his time in office. A number of journalists were physically and verbally assaulted while covering demonstrations in many U.S. cities in the spring and summer of 2020—a year that proved all too unnerving for people across the country as they dealt with a global pandemic, a contentious political climate, and natural disasters that seemed to ceaselessly wreak havoc on some coastal states. Some of these attacks on journalists will be highlighted in the following chapter, but one question that should be considered now is, were journalists and media workers assaulted because of heightened emotions due to a volatile year, or were they attacked because the president had been demonizing them for so long that people started to strike out? Both scenarios likely play into the mix, but from the examples above, a sitting president's—and now ex-president's—heated arguments against legitimate news organizations have certainly contributed to the media hate. The media are not blameless, of course, and have by some of their own transgressions weakened the public trust. Trump came along and stirred the embers.

For now, it is long overdue for the country to remember what reporter Eric Arthur Blair, better known as novelist George Orwell, observed: "Freedom of the Press, if it means anything at all, means the freedom to criticize and oppose." It is a truth that seems to have been forgotten—err, outright defamed—by many people in today's politically volatile world. Many people believe it is high time that the press is criticized and opposed, and there seems to be no dearth of those willing to take the low punches. A journalist's job—indeed, the role of the American press—is not to be a cheerleader for politicians, only insofar as the people's constitutional rights are defended and observed. The role of the press is to be a watchdog, not a lapdog. But when people start attacking the free press, trying to hinder and suppress its reporting, it's a frightful foreboding of a country losing its first freedoms.

The success of the American free press is tightly entwined with the sovereignty of the nation. As newspaper titan Joseph Pulitzer once said, "Our Republic and its press will rise or fail together."[13] But that hasn't stopped politicians, businessmen, religious crusaders, and crime bosses from trying to thwart the work of journalism. To them the press is a burden, and those who practice its ethics are annoying if not downright troublesome. It seems always to have been the case with America's intrepid reporters and eager publishers and editors but perhaps none so much as now.

Benjamin Harris is the first we know about on American soil who, because of what he published, drew the animosity of the powerful. Harris published the first broadsheet newspaper in the British-American colonies on September 25, 1690—and thereafter was silenced by Boston authorities after only the first edition was printed because he had published an article without authorization from the government. Ever after, nosy news writers have stuck their honkers in places where other citizens have not dared. Harris's paper, called *Publick Occurrences Both Foreign and Domestick*, was a far cry from the artfully designed newspapers of today—by today's standards it was more like a newsletter—nor was the writing anything to brag about, but it did what journalism was supposed to do: make people uncomfortable and spark controversy.

"Journalism," said former *Washington Post* publisher Philip Graham, "is the first rough draft of history."[14] But first and foremost, it must be a watchdog, the very reason reporters continue to be critical of those in power.

That is their job.

And then there is this: "To announce that there must be no criticism of the President, or that we are to stand by the President, right or wrong," said Theodore Roosevelt, a president himself, "is not only unpatriotic and servile, but is morally treasonable to the American public."

"It's Our Calling and Duty"

As seems to be the case more often than not, journalism is a thankless job. You don't have to usually look far to hear the praises offered to agricultural workers, healthcare personnel, firefighters, law officers, military veterans and soldiers. But rarely, if ever, do you hear anyone acknowledge the good work of journalists, no matter the beat or news organization. Instead, these defenders of the First Amendment get the rub: "enemy of the people."

Still, a journalist knows her or his obligation—and it's not what many people seem to believe it is: only to meet a deadline and sell their news product. One of the great newspaper publishers I have had the pleasure of working with exemplified in a text message to me the feelings that, I believe, many journalists share.

Early in 2020, shortly after the coronavirus pandemic was declared, reporters in my newsroom were sent home to work remotely unless stories called for them to be out in the field. I texted my publisher on the evening of March 20, thanking him for the way he was leading the newsroom during the pandemic, putting in long hours to make sure everything ran smoothly and everyone remained connected and at the top of their game while giving reporters the freedom to do their jobs without micro-oversight. We were all feeling a little burned out, to say the least, as increasing numbers of COVID-19, the respiratory disease caused by the coronavirus, were being tallied daily by healthcare officials and governors. Reporters were overwhelmed trying to keep up with these and other developments. In response to my text, Korrie Wenzel, publisher of the *Grand Forks Herald* and *Prairie Business* magazine in Grand Forks, North Dakota, responded: "Thanks Andy. Busy times but it's our calling and duty, I figure. We'll always remember this. And thanks for the work today." Korrie's words touched me because, outside of that perspective and duty, journalists across the country were being called sensationalists, fearmongers and enemies of the people by the very citizens they were trying to serve.

They might not always wear protective gear, but many journalists, like firefighters, law officers and soldiers, have often, and continue to, put their lives at risk. Like these other public servants, journalists also wear a badge of honor: the press badge. For many, it is not just an office job, but even when it is, there exist many hard knocks of the profession besides paper cuts. There are long hours and weeks, constant deadlines, and being in a position where, if a reporter or editor makes an error, everybody seems to know about it.[15] What is harder still is working in a profession that many people, attested to by the volatile hate of reporters spread by some people on social media and in the halls of Congress, seem not to understand.

The American public needs to become educated—to relearn what it seems to have forgotten—about the role of the free press. Otherwise, we stand in jeopardy of losing one of our first freedoms. If we lose that, it puts all of our other freedoms at risk, including the right to worship and petition the government for redress of grievances. And as we all know, many people have died on the battlefields defending American freedoms, including intrepid reporters and foreign correspondents.

From the News Beat to the War Zone

Journalists the world over have died while covering conflict, including American journalists over the course of many wars. From the Crimean War in the 1850s to the War on Terror in Afghanistan and Iraq in this century, reporters have been there to give eyewitness accounts of the battles and procedures of conflict and their effects. Death for some of these intrepid scribblers has come in different ways: while embedded with troops, kidnapped and slain by militants, or unintentionally killed or maimed by being at the wrong place at the wrong time. Each of them, however, was in or near the war zones because they believed it was important for them to document the historic episodes for their country, the world, and for future generations.

Some of the American journalists who have died while reporting in conflict areas since 9/11 include Michael Kelly, who died at the age of 46 in 2002 while stationed in Baghdad during the U.S. war with Iraq. Kelly, who was editor-at-large for the *Atlantic Monthly* and a columnist for the *Washington Post*, was embedded with the U.S. Army's 3rd Infantry Division when he was killed while riding in a Humvee on the outskirts of Baghdad. While trying to avoid Iraqi fire, the vehicle went off the road and into a canal, trapping Kelly and the driver under water. Both died at the scene.

Thirty-nine-year-old David Bloom, co-anchor of NBC's Today Weekend Edition, was also embedded with the Army's 3rd Infantry Division during the war. While he died from a medical condition known as a pulmonary embolism, doctors believed blood clots had formed in his legs due to the long hours he spent immobilized in the tight confines of the Humvee—or which the reporter liked to call his "Bloom-mobile" because it served as his studio away from the office and where he'd transmit images from the war zone. If he hadn't been there reporting for his country, perhaps he would not have developed the clots.

Also in Iraq was Elizabeth Neuffer, 46, who died while on assignment for the *Boston Globe*. Her death was caused by another vehicle accident but one that likely never would have happened if she hadn't been there reporting on the war's aftermath and the possible future of Iraq. Neuffer was returning from an overnight trip to Tikrit when the driver she was riding with struck a guardrail near the town of Samarra, about halfway between Tikrit and Baghdad.[16]

None of the above tragedies were caused by direct assaults on the journalists, but the reporters nonetheless died for putting themselves in harm's way because they believed the wartime events and issues were worth documenting.

The journalist perhaps most remembered for dying early in the war on terror is Daniel Pearl. In early 2002 Pearl, then 32, was the South Asia bureau chief for the *Wall Street Journal* and stationed in Pakistan. He disappeared on the evening of January 23 in Karachi, the country's capitol, while going to meet a source. Among the topics he was investigating was the possible connection between al-Qaeda and Richard C. Reid, later dubbed the "shoe bomber" after he was arrested for having explosives in his shoes on a flight from Paris to Miami. Pearl was planning to meet with Sheikh Mubarik Ali Gillani for an interview at the Village Restaurant in downtown Karachi, but he never made it to the restaurant. He hailed a taxi and was never seen again—except in disturbing photos and videos by his captors. As investigations into Pearl's disappearance progressed, it was revealed that the journalist had been kidnapped by militant members of the National Movement for the Restoration of Pakistani Sovereignty. In exchange for Pearl's life, the group demanded that the United States release Pakistani nationals it had detained as terrorists held at Guantanamo Bay in Cuba and that it stop sending fighter jets to the Pakistani government.

"We will give you one more day. If America will not meet our demands, we will kill Daniel," the group wrote in an email to Pakistani and Western media. "Then this cycle will continue and no American journalist could enter Pakistan."[17] In the email were photos of a handcuffed Pearl, a gun pointed at his head; in another image he was seen holding a newspaper.

As dire as the situation was, the U.S. stood by its vow to not negotiate with terrorists. Demands and pleas for Pearl's release continued, however, and U.S. and Pakistani intelligence officers tried tracking the kidnappers.

Pearl's wife, Mariane, who was pregnant with their first child at the time, went on television to plead with the terrorists to release her husband and the father of their unborn child. His editor at the *Journal* also tried to sway the militants to release Pearl, but all of these efforts proved unsuccessful. Eventually the kidnappers released a shocking and disturbing video of Pearl's gruesome death.

Journalism Can Be Hazardous to Your Health

Pearl's death—a beheading—was shocking in its brutality, but it also shocked the country in another way: American reporters just don't get killed like that. That's not to say that reporters from other countries haven't met violent endings; they have been faced with those types of fears and threats for decades. But the United States traditionally has fared better than other countries when it comes to the number of journalists killed either while on reporting assignments or specifically targeted because of their investigations. According to the Committee to Protect Journalists (CPJ), an international media watchdog group, a combined total of 30 journalists were killed in countries across the globe in 2020—"including 21 reprisal murders, up from 10 murders last year." Reprisal murders, meaning journalists who were "singled out for murder in reprisal of their work."[18]

Thirty journalists. That's a far cry from the number of people who lost their lives in other professions. Loggers, fishermen and roofers, and law officers—listed as some of the most dangerous jobs, to name a few—have far more fatality rates every year. But, with the exception of police officers, these workers usually do not face targeted attacks. Journalists do, and the threats are compounded in other countries where press freedoms are on shakier ground than in the U.S.

"It's appalling that the murders of journalists have more than doubled in the last year, and this escalation represents a failure of the international community to confront the scourge of impunity," CPJ Executive Director Joel Simon said in a news release on December 22, 2020, announcing the year's numbers.[19] Countries that had significant numbers of journalist murders included Afghanistan and Mexico, the latter having been for years the most dangerous country for journalists in the western hemisphere because of its high number of "violent drug traffickers and entrenched corruption." Worldwide, according to CPJ, "criminal groups were the most frequently suspected killers of journalists."[20]

Threats of retaliation, suppression and violence—which have been going on for years in many countries—haven't stopped journalists from doing their due diligence reporting the misdeeds of their societies. Take

Lydia Cacho, for example, a journalist and activist in Mexico who told her staff in 2004 that they needed to make alternative editorial plans in case she was killed. Cacho, who made a name for herself investigating sexual abuse and other types of violence against women and children, has been a controversial figure in Mexico for years. She started receiving death threats after publishing a book titled *Demons of Eden*, which uncovered a child pornography ring in Cancun. But still she continued her reporting ventures. Making alternative editorial plans in a worst-case scenario was something she and her staff had learned to live with. "Because that's what you have to do—we are in a high-risk job, and if you don't accept that, you could be killed and nothing would be done," she told *Mother Jones* in a May 2007 article.[21]

Journalists and media workers in other supposedly free countries also have faced growing fears as their governments try to stifle and shutter news outlets. "The big concern now is that the problem is no longer limited to the two dozen or so totalitarian regimes that have dismantled free media," according to a November 29, 2017, report by *The Guardian*. "Independent journalists are under siege in a growing cohort of supposedly freer countries such as Brazil, Turkey, Mexico, Kenya, Poland, Hungary and Cambodia."[22]

One bright note: according to the CPJ report in December 2020, only three journalists had been killed in combat or crossfire that year, the fewest since 2000. This was due in part to the worldwide coronavirus pandemic, which caused travel to be restricted. Each of the three journalists had been killed in Syria by suspected Russian airstrikes. The remaining 30 journalists killed that year were "killed on other dangerous assignments that turned violent, such as civil unrest in Iraq and Nigeria."[23] By year's end CPJ said it was still investigating the deaths of at least 15 other journalists in 2020 to determine whether journalism was the motive.

Back in the United States, journalists have historically fared pretty well, not having to deal with the types of suppression tactics and violence that reporters in other countries have been facing for decades. But the monster in the closet opened the door wider in recent years, pushing American reporters farther into the danger zone. In 2018, Reporters Without Borders listed the United States for the first time as one of the top five countries most dangerous to journalists. It was a high-fatality year for U.S. reporters, including four journalists and a newspaper sales rep who were shot in their own newsroom in Annapolis, Maryland. A total of 56 were killed worldwide that year.

Thankfully, no journalists were killed on American soil in 2019—though a total of 29 were killed in other countries.[24] The year 2020, however, saw an increase in the number of U.S. journalists physically attacked, arrested or detained by police while doing their jobs legally and professionally. A number of assaults on journalists were again made in early 2021. Instead of condemning these acts, many in the public cheered at press suppression or did nothing to speak up against it. Both the volatility toward the press by politicians and the public and their lack of defaming such actions have sadly helped entrench a new set of societal values, which, if left unchecked and uncorrected, could have significant ramifications not only for journalists and the free press but what we've known as a free and fair democratic society.

The Hardest Knock of All

Journalists know they put themselves at risk when reporting in battle zones, but the determination of war correspondents is the same that reporters share when reporting about issues at home, whether it be uncovering crime and conspiracy or reporting on business and education issues or the local happenings of city and county government. It also is the same when a reporter covers a president's administration. Sadly, some of these daily beat reporters face dire threats.

Often, journalists sacrifice family time to cover breaking stories and meet other obligations of producing news. It takes its toll over time, especially when such sacrifices are not appreciated by the news-consuming public who often "questions our motives," writes Roger Ledger. "But rarely are American journalists killed for asking questions and seeking truth." Reporters get a reality check about the dangers of their job when they hear something like the tragedy that befell Pearl, "who was doing the same thing we do every day: reporting a story."[25]

The death of a journalist is the most drastic form of censorship. It is the hardest knock of all in a profession full of hard knocks. Greeley was right—journalism can kill reporters. Yet knowing that threat, reporters continue to put themselves at risk to uncover facts and tell the truth, insofar as it is possible to gather, to a weary and leery public they believe has a right to know. Such is a journalist's job; it is not to fabricate facts or lessen them or shun them or belittle them but to reveal and expound them, and then, as the saying goes, let the chips fall where they may. Unfortunately, some of those chips have fallen hard and heavy on reporters, some of them with fatal results.

The other chapters in this book will discuss some of the hot-button topics related to today's news media while also profiling some of the reporters who, like soldiers who have died on a battlefield, made the ultimate sacrifice for truth's sake. One of them was Ruben Salazar, a Mexican American journalist who was killed by police in 1970 while covering a rally to protest the Vietnam War.

Ruben Salazar, 1970
Los Angeles Times & KMEX-TV

Perhaps the day looked something like this: Thick contrails of smog hugged the skyline of the City of Angels, filling the atmosphere and giving a burned-brushed look to the tall buildings that reached heavenward, as if the buildings were trying to grasp the fresher air above the man-made haze.

Below, on the streets of East Los Angeles, a crowd was forming that would eventually grow to some 30,000 people. They had come to participate in a rally to protest America's involvement in an overseas conflict that the country had made its own. The gathering place was at Belvedere Park, but participants would eventually wend their way to Laguna Park. What was meant to be a peaceful protest, as sometimes happens when many are gathered, started to turn more volatile as emotions flared. Some people in the crowd became unruly and destructive. Businesses began to be vandalized, which did nothing to help the protesters' cause. Law officers responded, and the rally grew more contentious. By the end of the drama, three people would be dead, including a member of the news media.

Though this might sound like something taken out of the pages of the year 2020, when journalists were assaulted and arrested while doing their jobs on the streets of America, this episode happened 50 years earlier, on August 29, 1970.

To understand what happened that day we must first know a little something about the Vietnam War and the United States' involvement in it. The rally in East Los Angeles was organized by the National Chicano Moratorium Against the Vietnam War, which opposed the deadly overseas conflict that continued to take the lives of young men who went to fight the jungle battles for old men in armchairs in Washington. It was America's most controversial war up to that time, spanned the administrations of several U.S. presidents, and cost the lives of more than 58,000 Americans.[26] The United States' involvement in the war began in the 1950s, but the genesis of the conflict began many years earlier when blood and carnage seemed to reign across the globe during the Second World War. It seemed that humankind was never to have peace, and the U.S. was hopscotching from conflict to conflict—the Second World War, where battles played out on many theaters and then the Korean War and now Vietnam.

Vietnam, a small country located off the China Sea not quite 2,400 miles from Japan, had been occupied by the French Empire but changed hands in September 1940 when Japan's Emperor Hirohito invaded Vietnam.

This was a boon to Japan because now that it was in control of the smaller country it could close Vietnam's southern border to China, a country it had been fighting since 1937.

Ultimately, over the years Vietnam would become the eye candy for many countries seeking its control. France tried to regain its authority there in 1954 but failed in its attempt to do so. What was left was the Geneva Treaty, which split Vietnam along the 17th parallel. The dividing of the country gave birth to North Vietnam and South Vietnam. The North became occupied by Ho Chi Minh, leader of the communist resistance army called Vietminh, and the South was overseen by Ngo Dinh Diem, who held capitalist ideas. The differences of the two political ideologies— communism and capitalism—are about as far apart from each other as the moon is from the sun, and it was easy for the United States to choose its side. This cold war of ideologies would last for decades between the U.S. and its perceived communist enemies, but before the climate improved, a more vicious conflict would ensue. By 1958, North and South went to war, setting the groundwork for the United States' escalation in the Vietnam conflict just a few years later.

The political climate was on the verge of changing in the U.S. as well. By 1961, John F. Kennedy ascended to the White House after beating Richard Nixon in a close-knit presidential election. Kennedy, 43 at the time, was inaugurated as the 35th president of the United States—succeeding Dwight D. Eisenhower and becoming the youngest elected individual to take the oath of office.[27] Just a few months later, on May 11, 1961, President Kennedy sent about 400 Special Forces members and some 100 military advisors to South Vietnam. It has been said that he also ordered a "clandestine warfare against North Vietnam" and called "South Vietnamese forces to infiltrate Laos to locate and disrupt communist bases and supply lines there."[28]

Kennedy's political reasoning, which had also been his predecessors': If South Vietnam fell to communist rule, it would bode ill for the U.S. and its allies. Tensions continued to escalate, and more troops were sent overseas in 1963. A year later North Vietnamese attacked U.S. Navy crews at the Gulf of Tonkin, a deliberate assault that escalated tensions with the West.

It was a war that, for the United States, lasted for years—ending in 1975 when that April the North Vietnamese Army took control of the Presidential Palace in Saigon—but would remain controversial long after it had ended. With all due respect to those who fought in the conflict, doing their country's bidding without knowing the full details of the war, it remains one of the United States' dark spots, not only by the politically motivated maneuverings that spanned several presidencies and cost the lives of tens of thousands of people but by how the returning soldiers were often treated by their government and, in some instances, the American public.

American troops began arriving home to a baffled and bewildered government that showed little respect for the soldiers who risked their all for the Stars and Stripes. The war may have been over, but for the soldiers who returned, new battles percolated. For many, the traumatizing effects of their experiences, both during and after the war, would last a lifetime and bring new wounds that would never heal.

Looking at it from another perspective, the war with Vietnam damaged the U.S. economy, weakened military morale, and undermined America's commitment to internationalism, all which took years to recoup.[29] In some instances, it never has healed from the damaging effects of the Vietnam War, and it has loomed a big shadow in the country's other foreign conflicts.

A controversy while the war was raging was that many U.S. citizens seemed not to understand their country's involvement. They deemed it a senseless war, a foreign conflict in which Americans died for no good American cause. As the number of young men sent home in body bags grew, so did the protests. In late August 1970, the rally in East Los Angeles, led by the National Chicano Moratorium Committee Against the Vietnam War, was to protest the war generally but, more specifically, the disproportionate number of Latinos who were being sent overseas and killed in a conflict many believed America should not involve itself with.[30]

Who would have thought that on this somber day in 1970's America that the war would claim three more casualties, including 40-year-old Mexican American journalist Ruben Salazar, "the most prominent Latino journalist of his day."[31]

Born to Be a Journalist

If it is true that some people are born as types, with natural abilities that only need to be tapped in this life—finding the middle ground between innate talent and developed skills—then perhaps Ruben Salazar was one of these people. To become an expert at either natural talent or skilled technique, one must practice and learn—and learn to practice—to bring to the forefront those abilities that will best serve him or her well and those of their associates. Salazar was a person who seemed to possess innate capabilities that would serve him well as a journalist. Eventually, through education, practice and life experience, he learned skills to enhance and hone those natural talents.

Salazar, born March 3, 1928, in Ciudad Juarez, Mexico, was raised and received his first forays into journalism in El Paso, Texas. In the mid–1940s while attending Texas Western College (now the University of Texas at El

Paso), he wrote for the school newspaper, often flavoring his articles with his own observations on campus and, at times, putting himself into his articles.[32] Like any young reporter, he likely thrilled at seeing his name in print for the first time, and like most reporters after learning their chops, he later thrilled at tackling the harder, more serious stories of a seasoned journalist—the kind of stories that cause people to take notice and that initiate change.

For reasons unknown, Salazar took leave of school for a few years to work with his father and serve a stint in the U.S. Army, but he returned to school in 1952 to complete his degree, which came two years later, in 1954, when he graduated with a bachelor's degree in journalism—not an insignificant feat for a young Hispanic man in 1950s' America. By this time, he had found his voice as a journalist—a voice that spoke up for those in society who had a difficult time finding their own—and he went to work for the El Paso *Herald-Post*. While there, two stories in particular seemed to catch people's attention and perhaps set him on the path that would later lead him to the Golden State and his fate there not quite 20 years later.

Posing as a vagrant, Salazar got himself arrested for a story he hoped to write about the plight of inmates at the El Paso Jail, where it was alleged that the jail's guards did not treat the prisoners well. His efforts paid off: Salazar was arrested and spent time behind bars. According to his story titled "I Lived in a Chamber of Horrors" that ran on May 9, 1954, he saw up close and personal that the rumors he had heard were true.[33] Among the troubling things he witnessed were jailers who did not provide proper food and sanitary conditions to the inmates, including those who were medically compromised. The story, like all good journalism, was likely an eye-opener to its readers.

Another brave article by Salazar was one he published a few months after his piece on compromised inmates, this time focusing on would-be jailbirds. Still using his undercover guise, the reporter pretended to be a drug addict in search of his next high and came away with a story that shed light on an infamous drug dealer and a heavy-handed look at the painful peril of drug addicts.[34] When the story was published, it caught the attention of not only an interested citizenry but essentially, according to some rumors, put Salazar on the books with state and federal law officers.

"The El Paso division of the FBI immediately took note of both articles, thus putting Salazar on FBI and police radar," according to an article by KCET, an online and broadcast group in Southern California that has covered much of the Salazar case. "They too would also remain in Salazar's attention as he would continue to report on law enforcement's contentious relationship with the Mexican American community."[35] Whether true or not, Salazar kept doing what he did best: digging into stories that told the social injustices of the communities in which he lived and worked. His career and reporting pursuits eventually took him to California.

"Salazar's work came full-circle when he began writing columns for the *Los Angeles Times* in 1970," according to one article as part of the Ruben Salazar Project by the University of Southern California. "From the beginning of his career to the end in 1970, Salazar's work was always infused with an emphasis on marginalized groups and education."[36]

More so, perhaps, he was deemed a poignant personality event then. Gustavo Arellano, writing in an August 23, 2020, piece in the *Los Angeles Times*, explained that back in those days he expected to see "Salazar the revolutionary, when Salazar the reporter was even more radical." Years have codified the experience. "Now, I see a journalistic John the Baptist. A voice crying out in the white wilderness that was the *Los Angeles Times* in the 1960s, making way for better coverage of Latinos to come—and for more Latinos to cover them."[37]

The Beginning of the End

Salazar was hired by the *Los Angeles Times* in 1959 and dove with gusto into the stories of his new community that comprised nearly 3,000,000 people at the time, focusing his attention on the Latino community. As he further cemented himself in his role, he eventually obtained his own column. In one piece he was critical of Los Angeles Police Chief Ed Davis, claiming the police chief had said derogatory things about Mexicans. Apparently, this wasn't the only blight on his relationship with the local police department.[38] The police department responded, saying Salazar had "fabricated information from an off-the-record event. The column also appears to have prompted the LAPD to open a file on Salazar."[39]

This was a prelude to what was to come, when it had been alleged that he believed he was being followed during the last community event he would cover. In 1970 he left the *Times* to work as the news director at KMEX, a Spanish-language television station.

The 30,000 people who showed up for the rally at Belvedere Park started marching through the streets of LA toward Laguna Park, a little more than three miles distance. Salazar joined the crowd, as he had done similarly on other occasions, to be an eyewitness to the unfolding events. In this he was not without bias, for the Latino causes were important to him.

As the crowd grew rowdier and reports of vandalism were called in to authorities, police officers showed up in riot gear and with batons and tear gas at the ready. As the crowd dispersed, Salazar and a media colleague,

Guillermo Restrepo of KMEX, pushed through the frenzy, hurrying along the streets until, according to reports, they came to the Silver Dollar Café. During their trek Salazar was apparently unnerved and kept looking over his shoulder. When asked why he seemed so agitated, Salazar told Restrepo, "They're following us."[40] The pair slipped into the café to use the bathroom and grab a quick beer, allegedly followed by Los Angeles County deputies. While Salazar sat at the bar, one of the deputies fired a tear gas canister inside the establishment, hitting Salazar with a fatal blow to the head.

The incident did nothing to help race relations in the community, nor did the protest change the number of Latinos sent overseas. But, like the Vietnam War the rally-goers had been protesting that day, it did cause more controversy.[41] Many believed the death of the high-profile journalist was not by accident. It didn't help that the deputy who fired the canister that killed Salazar, later identified as Thomas Wilson, said he was unaware and unconcerned at the time about what projectile he had fired into the bar.[42] A coroner's inquest ruled the incident a homicide, but Wilson was never prosecuted for the crime. However, another report done some 41 years later, after an examination of the Los Angeles Sheriff's Office records by the Office of Independent Review, a civilian watchdog group, determined that there was no evidence to prove law officers intentionally surveilled Salazar or targeted him.[43]

Then why did a deputy shoot a canister into a bar shortly after Salazar had entered? Rumor said two men had entered the bar with guns, but that proved false. In short order when police told the building's occupants to leave the establishment but they failed to do so, the projectile was fired.[44]

While time may have dimmed the details of what really happened that day, it has not diminished the legacy of Ruben Salazar, one of the country's bright spots in minority journalism. He has remained in the hearts and minds of Latinos and journalists ever since. Not quite a full month after Salazar was killed, Laguna Park, where the rally had ended, was renamed the Ruben Salazar Park in honor of the slain journalist.[45] Forty-four years after he died, in summer 2014, a group of citizens that included Rosalio Munoz, who helped organize the former antiwar protest, installed a commemorative plaque at the park celebrating Salazar and his work.[46] That same year director Phillip Rodriguez released a documentary film called *Ruben Salazar: Man in the Middle.* And in the summer of 2020, 50 years after his death, the news media remembered him in several reports.

The case of Salazar reverberates today as Black communities and other minority groups speak out against police brutality and racism. He will continue to be remembered as one of America's journalists who died for speaking truth to power, and his legacy will remain bright for anyone seeking social justice. As another journalist wrote of Salazar, he "deserves to be remembered not as a victim of murder or a tragic accident but by his words and deeds. He inspires as the first Hispanic-American mainstream journalist who found his authentic voice, told the truth as he saw it, finally mending his divided heart."[47]

2

Unprecedented Times

I am ... for freedom of the press, and against all violations of the Constitution to silence by force and not by reason the complaints or criticisms, just or unjust, of our citizens against the conduct of their agents.—Thomas Jefferson

The year 2020 was one for the history books, a year that many have marked as unprecedented. Those unprecedented times had their genesis at the tail end of 2019 when a novel, or new, coronavirus that causes a respiratory infection was first reported in a human in Wuhan City, China. That started the snowball that was tossed down the hill only to gather momentum and become bigger and deadlier as it rolled. Within just a few months, as the virus traveled across oceans and continents and the infection rate and death toll continued to rise, the World Health Organization declared a worldwide pandemic.[1]

The virus, dubbed COVID-19, may cause mild symptoms for most people, according to the Centers for Disease Control and Prevention, but it can make other people, especially the elderly or those with compromised immune systems, severely ill. As has been reported with catastrophic numbers, it also can cause death. Because it is a virus and not a bacterial infection, it cannot be treated by antibiotics. At the time the pandemic was declared, there were no vaccines to prevent against it. The public health crisis crossed boundaries, affecting many other aspects of life, impacting people's daily routines and work habits. During the pandemic employees were sent home to work, many were laid off, some businesses shuttered their doors or closed temporarily, travel was restricted, and our very way of life was altered.

But no one knew for how long.

As people donned masks and social distanced, others threw health guidelines to the side and said the coronavirus was overblown by the news media and the political left, whom they said sensationalized the number of hospitalizations and fatalities from COVID-19.[2] Instead of the country coming together under a national crisis, it seemed instead to be pulling apart. The worldwide health emergency revealed how divided the country really was at the time. The guidance from medical science experts was belittled by many, including at times by the president, and mask-wearing and social distancing seemed to become a political issue.

People began to look to the future, but unsure of what that might look like they adopted descriptions such as living in the "new normal." But even as the words fell from lips, people still wondered what that meant. What was the new normal? Would it be a permanent new normal or a temporary one? Was the increased tension among the right and left part of the new normal? What did the future hold?

The forecast became even more bleak as summer approached.

Journalists Under Attack

Over the coming weeks other events would compound the heaviness many people were already feeling. Not only were thousands of lives being taken because of COVID-19, the respiratory illness caused by the coronavirus, but another life was senselessly snuffed out when a Minneapolis police officer forced his knee onto the back of the neck of a Black man while he lay on his stomach on the streets of the city of Mini-Apple. George Floyd, a 46-year-old Black man, was arrested on May 25 for allegedly using counterfeit money at a local business. As Floyd lay handcuffed on the ground in broad daylight, one of the four police officers at the scene, Derek Chauvin, pressed his knee onto Floyd's neck and kept it there for nearly nine minutes, despite Floyd choking out sobs that he could not breathe. The incident was recorded by bystanders and broadcast on news outlets and social media for all the world to see this instance of police brutality and unbidden racism in America. Floyd died at the scene because of the knee press, and Chauvin was tried the following spring and found guilty on three charges: second-degree unintentional murder, third-degree murder and second-degree manslaughter.

The killing of Floyd by a sworn officer of the law, done in broad daylight on a public street in America, brought back decades of memories of hate and racial injustice, and people soon took to the streets to protest systemic racism and call for police reform. Many had shouted to defund the police. While the latter is an extreme measure that would likely do more harm to the country and communities than good, emotions were at their peak. Floyd wasn't the only Black man killed in recent years by law officers; there also was 18-year-old Michael Brown, fatally shot by a police officer on August 9, 2014, in Ferguson, Missouri; 25-year-old Freddie Gray, after being arrested by police on April 12, 2015 in Baltimore, Maryland, died a few days later on April 19, due to spinal cord injuries believed to have happened during travel while in police custody; and 26-year-old Breonna Taylor, shot by police on March 13, 2020, after being awakened in her own apartment. When Floyd was killed, the boiling pot of racism exploded, and people took to the streets, marching and petitioning for change.[3]

The protests, which expanded to many cities across the country, started out peaceful, but as happens when emotions are on edge and anger overtakes our better selves, some of the protests turned to rioting and looting. It also was alleged by witnesses in a number of reports that demonstrators from outside the respective areas showed up to initiate the deviant behavior and violence. Many businesses were vandalized in Minneapolis and elsewhere, police vehicles were torched, and chaos and disorder seemed to flood America's otherwise peaceful streets. And then on the morning of May 29, another shameful incident happened, unlike anything the country had ever seen: three journalists were arrested on live television in Minneapolis while doing their jobs as the world watched. It was a blatant attack on the U.S. Constitution and the First Amendment.

The journalists were from CNN, one of the national media outlets that was a favorite of President Trump's to verbally bash.[4] It was a surreal time in the country's history: first, the murder of an American citizen, pinned to the ground by police in broad daylight and captured in recordings, and then the arrest of the three journalists, who were doing their jobs professionally and legally, during a live broadcast. This was followed by the assault and arrest of a number of other press professionals over the ensuing days.

Amidst the unrest in many cities, journalists were there as eyewitnesses to report and document the historic episodes taking place across the country. That was their job. As unbelievable as some of the things that were happening and which the country witnessed on television and the internet, the drama became even more shocking when journalists began to be arrested and assaulted by badge-carrying lawmen in other states. It was as if the arrests in Minneapolis signaled to the other officers that journalists were now targets to suppress. During the protests, police weren't just carrying their badges. Law officers carried clubs, shields, rifles, tear gas and smoke screens, with some of those tools being used against peaceful demonstrators as well as reporters and photographers. Not only was the country reeling from the coronavirus pandemic and the national street demonstrations—let's be frank, some of it *was* rioting, a criminal act, but not all of it— but now was a blatant move, another unprecedented event that pulled at the threads of democracy. It was a deliberate attack on press freedom.

"A CNN reporting team was arrested live on television early Friday while covering the protests in Minneapolis, an extraordinary interference with freedom of the press that drew outrage from First Amendment advocates and a public apology from Minnesota's governor," *The New York Times* reported on March 29.[5] The arrest of the three journalists occurred while the network's camera was still recording. Reporter Omar Jimenez, producer Bill Kirkos and photojournalist Leonel Mendez were in police custody for about an hour before being released, but the damage had already been done. In the ensuing days the country would witness more journalists being assaulted and arrested for doing their jobs.

Safeguarded by the Constitution, it is a journalist's right to document public events. This time, however, reporters weren't being safeguarded. They—and the whole First Amendment—were being attacked, and this time it was the whole world that was the eyewitness. Was this really happening in the United States of America, the country that is supposed to be the bastion of freedom-loving people everywhere? The attacks were not only against journalists; they were against the very foundations of American democracy. Such actions put the whole First Amendment at risk.

"When a journalist is arrested at a protest, the free and fair gathering of the news is arrested, too. That's one of the reasons why these infringements on press freedom are relatively rare in the United States—and why Friday's brief arrest of a CNN crew in Minneapolis was so egregious," reads a report published later the same day the CNN crew was arrested.[6]

"Freedom of the press protects the right to collect and disseminate news, but the right is not absolute," reads information from the Reporters Committee for Freedom of the Press. It explains that journalists are subject to the same laws as citizens and "do not have a special right of access to sources of information. However, police may not arrest a reporter or deny access simply to retaliate for negative news coverage or to prevent reporting on a public demonstration."[7]

And yet live video from the scene clearly shows that Jimenez and his team were not interfering with police officers. As police dressed in riot gear and armed with shields approached, Jimenez can be heard telling officers his team would move back to wherever the police wanted them to go. Instead, the reporting team was arrested. According to the Reporters Committee, "police cannot arrest journalists in retaliation for negative coverage or to prevent reporting on a public demonstration."[8] And yet that seems to be what happened.[9]

It didn't stop there. During the protests it was reported by a number of news organizations and captured in live recordings by the journalists themselves, or by protesters, that field reporters had either been arrested or assaulted by law officers, in some instances both. Freelance journalist Linda Tirado, who was in Minneapolis covering the protests, was hit in the face with projectiles fired by police and as a result was hospitalized and left partially blind in one eye.[10] But it wasn't just police who were doing the assaulting. Some protesters also attacked journalists or in other ways tried to prevent them from doing their jobs.

"It's a scale that we have not seen before," Kirstin McCudden, managing editor of the U.S. Press Freedom Tracker, told *Time* in a June 4, 2020, article. "It's unprecedented in scope without a doubt." She said while protests are no doubt "incredibly dangerous places for journalists," what set the 2020 protests apart was that journalists in many instances were being deliberately assaulted and arrested.

In the midst of the chaos some people wondered why journalists were putting themselves at risk. A non-journalist friend of mine said maybe it was time that reporters put away the press badge when they cover an event like the protests; do it while undercover. "Don't display press credentials," he said in essence, "don't allow people to know who you are. Hide the camera or microphone. Put away your notepad."

I know my friend meant well, but it was a philosophy that I couldn't get behind. The press credential is a badge of honor, not something to shun or hide. A reporter has the constitutional right to cover protests, dangerous or not, and it is imperative that others know the reporter is there to document the event. As the *Los Angeles Times* editorialized on June 2, "Journalists know that when they cover chaotic and dangerous events, a press credential is a thin shield against the bullets flying and batons swinging around them." But during the spring and summer of 2020, journalists were themselves targets. "Whatever you think about the fourth estate, news reporters serve as the public's eyes and ears on the events shaping the world."[11]

Even after the riots, and as peaceful protests continued, some law officers in cities were still telling journalists to vacate the scene or be arrested. Some of the peace officers used more than words, such as when a deputy charged and tackled a reporter to the ground in Lincoln, Nebraska. Chris Dunker, a reporter for the *Lincoln Journal Star*, was wearing a neon vest with the word PRESS printed on it and was carrying his press credentials on the evening of May 31 while livestreaming a protest in downtown Lincoln when, according to video captured at the time, a deputy ran toward Dunker without saying a word and threw him off his feet. Two deputies pinned him to the ground and handcuffed him.[12] While Dunker received only a scraped elbow and knee, the more flagrant injuries to this injustice run deeper and will take longer to heal.

Likewise, two Associated Press reporters were shoved by police and called expletives while covering protests in New York City. While documenting the scene in lower Manhattan, video journalist Robert Bumsted and photographer Wong Maye-E were surrounded by about a half-dozen officers, with one officer telling Bumsted he didn't care that he was a member of the press.[13]

And that's the problem journalists find themselves in today. People, even those who have taken oaths to serve and protect, don't seem to care anymore about protecting press freedom. If left unchecked and allowed to perpetuate, where will this take us as a country?

Compounded Problems

Journalism had already been reeling for a number of years due to increased digital competition, budgetary cuts, and newsroom shortages. A world full of smartphones and social media where everyone is their own citizen reporter compounded the problem for legitimate news organizations, and the public's trust continued to decline, but perhaps none so much since the 2016 presidential election.

Republican presidential candidate Donald J. Trump, a television celebrity and business-tycoon-turned-politician,[14] began early in his campaign to discredit the national press. It was easy for his supporters to jump on the bandwagon and shout through social media the same drivel that Trump was tweeting and shouting at his own rallies. These lamentable actions increased once Trump moved to the White House.[15]

Media distrust did not happen overnight, nor is it the result of any one person or event. It is the result of slow accumulation over years of mistrust fueled by party politics, increased digital technology that has created an overwhelming number of media voices, much of it unchecked, and the transgressions by fully credited news practitioners. Tweets and verbal attacks by a sitting president only fan the flames of mistrust, causing many to further question the validity of legitimate news organizations and journalists.[16]

All of these issues combined have brought us to the point we're at today, where journalists are treated harshly and disrespectfully. If the example of a president of the United States is to call names and denigrate the news media, calling journalists the enemy of the people, what's to stop others from doing the same? If he is to promote through his rhetoric and cheap-shot videos that it's OK to punch a CNN reporter, what's to stop people, even law officers, from enacting those things out on the streets? If words matter in one instance—such as a president complaining about the words in a news article—then they matter in other instances, such as when the president of the United States says journalists are scumbags. Was Trump's big glitch against the news media a play at tit for tat for reports that have been unfavorable to his administration? Or was it something more sinister?

Trump may not be the sole cause of the current media hate and distrust, but he certainly has fueled it, perhaps even inciting the volcano that in May 2020 seemed finally to have erupted when journalists began to be arrested and assaulted on the streets of America.[17] What happens after a volcano erupts? It scorches, burns, and leaves a scarred landscape that takes years for it to regrow.

By the time the presidential election arrived on November 3, there had been 229 journalists who had been attacked in the U.S. in 2020, according to U.S. Press Freedom Tracker. Seventy-five journalists had been arrested while covering protests and riots. Twelve journalists had their equipment searched or taken away, and there were 64 reported cases of damage to journalists' equipment, including one vehicle driven by a news crew that was getting ready to leave the scene of a demonstration in Louisville, Kentucky, when a young assailant threw a large rock at the vehicle, damaging its hood and windshield.[18]

On June 14, 2020, a reporter for Unicorn Riot, a nonprofit media organization, was repeatedly hit while filming protesters who said they were defending a statue of Christopher Columbus in Philadelphia. On July 12, 2020, a *New York Post* reporter was video recording protesters when he was hit with a slab of wood during a demonstration to cut police funding at the City Hall in New York City. The assailant knocked the cellphone out of the journalist's hand and struck him in the face with the board.[19] And the list goes on.

While all of this media hate was continuing, and just one week before the election, President Trump expressed another rant against the news media. He posted on his social accounts on Wednesday, October 28: "The USA doesn't have Freedom of the Press, we have Suppression of the Story, or just plain Fake News." He was upset because he believed more should have been reported on the Biden family and an alleged laptop that supposedly contained incriminating evidence about Biden's son, Hunter, and his dealings with China. "So much has been learned in the last two weeks about how corrupt the Media is, and now Big Tech, maybe even worse." He ended his tweet by writing: "Repeal Section 230!" of the Communications Decency Act, which, in part, says, "No provider or user of an interactive computer service shall be treated as the publisher or speaker of any information provided by another information content provider."[20]

It was claimed by Donald Trump and his allies that Joe Biden's son, Hunter Biden, allegedly used his father's influence to make business deals in China and the Ukraine. The efforts put money in the Bidens' coffers, they said, and there was evidence to prove it—namely the laptop that contained incriminating information. Few news organizations, including Fox News and the *Wall Street Journal*, were allowed access to key documents. What they found wasn't quite what Trump had alleged. "Leaving aside the many questions about their provenance, the materials offered no evidence that Joe Biden played any role in his son's dealings in China, let alone profited from them, both news organizations concluded," NBC News reported.[21] Does that mean the investigation is conclusive? No, but the same report points out one of the problems. "Most mainstream news organizations, including NBC News, have not been granted access to the documents." After repeated efforts through various means, including email, phone, and even certified mail, its requests were denied.

The Big Push

There seemed to be a real battle going on between the president, the public, and the news media. It was the big push leading up to the presidential election on November 3—an unprecedented election in which more than 150,000,000 people cast their ballots. More than 81,000,000 of the votes went to Joe Biden, while some 74,000,000 went to Donald Trump, both impressive numbers. Biden also won the electoral college votes, 306 to Trump's 232, but Trump had called fraud, and he and the Republican National Committee contested the election results in the courts. That was his right, of course, but when the courts came back and said there was no evidence of mass voter fraud, Trump still incited his base with words that attacked America's voting system—a prime element in any democracy. He and his supporters cried foul at mail-in ballots—a fight Trump had preempted when a year before the election he said if he lost the election, it would only be because it was a rigged election. In fact, Trump has had a history of calling elections rigged.[22]

When Obama won his second term in office, Trump said it was a "sham." In 2016 when Trump was contending for the Republican nominee and lost the Iowa caucus to Senator Ted Cruz by three percentage points, Trump said it was stolen from him. He also cast doubt on the 2016 presidential election, tweeting that it was "absolutely being rigged by the dishonest and distorted media pushing Crooked Hillary—but also at many polling places—SAD."[23] When that same year he won the presidency by winning more electoral votes than Clinton, it still apparently wasn't enough for his ego. He claimed falsely that he also had won the popular vote.

By the year 2020, the Constitution was hanging as if by a thread. It was only to get worse. Trump negated the court rulings, and at his beck and call his supporters seemed to believe the whole of the country's longtime institutions were in a conspiracy against the president, pushing him out of office. The sitting president was basically saying that America's democratic institutions were a big hoax. In the name of patriotism shouted by Trump, they supported his unfounded attacks of the election results. Many others saw through the lies and viewed Trump as an egomaniac attempting to usurp the Constitution, voter privileges, and remain in power at all costs.

Those costs were drastically seen on January 6, the day Congress had gathered to count electoral votes, a ceremonious event mandated under the Constitution.

After speaking to an assembled crowd in DC that morning, Trump encouraged his supporters to walk to the capitol and let their voices be heard. If you read or watch his speech, he does not tell those who had gathered to hear him to storm the capital, but he does tell them to let their voices be heard loud and clear and that the country must be taken back by force, something he had been saying, in essence, for weeks. What happened was a nefarious siege on the People's House.

The events on January 6 were a physical display of what had been happening for the past several years: the erosion of trust, not only of the news media but of our other legacy institutions—Congress and our courts of law. It was a huge, unsightly rip in the fabric of democracy.

I feel inclined not to relate the tragedy we saw as a country that day in early January, but only when the siege was over, when the capital had been cleared and the legislators went back to work, many of Trump's followers found every excuse they could to defend the president. It wasn't Trump supporters who stormed the capital, they reasoned, it must have been Black Lives Matter protesters. Trump, however, knew who these people were. He had called these insurgents "patriots" and said he "loved" them. Trump was reckless, a president gone rogue in the waning days of his power. And what his supporters did ... it was blind faith on a massive scale. (The following May, Republicans in the Senate voted against establishing a commission to investigate the nefarious act not seen since the days of the Civil War. One can only wonder what they were trying to protect.)

It didn't matter anymore what was reported by the news media about Trump because to his followers the news media was corrupt. No matter what was reported—no matter the evidence laid out before the public—they wouldn't believe it if it contradicted with their already-enshrined political beliefs. It started there, with the news media and the name-calling (fake news, enemy of the people), but it escalated to believing the presidential election was rigged and stolen from Trump to storming the nation's capital.

When the storm ended that day, did Trump and the people who stormed the capitol have blood on their hands? A woman had been shot inside the capitol building and later died of her wounds. A capitol police officer also died while trying to defend the capitol. In all, five people died because of the insurrection at the nation's temple.[24]

That evening I had a discussion with a family member who was defending Trump and saying she wouldn't be surprised if BLM protesters were involved. I said, no, these were Trump supporters whom he praised in a video he shared on Twitter (which was later removed). "It's documented," I said, "Watch it." Her response: "I don't need to because I believe what I believe." That's fine I said. Believe what you want. But facts are facts.

And that's the problem. No one wants to believe facts anymore when they contradict their personal beliefs. Facts, truth, do not seem to matter anymore because everyone has their own version of perceived truth. It is that perception that led people to the capitol on the morning of January 6. But the fact is—facts speak for themselves, which helps us get closer to the truth of what really happened.

Long Live the News Media

While the news media were reporting on the happenings at the nation's capital, they also were vehemently attacked. This is what I saw while watching it on TV: while filming the chaos, a Trump supporter walked up to a CNN cameraman and flashed two middle fingers at him, shouting profanities at the cable network during the live broadcast. One reporter at the scene said on camera he was unnerved to be among such a crowd, fearing he could be assaulted. His crew back in the studio, who were asking him questions, told him to be careful. These were nothing compared to what other journalists had experienced.

Pro-Trump rioters were seen destroying journalists' equipment, shoving and berating reporters, and calling networks and reporters foul names. "Mob of Trump supporters swarm the media near the US Capitol," tweeted NBC's Shomari Stone, showing a video of rioters breaking, vandalizing, and stealing equipment. "They yell what Trump frequently says, 'the media is the enemy of the people.' They destroy equipment and chased out reporters. I've never seen anything like this in my 20 year career."[25]

The New York Times headlined a story the next day, "Murder the Media"—the same words that rioters carved into a door at the U.S. Capitol. They had heard earlier that morning Trump once again call the press the enemy of the people.[26] But what did he call those who stormed the capitol? He called them "patriots" and "special" and even expressed his "love" to them in a video he posted to his social accounts while the mob continued to desecrate and vandalize the nation's temple. Those with more levelheaded thinking said we should call these trespassers what they really were: vandals, rioters, insurrectionists, domestic terrorists. Trump had called BLM protesters "thugs," but he called these trespassers "patriots."

"'Murder the media' was carved into the U.S. Capitol today," Samantha-Jo Roth, a reporter and correspondent for Washington, DC–based Spectrum News, tweeted on January 6. "There are no words to express how disturbing this is. A free press that's able to hold those in power accountable is what makes our democracy work."[27]

At least two journalists from the *Washington Post* were arrested and then released while covering the attack. Demonstrations occurred at a number of state capitols across the country as well, with some journalists covering these events also being assaulted. At the Utah State Capitol in Salt Lake City, a *Salt Lake Tribune* photographer was pepper sprayed by a protester.[28] Salt Lake City Mayor Erin Mendenhall tweeted: "An assault on a journalist is an attack on freedom of press and democracy. This is unacceptable, and should not be allowed to go unchecked."[29]

It was the volcano that had finally exploded. "The United States on Wednesday," the Associated Press reported the day after the insurrection, "seemed at risk of becoming the very kind of country it has so often insisted it was helping: a fragile democracy."[30]

We are now dealing with the scars of the scorched and burned land.

What's the New Normal?

I remember when I first heard about the three CNN journalists being arrested. I was sitting at my desk, working on a story for a magazine. My gut, which in some ways was already tied in knots by the escalating coronavirus pandemic and the riots taking place, tightened, and I felt a sickening feeling come over me. It was a surreal moment for me, as I'm sure it was for many others who were watching the scenes unfold. After watching the arrest in real time, I searched news articles about the incident. Before long stories began popping up about the incident, and before long many others followed about other journalists being arrested and/or assaulted by law officers.

I felt like I was living in a dystopian novel, the beginning of the end of our democracy. What could I do, what could anybody do, to fight against the totalitarian state? For this, the arresting of journalists for doing their jobs, was exactly what such a state would do. You don't arrest people for doing their jobs—unless, of course, they're journalists in the era of Trumpism.

The president did not arrest the journalists, but it was under his watch that the volatility toward reporters led to this moment—a moment that will live in infamy. But was this only a dark *moment* for journalists, one they would eventually pass? Or was this the beginning of a new way journalists would be treated going forward? Was it part of the new normal?

By the time April 2021 arrived, almost a year after the riots of 2020, it seemed as if it was a new trend. By now Trump had been out of office for a few months—though he had set up shop in Florida and continued to send out missives, including calling the news media fake and the election stolen—but journalists were once more on the scene of yet another protest because of a police shooting and were once again assaulted by law officers in Minnesota.

That spring there was another police shooting of a Black man on April 11 at Brooklyn Center in the North Star State. Twenty-year-old Daunte Wright was shot by a law officer in what police described as "an accidental discharge" after police stopped him for having expired registration tags on his car, according to reporting by the Associated Press at the time.[31] They attempted to arrest him for an outstanding warrant when the gun was fired. Police said the officer who had shot Wright was reaching for her taser but accidentally pulled her firearm instead.

When demonstrators took to the streets to protest, the news media was once more assaulted by law officers—for doing their jobs. Some of the reported mistreatment of journalists this time included the following: a CNN producer was grabbed by her backpack and thrown to the ground by state troopers.[32] A freelance photographer said he was punched in the face by a police officer, who then tore off his credentials, forced him on the ground, and pressed a knee into his back.[33] A Today videographer tweeted he and other reporters were forced to lie on their stomachs while police photographed them and their credentials before letting them leave.[34]

These are representative of the many more instances of journalists who received harsh treatment by police officers while covering the protests. According to a letter by Attorney Leita Walker to Minnesota Governor Tim Walz and public safety officials in the state, there had been "multiple instances of journalists being harassed, assaulted, or arrested by law enforcement officers while covering protests in Minnesota."[35]

CNN's Miguel Marquez tweeted a few days later, on April 18, that forcing reporters to the ground and photographing their faces and IDs were things he had only seen "in Afghanistan when US forces were trying to control a local population." In the same thread he continued: "Some in law enforcement clearly view reporters as part of the problem and are trying to force us to commit to their controls regardless of basic rights."

Governor Walz came out in response to the police treatment of journalists, saying on social media: "A free press is foundational to our democracy. Reporters worked tirelessly during this tumultuous year to keep Minnesotans informed." He said he met with "media and law enforcement to determine a better path forward to protect the journalists covering civil unrest."[36]

One could ask if this was a problem with Minnesota law officers instead of a national bent against journalists, but similar scenarios, as what happened in the summer of 2020, seemed to play out in other states.

A month after the Daunte Wright shooting, on May 19, two reporters from *The Staunton News Leader* were detained by police while covering a protest in Elizabeth City, North Carolina. The protest was in response to yet another shooting of a Black man, Andrew Brown, Jr., by law officers on April 21. The prosecutor's office said the shooting was justified and that none of the Pasquotank County Sheriff's deputies would face charges.[37] The protests started, and so did police action against journalists.

Once again, the question: are these types of assaults and suppression tactics on journalists the new normal?

If the mantra holds true and the evil deed, "murder the media," comes to pass, we can say goodbye to democracy as we know it. If, however, we promote the motto by our own actions that "long live the media," we have a chance to retain our freedoms for future generations.

Yet it is not just the blatant and physical assault on journalists that we need to worry about. There is another kind of assault that is just as sinister. On May 7, 2021, the *Washington Post* reported the findings that while Trump was in office, his Justice Department had secretly obtained a *Post* reporter's phone records.[38]

Where Do We Go from Here?

The press is not the sole thread that upholds our constitutional way of life. The Constitution in its entirety, though not a perfect document, is a testament to freedom-loving people everywhere. It is mankind's best hope for democracy. There is a reason freedom of the press—along with freedom of religion, speech, peaceably to assemble and petitioning the government—is listed among the country's first freedoms. They serve as the bulwark, the sentinels that safeguard so many of our other rights. The press is at the forefront of that fight, but it can defend our rights only as it remains free without suppression tactics or infringement by government entities.

Those who share the same sentiments about journalists as Trump find themselves in a precarious situation, whether they know it or not. The Constitution, including the First Amendment, either protects all or it protects none. As Jan Neuharth, chair and chief executive officer of the Freedom Forum, said, the public apparently needs to be better educated about their own constitutional rights and then to properly stand up for them.

Neuharth, in a letter dated January 5, 2020, on the organization's website, said any attack on journalists is reprehensible, no matter who it comes from. "We encourage all who wish to add their voices 'peaceably to assemble, and to petition the Government for a redress of grievances,' protected by the First Amendment, with journalists present in their constitutional role as observers and reporters on behalf of us all."[39]

Don Bolles, 1976
The Arizona Republic

There was nothing special about the white Datsun that sat in the parking lot of a hotel in Phoenix, Arizona—except for the six sticks of dynamite that lay beneath it on the morning of June 2, 1976. The car's owner, a reporter named Don Bolles, was inside the Hotel Clarendon to meet with a source. Before he went to the hotel, he left a note on his desk at the state capitol where he was working that day, saying he would be gone for a while.[40] His appointment at the hotel was slated for 11:30 a.m. He arrived early and waited in the lobby for a number of minutes. Bolles then was summoned to the phone. His source called, telling the reporter he would not be coming to the hotel after all.

Bolles, who worked for *The Arizona Republic*, had been a reporter for most of his working career and knew that sometimes sources backed out of interviews. But this is one he was looking forward to. Now he perhaps wondered what the goose chase was all about.

After hanging up the phone, Bolles exited the hotel and walked back to his car, the sun still climbing in the Arizona sky. Noon was approaching, and that meant lunchtime for many people in the bustling city. Bolles already had a luncheon he wanted to get to after his planned meeting with his source, but now that his source had cancelled, that left him with more time on his hands.[41] Whatever plans he came up with to fill the time before his luncheon, they drastically changed as he approached the car, opened the door and sat behind the steering wheel. He turned the ignition, the car started, and he started to back out of the parking stall. Another person watching the journalist from a nearby location pushed a button on a device—and Bolles's whole world exploded.

It was 11:34 a.m.[42]

The bomb—six sticks of dynamite attached by magnets to the underside of the car and which investigators later discovered had been detonated by remote control—didn't kill Bolles immediately. The explosion, which blew a gaping hole in the floorboard and knocked the front door open, caused Bolles to crawl from his vehicle, where he struggled on the hot pavement, bleeding, limbs akimbo, and in more pain than he ever thought was humanly possible.[43]

Why was this decent, unassuming man targeted in such a ghastly way?

The answer is the same as it is for other journalists who are targeted for assassination: because he sought to bring darkness to light by the facts of his reporting. Even as Bolles suffered on the ground, he muttered words that gave clues to his would-be assassins and the story they were trying to suppress: "John Adamson." "Emprise." "Mafia."[44]

The Journalist's Path

The idea of becoming a journalist was perhaps ingrained into Bolles's mind at an early age. He grew up in Wisconsin, where his father worked as a reporter for the Associated Press. It's not difficult to imagine a young Bolles hearing about his father's adventures in storytelling, about the role and responsibilities of the newspaper world. In those days, at least in Hollywood's portrayal of the newspaperman on the silver screen, reporters were craggy fellows who wore fedoras and long coats and with cigarettes hanging from the corners of their mouths, resembling much the private detective. This stereotypical image added mystique to being a news chaser. The reality was likely similar, only much different. Journalism has its high-water marks in which reporters uncover the big story, but much of the day-to-day grind isn't quite as glamorous. In the movie *All the President's Men* there is a scene that shows Carl Bernstein and Bob Woodward, played by Dustin Hoffman and Robert Redford, respectively, sitting in a library rifling through index cards. As the camera's lens focuses on the journalists, it moves upward. The two finally appear as ant-sized people in a large room of many other people sitting at a circular desk doing mundane work. It's a great scene that depicts the dreary legwork that goes into journalism. The movie also depicts the two reporters making phone calls and knocking on doors.

The payoff for any journalist is when the story is printed or broadcast and prompts discussion and change. It's the payoff that makes the tedious hours spent in journalism worthwhile, and perhaps as a young man Bolles saw that payoff with his father's work.

For whatever reason, Bolles found himself on the same career path as his father. When he became of age, he enrolled at Beloit College in Beloit, Wisconsin, where he edited the campus newspaper. After graduating with a degree in government, he did a stint with the U.S. Army before embarking on his career in the newsroom.[45] Following in his father's footsteps even more closely, he landed a job covering the sports beat for the Associated

Press. It was the start of a successful and adventure-filled career as a newsman in journalism's prime.

Always a sports fan, by the time he landed at *The Arizona Republic* in 1962, he now turned his pen to the deeper, more investigative stories of journalism. The story that ultimately led to his death was one he needn't have pursued, because by the time he went to the Clarendon, he had been assigned to cover politics at the state capitol.[46] As he had demonstrated time and again, however, he was first and foremost an investigative reporter. He could no more ignore investigating this story than a priest could dismiss his evening prayers.[47]

Bolles had been in the business long enough to know something else: journalism, especially the investigative kind, does not make friends easily, though it might make a few enemies along the way. Such was the case with Bolles. He was neither timid nor afraid to ask the tough questions, to dig and uncover, inquire and find answers. He never shirked his responsibilities, even when his enemies mounted their attacks. It was this dogged determination that earned him the respect of his colleagues; it also is what ultimately led him to the Hotel Clarendon on that fateful morning in early June 1976.

The Beginning of the End

Bolles went to the hotel to meet a man named John Harvey Adamson, who claimed he had information that linked U.S. Senator Barry Goldwater and Congressman Sam Steiger to a land fraud scheme, something Bolles had been investigating for several years. Bolles wasn't duped easily; he knew Adamson wasn't trustworthy, but a good reporter is always curious. He figured meeting with the source might lead to some new clues.[48]

Bolles hopped in his Datsun and drove to the hotel for his meeting with Adamson. While waiting in the lobby, the reporter received a phone call from his source, telling him he was not going to come to the meeting after all. Figured. Like Bolles had surmised earlier to his wife and editor, Adamson wasn't trustworthy.[49] Bolles checked his watch, exited the hotel, and walked to his car.

After the bomb exploded, and with Bolles trembling on the edge of death, he allegedly repeated the three words that gave investigators clues to his suspected assassins. Later, during lucid moments in the hospital, he told them further of his suspicions and more about the story he was seeking to uncover.[50]

Eventually police arrested Adamson, who named three others in the conspiracy: Max Dunlap, a Phoenix contractor; Kemper Marley, a known mob member; and James Robison, whom Adamson said had detonated the bomb. The investigations of these individuals continued, which eventually led to the imprisonment of Dunlap and Robison, but investigators couldn't find any evidence linking Marley or the mafia to the crime. Adamson, in 1977, testified to second-degree murder, the same year he testified against Dunlap and Robison, and both were charged with first-degree murder. Their convictions were short-lived, however, when they were overturned the following year. Later, both were recharged. But for at least one of them, prison time was not to last. Robison was acquitted in 1993. Dunlap, after his retrial, was once again charged with first-degree murder. He was the only one of them to die in prison. Adamson, who had been charged with first-degree murder in 1980 and sentenced to death after he refused to testify a second time after Dunlap and Robison's first acquittal, received a break when the Arizona Supreme Court overturned the sentence. By 1990 Adamson had changed his mind and agreed to again testify against Dunlap. For his cooperation to do so he received a reduced sentence. He was released from prison in 1996. All three have since died.

As for the reporter, Bolles languished in the hospital and suffered tremendously from his injuries.[51] Both of his legs and one arm had to be amputated in an effort to save him, but in the end it was to no avail. Bolles died 11 days after the bomb exploded. He left behind a wife and children, colleagues and friends, and a community of journalists all over the country who would long remember him for the extraordinary journalism he accomplished. By the time of his death at age 47, Bolles had 14 years of investigative journalism under his belt.[52] His legacy continued after he took his final breath.

The hit on Bolles sent reverberations throughout the Grand Canyon State and the nation's journalism community. Newshounds from near and far were saddened and angered that one of their own—and surely one of America's most respected press members—had been specially targeted for assassination. There also was the fact that Bolles's killing meant his reporting investigations were on target. If anything, his death only heightened those efforts by a much larger team of reporters and law officers. Journalists flooded into Phoenix to pick up where Bolles had left off in what amounted to a massive team-reporting project rarely, if ever, heard of in the U.S. The journalists produced a 23-part series exposing corruption at the highest levels of Arizona politics.[53]

Legacy of a Newsman

Today's up-and-coming journalists may not be familiar with Bolles's story, but the industry itself has not forgotten, especially his former newspaper, *The Arizona Republic*, which has continued to report and uncover new details about the tragic episode that cost the life of one of America's finest journalists. Since his passing, the *Republic* and its army of dedicated journalists have done a number of stories about their slain colleague, honoring him in a way Bolles would have appreciated: through investigative journalism.

It is important that such work continues, not only for Bolles and his family but for truth's sake, because there yet remain many unknowns about the story he was seeking to uncover. As sometimes happens in high-profile cases, conspiracy theories get thrown into the mix. It was alleged at one time, for instance, that Bolles's notes were removed from his desk shortly after his passing, though others have said that was not true.[54] In a report by a different publication, it was said that the "police investigation was sloppy and highly compromised."[55] And in 2019 it was reported that "long-forgotten tape recordings and documents" were still being discovered.[56]

Kudos to *The Arizona Republic* and daring news outlets everywhere who never raise the flag of surrender but instead position their own armaments to confront the war party, no matter how daunting or exasperating or however long the road. Investigative journalism, as the *Republic* has demonstrated time and again, is much needed today, and Bolles's story serves as a reminder and as a testament not only of its value and impact but of its risks. As a June 16, 1976, editorial in *The Michigan Daily* intones, "Don Bolles was killed solely because he sought to uncover and print what the public has a right to know—the truth."[57]

Journalism once was viewed as a noble profession, perhaps even a prestigious calling to help reform and rejuvenate society. In many communities, local reporters were viewed as community celebrities, at least quasi so. Those days seem to be over as the public's perception of newsmen and women may have changed over time. "In Bolles' day, suffering in service to journalism got you labeled a hero," writes EJ Montini in *The Arizona Republic*. "These days, it's likely to mark you a traitor or even land you in jail."[58] Journalists today have been branded as perpetrators of fake news and enemies of the people.

On the opposite side of the aisle there are those who won't let journalism—or Bolles's memory—die an ignominious death. It is in that memory where we find the value and haunting tributes of this still-noble profession we call journalism. It is a profession, especially the investigative kind, that still has the power and means to influence public opinion, prompt change at the highest levels, and alter the course of history. It has the power for great and lasting impact on communities and countries.

Besides the continued conversations and news reports in memory of the slain journalist, Bolles has been remembered in other ways. The Hotel Clarendon was named by the Society of Professionals as a historical marker, and a bust of Bolles has greeted visitors in the hotel's lobby for years. In 2017 the Don Bolles Medal was established to recognize investigative journalists and the exceptional work they have done without intimidation or fear.

As for the white Datsun that Bolles drove to the hotel that day five decades ago?[59] It had for a time been on display at the Newseum, a museum about journalism, but since the site closed its doors at the end of 2019 due to financial setbacks, the car, as with other items from its collection, were moved to storage.[60] Hopefully it one day will again be on display as another reminder of the terrible cost that some journalists pay for seeking the truth.

For now, time marches ever onward. Emblems may be packed away, but memories remain. We now live in politically contentious times not seen in decades, and our multi-digital world has not helped lessen the chaos. "Newspapers fight to stay relevant," reads another article by *The Arizona Republic*. "The institutions journalists cover build higher walls around themselves. The people in power try to dismiss the free press as fake or as liars. But what happened that morning, at 11:34 a.m., remains a constant: An American journalist was murdered in pursuit of the truth."[61]

3

The First Amendment
and the Fourth Estate

Freedom of the press is not just important to democracy, it is democracy.—WALTER CRONKITE

The epigraph quote by famed broadcast journalist Walter Cronkite sets the tone for the chapter. Perhaps this truth was no more apparent than it was during the summer of 2020 when news media were verbally assaulted by a sitting president and physically attacked by police during nationwide protests over the death of a Black man while in police custody in Minneapolis. That summer in America resembled something from a dystopian novel, not the real life that we had come to expect in the United States.

Sadly, it was all too true and brought this thought to my mind: What would the country look like if it didn't have an independent press? In this contentious age when the news media is constantly belittled by a barrage of derogatory epithets such as "fake news" and "enemy of the people"—those are fightin' words, some might say—many people actually believe the country would be better served without its legacy journalism institutions. That belief itself is a troubling sign of where we are at today.

Where would we be without the watch-doggedness of the news media? The answer comes not from sarcastic rants on social sites but perhaps is gleaned better from an episode of the classic television show, *The Twilight Zone.*

In the episode titled "The Obsolete Man," a librarian played by Burgess Meredith is on trial for what TV viewers are led to at first believe is a heinous crime. The man in the shadowed room stands before his accusers at the end of a long table while a judge on a high pedestal looks down, denouncing the man's crime: for being a librarian, an obsolete profession in the totalitarian age. As a biased jury looks on in the shadowed recesses of the makeshift, warehouse-looking courtroom, the man awaits his judgment: he is to be executed within the next 48 hours. The one gracious offer he is granted by the court is that he can determine how and when he will die.

You'll have to watch (or rewatch) the last of the season two episode to find out the rest of the story, but as you can tell, this was the fictional story of a society gone amok. Perhaps it seems extreme to share this scenario here—as a country, we haven't digressed that far—but in shades and shadows, much like those in the episode, this is what it often is beginning to feel like to be a journalist when confronted with the taxed minds of a great many people: obsolete in the twenty-first century. Their very accusers are the same people journalists try to serve by bringing them the news of the day, important facts that will help the citizenry make better decisions.

Here is one real-life example of many. In March 2020, while gathered for a press conference at the White House, one of the broadcast reporters in attendance asked President Donald Trump what he had to say to the American people to help lessen their fears about the coronavirus pandemic. This was early in the pandemic when new things were still being discovered about the virus. Businesses were closing their doors, people were being laid off from work, unemployment filings were skyrocketing across the country, and the infection rate and death toll continued to climb. Many wondered what the future held for them and their country. During a press conference at the nation's capital, Peter Alexander, White House correspondent for NBC News, asked the president a direct question: "What do you say to Americans who are scared? Nearly 200 dead, 14,000 who are sick, millions, as you witnessed, who are scared right now. What do you say to Americans who are watching you right now who are scared?"

Trump: "I say that you're a terrible reporter, that's what I say."

It was a direct question—a legitimate question, asked professionally, similar to other questions that could be asked during times of crises, and it gave the president of the United States the chance to help soothe the concerns that many Americans across the country were feeling. Instead of taking the high road and doing what a president should do, Trump, instead of answering the question, called Alexander a "terrible reporter" and then said, "I think it's a very nasty question, and I think it's a very bad signal that you're putting out to the American people. The American people are looking for answers and they're looking for hope. And you're doing sensationalism, and the same with NBC and Concast—I don't call it Comcast—I call it Concast. … Let me tell you something, that's really bad reporting. And you ought to get back to reporting instead of sensationalism."

The press conference was broadcast live for all of the country to see. My company's news staff was sent home to work during the rapidly growing virus concerns, and my remote office was a two-bedroom apartment in North Dakota. While working in my makeshift office, I had the press conference turned on the television, trying to glean my own understanding of the unfolding crisis our country was experiencing.

And then I heard Alexander's question and Trump's response.

I knew how Trump sometimes treated reporters, calling them names during live broadcasts, but I didn't expect this.

The clip was later posted to YouTube, and some shared it on social media, including one of my Facebook friends, who said she was appalled that someone who took the oath of office to defend the Constitution would respond so negatively to a reporter during a time of crisis, especially in response to the question that was asked so the president could allay some of the fears that many were feeling. Most of the responses on this Facebook post, I later saw, sided with the president. One person commented that Alexander had "baited the president" with his question. Reading these responses deepened my understanding—and my sadness—by how much today's news media is harangued and despised, more so it seems by at least one side of the political aisle.

While there has always been a fairly substantial amount of criticism of the news media by politicians, presidents and the public, it seemed like every day was a new low in relations between the president and the press. But, as the saying goes, "We hadn't seen anything yet!" Everything seemed to be building for years to the contest news practitioners faced during the pandemic and the next election cycle, trying to stay relevant in a world where legitimate press was attacked as being obsolete because everyone with a smartphone and social media account was now their own reporter, columnist, and media critic.

Much of these struggles remain.

It has been a long and arduous journey since the Founding Fathers drafted the Constitution, when they placed the rights of the press as one of the country's first freedoms. That doesn't mean the Founders didn't experience their own unwanted criticisms by sly wordsmiths and publishers with a bent to politick, but in spite of being harangued and judged by newspapermen, the constitutional fathers defended the need for an independent press. In 2020, we heard just the opposite—that the country would be better served without the news media.

Far from it, journalists and journalism are not obsolete.

The Fourth Estate

Under the U.S. Constitution are three distinct branches of the federal government: legislative, executive, and judicial. In simple terms, the legislative branch, or what is known as Congress and which includes the House of Representatives and Senate, makes laws; the judicial branch, which comprises the Supreme Court, district and municipal courts, interprets laws; and the executive branch—the president, vice president and cabinet and most federal agencies—carries out those laws. Each branch of government can change acts of the other branches. For instance, a president can veto legislation created by Congress and nominate heads of federal agencies; Congress may confirm or reject the president's nominees and can remove a president from office in exceptional circumstances; and justices of the Supreme Court, who are nominated by the president and confirmed by the Senate, can overturn unconstitutional laws.[1]

There also is a fourth, unofficial branch of government, sometimes called the Fourth Estate. The term "fourth estate" is attributed to Edmund Burke in 1787 when English journalists, acting as free agents without government oversight, were allowed to report on the goings-on of the House of Commons of Great Britain. He purportedly said at the time that "there were three Estates ... but in the Reporters Gallery yonder, there sat a fourth Estate more important far than they all."[2] The term has been adopted in the U.S. and refers to the free press or what often is termed the news media today, which serve as the last checks and balances of the U.S. government. Each of the other official branches of government serve as the first checks and balances on each other. The press also is so named because of its power to influence public opinion, which, as a government founded of, by and for the people, is where many changes by government often first begin.

The word press comes from the "printing press," enhanced by Johannes Gutenberg in 1440 when he invented moveable type and which was the means to distribute news to people thereafter. Because of the many mediums of news reporting and delivery today, the press refers to legitimate newspaper, digital, and broadcast reporters and outlets broadly referred to as the "news media" or sometimes "the media." The press, or news media, is a plural term and, as a whole, is one of the United States' most important institutions because it not only provides checks and balances to the three branches of government; it also provides insight and perspective into other aspects of life and the world in which we live. Its importance has been hailed, as Philip Graham made popular, by serving as "the first rough draft of history."

In our day Harold Holzer, in his notable book *The Presidents vs. the Press*, asks: "Does traditional press coverage remain the proverbial first draft of history, or has it been discredited forever by the mantra of 'fake news'?" He takes it a step further by asking: "Do facts still matter in an era in which a president's thousands of false statements have been exposed without ramification?"[3]

In the long haul and in the near term we must pivot facts as still important to our democratic values. And yes, the press remains the first rough draft of history for the obvious reason: journalists' credentialed role being eyewitnesses and recorders of world events. In many instances, they serve as our own eyes and ears.

The Early Printers

Humankind has always recorded its acts of bravery and deceit, its impressions and understandings of virtue and vice, of good and evil, of the rise and fall of great civilizations and of political graces and disgraces. We can turn to the writings of the ancients, the scriptorians, the early history buffs such as Polybius, Herodotus, and Flavius Josephus, who recorded their histories and, sometimes like journalists do today, eyewitness accounts on scrolls or parchment.[4] Some found other means to record the goings-on of their day through means more resembling the newspaper. Rome, in 59 BC, recorded information in the Acta Diurna, public records that were engraved onto metal or stone and displayed in public places in the city for all to read; the Dibao, or palace reports, was among the earliest forms of newspapering during China's Han Dynasty, 206 BC to 220 AD, which continued in one form or fashion over ensuing dynasties, including the Tang Dynasty, from about 618 to 907 AD, which distributed matters of importance from the courts to government officials in the form of written publications. This practice continued until the Qing Dynasty in 1912. In 1556 the government of Venice published the *Notizie scritte*, which were handwritten notices containing economic, military and political items. These early newsletters cost one gazzetta, a Venetian coin that eventually came to mean "newspaper" (or gazette). Germany in the 16th and 17th centuries had circulated a number of news sheets containing events in Europe, including battles and treaties. One publication, perhaps the first resembling anything akin to the newspaper as we know it, started in 1609, called the *Weekly Newes*.[5]

Traditionally, the history of news publications in the colonial states starts with the aforementioned *Publick Occurrences Both Foreign and Domestick*, published by Benjamin Harris in 1690. It comprised four pages, including items in what we'd call community news today, as well as gossip entries, including the last page that was left blank so that readers could fill in their own news and pass the paper along to the next reader.[6] It may have been America's first newspaper, but it also was the first to be targeted with an act of suppression. It was shut down after only the first issue because the British hierarchy didn't like what Harris had published.

Slowly, other daring entrepreneurial types with printing presses began publishing their own papers. In 1704 emerged the first regularly published newspaper, called the *Boston-Newsletter*. Published by John Campbell, which, besides news from the mother county, contained items of local interest including maritime arrivals and church sermons. James Franklin in 1721 started the colony's first daily publication, called *The New-England Courant*. The venture introduced a then future revolutionary to the world of news printing, Franklin's younger brother, Benjamin, who served as an apprentice. Not just a printer, his position also gave young Benjamin an opportunity to publish his own articles using the pseudonym Silence Dogood, a name whose identity his older brother did not even know.[7] Journalism frowns on using pseudonyms today, but in pre-revolutionary days it was a popular way to write opinion while trying to avoid retribution from government officials.

Benjamin Franklin, besides his many other pursuits as an inventor, continued in the publishing trade. In 1729, at just 24 years of age, he became publisher of the *Pennsylvania Gazette* and elevated its status by broadening advertising and readership. It was deemed one of the best newspapers published at the time.[8]

Other papers came and went, including John Peter Zenger's *New York Weekly Journal*, an important paper at the time because it criticized British rule, adding a spark that would merge with other flames to create a bonfire of freedom later on. Started in 1733, the *Journal* was harassed for its unfavorable articles, and Zenger was arrested in 1734 for seditious libel because he had published unfavorable news about the British governor of New York, William Crosby. He spent eight months in jail for his alleged crime, but the first battle for press freedom was won in the courts of law a year later, when a jury ruled that newspapers had the right to criticize government and its officials as long as the reports were true.

As time marched forward, so did the approach of a critical juncture in colonial history: severing ties with the Royal Crown. Revolutionists found a use for the printing press beyond the news of the day. With their newspapers and pamphlets, they continued to use it as a means for change, to inspire their readers—and as such, whole communities—to unite in planning their own future and not let it be dictated by an absentee government across the ocean. In some instances, publishers and writers used the press as a call to take up arms, thus cementing the notion that the first volleys of the Revolutionary War were not launched by cannon or musket but by the sharp words of the printing press.

The pen, and thus the press, had become by all intents and purposes mightier than the sword as it swayed public opinion and cemented notions. Press hounds such as Thomas Paine and Benjamin Franklin, with their newspapers and pamphlets, pushed for revolution. They got it, and the colonial states went to war with Britain. When arms were taken up in the cause of liberty, columnists and printers continued to pound the presses with words that served as a different kind of mortar. So impactful were newspapers in shaping public opinion and felling America's enemies, Dr. Benjamin Rush, one of America's Founding Fathers, wrote in a letter to General Nathanael Greene, that just one of them "would be equal to at least two regiments."[9]

The Press and the Founding Fathers

America's Founding Fathers, perhaps in part seeing its influence during the Revolution and what preceded it, knew the importance of having an independent press. They placed it as one of the new country's first freedoms in the Constitution's Bill of Rights in 1791. They knew that freedom to worship and to express were essential ingredients to a viable and healthy life and democracy. But this fairly new way to report the news of the day was more than a vehicle to express opinion; it was, the Founders knew, an important force within the emerging democracy they were trying to form and protect. The press would serve as additional checks and balances on government, hinting at it becoming an unofficial branch of government or the Fourth Estate.

The Founders saw its power even before the Constitution was drafted. During the Revolutionary War, Congress provided the Continental Army with a printer so it could pass information to the public. When the war was over and the Redcoats sailed back to Britain, newspapers continued to play an important role in educating readers about the happenings of government, including those printers who dared "publishing the Federalist and Antifederalist Papers, which provided a staging ground for the ideas that would form this country's Constitution."[10]

While printers and writers defended the colonies and their cause during the war, including their leader, General George Washington, some of them became cynical and later turned their favorable pens to writing scorn against Father George. As Holzer writes, a rocky relationship between journalism and the presidency has existed ever since, waning and waxing through all of the country's presidencies, starting with the first man to hold the office of president. This was especially apparent as Washington approached the end of his first term in office. In *The Presidents vs. The Press*, Holzer writes:

> Toward the end of Washington's first term, Americans, once relatively unified in the quest for independence, began splitting into warring political factions devoted to markedly different aspirations. Pro-Washington, pro–Alexander
> Hamilton Federalists pledged to strengthen the new national government,

regulate fiscal policy, and reestablish ties with Great Britain. The merging Democratic-Republicans, led by Secretary of State Thomas Jefferson and the father of the Constitution, James Madison, advocated smaller government and states' rights. Infatuated by the French Revolution, Jeffersonians favored America's mother country and embracing Enlightenment France. Federalists viewed recent upheavals there as a mobocratic threat to global stability, while populist Republicans regarded the French uprising as an inspirational outgrowth of America's successful revolt against England. Jeffersonians feared the imposition of a British-style class system here; Hamiltonians in turn dreaded a Jacobian-style reign of terror.

As the chasm widened, newspapers aligned with one or the other party ratcheted up their criticism of the respective opposition. In openly choosing sides, some editors abandoned original commitments to objectivity and embraced new roles as propagandists.[11]

The partisan press was born. George Washington—the first in war, first in peace, and first in the hearts of his countrymen—also was the first president to be both praised by the press and vilified in it.[12] It was a semblance of the journalism that would continue and only deepen as time marched on; it had, in effect, sprouted its wings and was now learning to fly.

As surefooted and commanding as Washington may have been on the battlefield, he was unsteady and thin-skinned when he read press reports unfavorable to his administration. He basked in the sunshine glow of praises but balked and belittled the negative stories. Of course, George Washington should not be faulted for these contrary sentiments. Almost anyone would feel much like he felt—including President Trump: happy when the news coverage is good and disgruntled when the coverage is bad. Washington, who had defended the press in his earlier days, begrudged it later in life, at one time even going so far as to say that the journals and newspapers of the day were useless. But these often were more heat-of-the-moment lapses than true convictions. Even after runabouts with bad press, he had subscribed to several papers and was often found sitting quietly in his home reading the latest editions.[13]

Thomas Jefferson, who became the country's third president and writer of the Declaration of Independence, was another one who adamantly defended the American press while, at times, still being scrutinized and scorned by it. After the favorable press soured, Jefferson was so disheartened by it that he once suggested that newspapers might consider dividing their content into four sections—or chapters, as he called them—including a chapter on what he perceived as lies—or what modern-day media critics might call "fake news."

"Perhaps an editor might begin a reformation in some such way as this," Jefferson wrote to John Norvell on June 11, 1807. "Divide his paper into 4 chapters, heading the 1st, Truths. 2d, Probabilities. 3d, Possibilities.

4th, Lies. The first chapter would be very short, as it would contain little more than authentic papers, and information from such sources as the editor would be willing to risk his own reputation for their truth. The 2d would contain what, from a mature consideration of all circumstances, his judgment should conclude to be probably true. This, however, should rather contain too little than too much. The 3d & 4th should be professedly for those readers who would rather have lies for their money than the blank paper they would occupy."[14]

Jefferson continued his rant, saying newspaper editors should forego "the demoralising practice of feeding the public mind habitually on slander," remarking that defamation of character had become such a part of newsprint "that a dish of tea in the morning or evening cannot be digested without this stimulant." He even suggested that in spite of the sensationalist topics, readers seemed to enjoy them and was, for so doing, part of the problem. "Even those who do not believe these abominations, still read them with complaisance to their auditors, and instead of the abhorrence & indignation which should fill a virtuous mind, betray a secret pleasure in the possibility that some may believe them, tho they do not themselves. It seems to escape them, that it is not he who prints, but he who pays for printing a slander, who is it's real author."[15]

In spite of these misgivings about news coverage, Jefferson, like Washington, remained true to his innermost convictions that an independent press would help the country retain its democratic values and virtues. Linda Barrett Osborne, in her informative book for young readers, *Guardians of Liberty*, explains it like this:

> The person the Founding Fathers feared most could abuse his or her power—and who needed to be watched closely—was the president. At the Constitutional Convention in 1787, the delegates hotly debated whether the country should have a president at all, and if so, how much power he should have. Charles Pinckney, a delegate from South Carolina, expressed the dilemma. He wanted a "vigorous Executive," but not one that could totally control "war & peace," which, he believed, "would render the Executive a monarchy, of the worst kind, to wit an elective one." In other words, even an elected president might assume the absolute powers of a king. In the end, the convention decided the United States should have one elected president, limited to his or her power by Congress and the Supreme Court. They also counted on a free press to keep an eye on the president.
>
> Because the way Americans feel about presidents and their politics varies widely, no president can count on only "good" press. So from the early days of our country, the amendment guarding press freedom put the president—regardless of his political party—and the press at odds with each other. If the news printed about the president was favorable, he liked the press. If it was negative or disapproving, he didn't. Most presidents have objected to news that does

not agree with them or shows them in a bad light. This was the situation when the United States was founded and it is the same today.[16]

As she also shares, it was Samuel Adams who said: "There is nothing so fretting and vexatious; nothing so justly TERRIBLE to tyrants … as a FREE PRESS."[17]

Other presidents became a target of press criticism, especially as more newspapers started operation, some publications leaning to the opposite side of the then-current administration. Presidents referred to these publications as the "opposition press." Yet all of them, at one time or another, have been both praised and pouted by the press. All presidents also have, at one time or another, and often more than once, been antagonistic to the news media. Joe Biden, for instance, responded negatively to a question by a CBS reporter when asked while contending for the White House in October 2020 what he thought of a report of his son Hunter Biden that appeared in the *New York Post*. "I know you'd ask it. I have no response. It's another smear campaign, right up your alley. Those are the questions you always ask."[18]

And yet presidents need the press, whether they want to admit it or not.

"The press surely helped bring down John Adams and Richard Nixon," writes Holzer. "It helped elevate Abraham Lincoln and Barack Obama, to name two, by emphasizing their inspiring personal stories. Yet the press has done little to inhibit Donald Trump, either because of his own mastery of nontraditional media, the establishment media's declining influence, a public inured to presidential misbehavior, or all of the above."[19] Presidents who come after the current administration and on down the line to the next president ad infinitum will be scrutinized and investigated and adored and shamed by the news media.

In many respects it is difficult to compare the press of today with the press of the founding era. Much has changed since the days of the moveable handpress, when it took days for news to travel across states let alone continents. Now news is delivered instantaneously, readily available to anyone with a smartphone 24 hours a day, minute by minute. And yet in today's changed environment some things have remained the same—journalism's importance and role as the Fourth Estate.

What form that news will take in the future is anyone's guess. What will not change is the obligation and impact of the press and the public's right to know—that is, of course, if press freedoms are still adored and defended in those upcoming years. As Holzer says, there is a "declining influence" with regard to big media, but that means local journalism's role in society is perhaps more important than it ever has been in the modern era's past.

The Proper Role of Government and the Press

What comes first, the chicken or the egg? The answer of government's founding is not a riddle: government was made for and by the people, not the other way around. Abraham Lincoln exemplified this during the now-famous Gettysburg Address in which he honored soldiers who had died, saying they gave the ultimate sacrifice so that "government of the people, by the people, for the people, shall not perish from the earth."

Think of those words for a moment. Soldiers fought so government of, by and for the people "shall not perish from the earth." The drastic outcome would be the same today if our democracy fails: it would perish not only from the United States but anywhere else the ensign of freedom has been held aloft. America is the bulwark and stalwart of democracy around the world, the staff and bright pinnacle of freedom everywhere, and its government is the vehicle of that democracy of, by and for the people.

Before Lincoln, Thomas Jefferson purportedly said: "When government fears the people, there is liberty. When people fear the government, there is tyranny." The proper role of government, in the simplest of terms, is to secure the rights and freedoms of its country's citizens. It is not to serve any one person, no matter who the president might be; it is to serve the country's citizens and of democracy itself.

Going back to the role of the Fourth Estate and the public's right to know, one of the ways democracy is best served is with a free, independent and aggressive press. If the press is doing its duty, it is holding accountable those in office while also defending the other rights of the Constitution, including the right to worship, speak, peaceably to assemble and petition the government—and doing all of these things without fear and intimidation by said government.

A Fifth Estate?

I remember attending a business college in 1993. One of the topics of class discussion was the World Wide Web, which was promised to revolutionize the globe and practically everything we did going forward. It would change our very lives, we were told. One segment of a class walked students through the means of accessing an internet page. "Type in www-dot before the name of the company or organization you wish to access," our teacher, in essence, instructed the students. "At the end of the name there is another dot, followed by either com, org, gov." It was, as you can see, a very basic introduction to a platform that would revolutionize the world and forever impact our daily lives. In the early 1990s people were still being introduced to the World Wide Web, as it was often referred, and its revolutionary status, and so an introduction to its accessibility was deemed essential. We learned of the great amount of information that could be easily accessed at our fingertips but also that it was a platform where many dark and devious sites existed.

Much has changed since then, including the technology to access the internet. Back then it was accessed through desktop computers with large, box-like monitors and by a telephone connection that would make funny, obnoxious noises whenever it tried to secure a connection. Access was slower, and sometimes those connections failed or would freeze while in use. The internet brought new convenience—such as the ability for students to access research tools and topics for papers and class assignments—but it also was frustrating in other ways, including the slow and noisy connections. Little by little—or sometimes by leaps and bounds, depending on how you look at it—things started to change. Before long, the past was clouded by the present; it seemed we always have had the internet with us. Especially it seems this way to those born since its advent, because they know not of the world before the triple-w (typing www is outdated in today's world of internet usage). Instead of heavy, boxy computer monitors, people now access the Net with their smartphones and tablets and slim-screened desktops. For those who grew up with the internet, it is difficult for them to imagine there was ever a time without it.

Where once people received their news strictly from newspaper, television and radio, now most people get their daily briefings through digital means, much of it through social media. But years after these platforms started, social media has remained a spontaneous and, except in rare circumstances, unvetted source of information—much of it *dis*information.

If indeed there is a fifth estate, it has not positioned itself responsibly. There is so much shared on social media that is not fact-checked or vetted, drawing people from their self-made silos into the foray of an already contentious society made even more unsure by the dross of fake news ever prevalent on its platforms. It is pertinent that the professional journalist remains ever-vigilant and stays at the top of her or his game by practicing the ethical standards of the profession and combats the elusive influence of a, right now, fake fifth estate.

A Country Without a Free Press

Through its fantastical fictional telling, *The Twilight Zone* and its five seasons tackled many of the challenges and fears of the 1960s, some which still might seem pertinent today, such as the episode about the Obsolete

Man. But we don't have to turn to fictional accounts to learn what happens to a country without a free and independent press.

In 2006 the Committee to Protect Journalists described North Korea as the most censored country in the world. It also listed nine other countries in its report, each whose news agencies were heavily controlled or influenced by the state. Those countries that allowed privately owned media outlets were still overseen by "regime loyalists." All of the news in North Korea, for instance, spins positivity, with media there saying the country "has never suffered famine or poverty, and citizens would willingly sacrifice themselves for their leader." As an example, the official Korean Central News Agency one time reported that Kim Jong il, the country's leader at the time, was "so beloved that after a deadly munitions train explosion in a populated area, people ran into buildings to save the ubiquitous portraits of the 'Dear Leader' before they rescued their own family members."[20]

As much as we all like positive news, the reality is that a press that is not willing to look at the hard truths, the sad misgivings of society, the shady or questionable goings-on of government officials is only a puppet press and not an independent press that can make positive change in the world. If people like Donald Trump and his "fans"[21] had their way, there would be no more *New York Times, Washington Post,* CNN or MSNBC, ad infinitum. Such a void would leave the country with officially sanctioned reporting, a continuous public relations spiel that only the current president wants citizens to know about.[22]

Talk about slanting the news! What bias! What a nightmare! That'd be something from a dictator's regime and not a democratic government—something that belongs only in shows like *The Twilight Zone.*

Celebrating Press Freedom

A day every year in May has been designated to celebrate the impact that journalism makes not only in the United States but across the globe. After a recommendation two years earlier, the United Nations General Assembly in 1993 declared May 3 as World Press Freedom Day to celebrate and promote the protection and safety of the press, discuss journalistic ethics, and to celebrate journalists who have died while reporting the news. On that day in 2021, while this book was being completed, I noticed many posts on social media that shared logos and memes about the day that honors journalists and journalism all over the world. The theme for the day that year was "Information as a Public Good."

Press freedom empowers news organizations to be able to investigate those in power, enables them to document facts, and allows the best information possible for the public good. The opposite happens when the press is censored.

"Journalism everywhere must be protected & be ethical & independent," the SPJ tweeted, one entry of many that I saw posted on social media that day to defend and honor reporters and their craft. Perhaps most stark for me was a cartoon by Ann Telnaes of *The Washington Post* which depicted a reporter standing to the left holding a microphone, her mouth stitched shut. In the middle was an equal sign and on the opposite side of that, on the right, was another figure depicted as being the public. Her eyes were closed.[23] If the media's mouth is shut, the public's eyes are closed.

In addressing the importance of journalism, President Joe Biden said on World Press Freedom Day in 2021 that "we celebrate the courage of truth-tellers who refuse to be intimidated, often at great personal risk, and we reaffirm the timeless and essential role journalism and a free media play in societies everywhere."

> Journalists uncover the truth, check the abuse of power, and demand transparency from those in power. They are indispensable to the functioning of democracy. Throughout the COVID-19 pandemic, journalists and media workers have been on the front lines to keep the public informed, at significant risk to their own health. And, at a time when the truth is increasingly under attack, our need for accurate, fact-based reporting, open public conversation, and accountability has never been greater.
>
> It is incumbent on all of us to counter these threats to a free and independent media, including physical risk and arbitrary detention.

Biden continued, saying that in 2020, according to findings by the Committee to Protect Journalists, "a record number of journalists were imprisoned globally. Online abuse and harassment of journalists, particularly women and journalists of color, continues to increase. Authoritarians are striving to undermine the free press, manipulate the truth, or spread disinformation even as a shrinking news industry is creating more and more 'news deserts,' areas without local media, around the world. These attacks are nothing less than a threat to democracies everywhere."

The United States must be different, as it has been over the course of its history. It must stay the course and continue to defend the rights of all people, including journalists' rights. As Biden concluded his statement, "Today, on World Press Freedom Day, we celebrate the fierce bravery of journalists everywhere. We recognize the integral role a free press plays in building prosperous, resilient and free societies. And we recommit to protecting and promoting free, independent, and diverse media around the world."[24]

Manuel de Dios Unanue, 1992
El Diario-La Prensa

When Cuban-born Manuel de Dios Unanue came to the U.S. with his family in 1973, he never imagined he'd be killed for doing the work of a journalist in, of all places, the one country on earth that, with its Constitution, vehemently protected journalists' right to report and publish. But when a man pulled a gun on him while inside a New York bar nearly 20 years later, on March 11, 1992, the 49-year-old man didn't have time to process that he was dead wrong. Within a matter of seconds, he was just dead—another journalist's life cut short because of the work he had been doing.

The tragedy proved all too bold that revenge crosses borders and oceans. Unanue, who devoted his efforts to uncover crime and conspiracy, was killed on orders from the highest-ranking members of the Colombian drug cartel for the stories he wrote about the crime organization.

Though more than 50 journalists had been killed in Colombia in the past decade, it appeared that the cartels' revenge had crossed to the United States.[25]

A good reporter knows and evaluates the risks he or she takes before embarking on a reporting quest, or they realize it once they have started the journey, but the revelations of those risks often do not change their course. That does not mean journalists should be careless, nor does it mean they have a death wish. Journalists should always make sure their own safety and the safety of their sources are paramount. There also is the complacent thinking that the dangers one has heard about befalling others would not befall them. But then it does, and the whole paradigm of the daily work routine is thrown for a loop.

And so is the cause of truth.

"Any murder is obviously a heinous crime, but when the victim is murdered not for revenge or out of passion but because he has reported on the truth as he has found it," Acting U.S. Attorney Mary Jo White was quoted in an article by the *Baltimore Sun*, "we all are very much the victims here."[26]

The Promised Land

Manuel de Dios Unanue, born in Cuba on January 4, 1943, immigrated to the U.S. with his family after fleeing their communist-ruled country in 1973. Cuba, a small country that sits just 90 miles from the Florida shorelines, was ruled by communist dictator Fidel Castro, who first served as prime minister and later its president. He had established the communist state after overthrowing the military dictatorship of Fulgencio Batista in 1950 and was a specter who haunted the West until he receded power when he handed it to his brother Raul Castro in 2008. During Castro's rule, many people went into exile in an effort to escape the oppressive government.

The Unanue family first migrated to Spain and Puerto Rico before coming to the United States. The family arrived in New York in 1973, and four years later Unanue became a working journalist, perhaps the perfect fit for someone of his character. He had seen dysfunction and oppression in his home country; it gave him a perspective and understanding of other people's plights. Journalism was perhaps the best way he could help facilitate change or in other ways do impactful, meaningful work. If the word of truth was indeed mightier than the sword, then Unanue would gladly take up arms in its defense. And so he did, writing forcefully against social injustices in his new country and against crime that affected his homeland.

He worked for a time at *El Diario-La Prensa* as a staff writer, but eventually he moved into the role of columnist, which, without the restrictions of a news reporter to remain objective, provided him the opportunity to better analyze issues important to him and criticize and call out those in authority. In 1984 he became the paper's chief editorial executive, a title he held for the next four years. His exit from the newsroom in 1989 was precipitated by critical coverage he had given of the city's mayor.

After his exit he could perhaps have found other paths to his next paycheck, but he had been bitten long before by the journalism bug. Once it bites, its infection only grows. Still wanting to effect change and call out corruption, he turned to other news mediums—talk radio and magazine publishing.

Exposing the Cartel

Unanue joined the field of broadcaster with a radio show called "What Others Try to Silence." By then he had narrowed his views, boldened his opinions, and seemed to be on a mission. He spoke against crime, often mentioning alleged drug dealers by name, something he continued to do with the two magazines he founded.[27] With print at his disposal once again, he also published photos of people in alleged criminal activities. It's not the sort of work that makes friends and influences people, though it did stir the ire of those whom he had broadcast and written about. Also, before he was fired from his previous job, he published a book in 1988 titled *The Secrets of the Medellin Cartel*, which further brought to light those who wished to remain in darkness. According to Rossana Rosado, city editor of the *El Diario–La Prensa*, "He was absolutely the most prominent American journalist to expose the cartels."[28]

The cartels didn't like what Unanue was writing and broadcasting, and members of the crime organization finally caught up with him on March 11, 1992. While relaxing at a restaurant in the Jackson Heights area of Queens, New York, a man with a hoodie walked up to him, brandishing a firearm, and shot the reporter twice, point-blank in the head. The gunman, later identified as 17-year-old Wilson Alejandro Mejia-Velez, said he received the hit order from John Mena, 24, who allegedly contracted the killing on behalf of the Cali cartel.[29]

In a report two months after the killing, a number of suspects had been arrested. "We now have in custody most of those directly responsible for this murder," Acting U.S. Attorney General Mary Jo White said at a press conference at the time. "It is believed the order for this murder came from the highest levels of the Cali cartel in Colombia."[30] She said it was believed that Unanue was killed because of his "vigorous reporting on the activities of the Cali cartel."[31]

As one writer expressed the sad episode in a column published in March 2018, some 16 years later, "It was the heyday of the Colombian drug cartels," whose influence extended to Unanue's community in New York and that having the courage to expose them had "sealed his fate."[32] The writer of the op-ed in the news publication *Al Dia*, Albor Ruis, further wrote how shameful it was that he did not see one story that year about Unanue or his journalistic work, this at a time when slain journalists and what they reported should have been more widely remembered. He said Unanue and his work have been "shamefully forgotten by those who, more than ever, should be following his example, expressing their admiration or, at least, paying their respect to his courage and sacrifice."[33] He also iterated something we all should remember: "His death was a grim reminder of how fragile freedom of the press is."[34]

Another writer intoned: "American democracy, and its cornerstone, the First Amendment to the Constitution, were affronted by Unanue's coward assassination in a New York restaurant, and it became a shameful memory for those who failed to protect the writer from violent death."[35]

4

The Public's Right to Know

When the public's right to know is threatened, and when the rights of free speech and free press are at risk, all of the other liberties we hold dear are endangered.—CHRISTOPHER DODD

The public's right to know is an important principle in any democratic society. It's a principle that, if honored, helps individuals and families make better decisions about the topics and issues that affect or are important to them. It is important for them to know about crime and safety issues in their community, for instance, about economic proposals that could potentially impact their own pocketbooks, and about the educational issues that affect their children. It is important for them to know business developments and employment situations, about travel dangers and restrictions, and about the happenings of their local government agencies. It is important for them to know about laws, policies, and what is happening at the nation's capital and with the country's president. It is important for them to know about the goings-on in the world, in relationships with other countries, and about conflict. In short order, the press plays a fundamental role in the public's effort to obtain proper information.

But beyond these surface items, sometimes it is important for citizens to know the deeper truths that those in power prefer to keep hidden. That doesn't mean intelligence secrets that, if publicly known, would jeopardize the country's safety or that of its allies, but it does mean the public has a right to know—as an example—that their president paid only $750 in income tax. Why? Because it holds those in power accountable, not to the press but to the American people.

The public's right to know is entwined with journalists' right to publish and broadcast without prior restraint or fear of reprisal. It means having access to facilities and material essential to communication and being able to distribute information without government interference acting under the law or by citizens acting in defiance of the law.[1]

To make clear, the First Amendment does not specifically mention the public's right to know, but some rights' protectors, including libel expert Harold Cross, have argued that "the language of the First Amendment is broad enough to embrace, if not require it."[2] In short, the press helps foster an engaged public. Part of that is by its multiple platforms and individual organizations (i.e., free and independent press outlets) that also facilitate public discussion.

Before he became vice president of the United States in the Donald Trump administration, Mike Pence spoke to journalists at the 2006 Freedom of Information Summit in Indianapolis, where he defended the public's right to know and advocated for the media shield law, which protects journalists against the compelled disclosure of their sources or the forcing of them to surrender their notes. He urged journalists to speak and write about the shield law not only "as a reporter's privilege" but "as the public's right to know."[3] He also said: "I think a free and independent press is the only check on government power in real time. And as a conservative who believes in limited government, I understand that the vitality of a free and independent press was precisely the reason for which our founders enshrined this principle in the Constitution."[4]

Too bad his boss set another example, but Trump has not been the only one. Other presidents, during their administrations, have made efforts to thwart journalist activity and, as such, hindered the public's right to know. The administration of President Barack Obama, for instance, named Fox News Reporter James Rosen as a co-conspirator in a leak about North Korea's nuclear program and targeted *New York Times* Reporter James Risen to reveal his confidential source during the leaked investigation of a former CIA officer.[5] Under President George W. Bush and while the war with Iraq was in full-swing mode, some journalists were censored in their reporting of the conflict. Others said the press had censored itself when it "bought the party line."[6]

These instances, just a few of many, beg the questions: What information does the public have a right to know? What information should be withheld from a curious citizenry? Not all information is important for public consumption. But where does one draw the line, and, ultimately, who draws it? Who is it that says what information is important for the public to have and what information is best kept from citizens? One study about editing gives the following example, which, in a different context, may be applied to the above questions:

> Perhaps you were warned by your parents to "think before you speak" when you wanted to direct everyone's attention to Aunt Mildred's bald spot during the family picnic. They meant that you should fit your comments to a sensitive situation. It was an early lesson in self-editing, involving an issue that even experienced editors debate when they grapple with the murky distinction between

public and private life in news coverage: Does this story's importance offset the negative effect its publication might have on the specific person involved? You posed the same question when you began to weight the momentous significance of Aunt Mildred's shining dome against consideration of her feelings and dignity. From an early age your internal editor begins to consider what kind of information is appropriate in a particular context and for a given audience.[7]

In some cases, journalists must "think before they publish." Is the information they are releasing for public consumption important to be known broadly? Are there things that should not be made publicly known? Luckily, journalists and editors have their own inside editor, their filter—or what otherwise is known as news judgment—to make these important decisions. That doesn't mean journalists haven't been wrong at times and their attempts backfired. But in other instances, journalism has ruled the day. From that exemplary teacher—*history*—whom we all can glean understanding, we learn that some information the government wanted hidden was information best served by revealing it to the public. Lucky for us, it was the journalists who made the call.

The Pentagon Papers

Remember the Pentagon Papers, that top-secret study about U.S. involvement in Vietnam that was leaked to the *New York Times* and *Washington Post*? U.S. Secretary of Defense Robert McNamara commissioned a study to look at the country's military and political involvement in Vietnam that spanned more than two decades, from the end of World War II to 1967 when McNamara commissioned the study. Officially called the "Report of the Office of the Secretary of Defense Vietnam Task Force," it became more popularly known as the Pentagon Papers when, in 1971, the *New York Times* published a damning series of articles based on their content. Among other things, the papers discussed how the United States had helped propel the conflict for its own benefit.

No wonder the papers were classified as top secret. The only problem was, one of the individuals who worked on the study, a military analyst named Daniel Ellsberg, believed the information the papers contained should be made known to the American citizens, many who had sent their sons to fight in the war. He believed the citizenry had a right to know about, among other things, how the government helped to overthrow and assassinate South Vietnamese President Ngo Dinh Diem in 1963 and how the report contradicted official government statements about the U.S. bombing in Vietnam. The report said the bombing had no significant impact on the enemy's will to fight, and yet the bombings continued.[8] If you haven't read the Pentagon Papers, it is an eye-opener even after all the years since their publication.

By 1971, Ellsberg, then working as a senior research associate at the Massachusetts Institute of Technology's Center for International Studies, had become disillusioned with the war and went to *New York Times* Reporter Neil Sheehan, who had further persuaded Ellsberg, saying "that Americans had a right to know how the government, especially the president, had made crucial decisions involving the war."[9] Ellsberg, his conscience nettling him, decided it was time the public learned what their country's leaders were doing and saying behind the scenes. He took the information—which he secretly copied piecemeal—to Sheehan. The *Washington Post* also had obtained information about the top-secret papers.

When the articles were published, the U.S. Department of Justice requested a restraining order against further publication of the material by the newspapers, saying publishing such information was detrimental to the country's national security. The legal fight wound up in the Supreme Court, which ultimately ruled 6–3 in favor of the newspapers and, in so doing, the people's right to know. It had ruled that the "government had to prove harm to national security, and that publication of the papers was justified under the First Amendment's protection of freedom of the press."[10]

Supreme Court Justice Potter Stewart wrote: "In the absence of the governmental checks and balances present in other areas of our national life, the only effective restraint upon executive policy and power in the areas of national defense and international affairs may lie in an enlightened citizenry—in an informed and critical public opinion which alone can here protect the values of democratic government."[11]

The Watergate Exposé

It was a Saturday morning, a time to sleep in, but then the phone rang, stirring a groggy Bob Woodward from his slumber. It was the city editor on the line, passing along an assignment to the reporter who had been at the *Washington Post* for only a few months. There had been a break-in during the night at the office of the Democratic National Committee, located in the Watergate complex in Washington, DC, and several people had been arrested.[12]

It was June 17, 1972, and the phone call altered the course of Woodward's career and that of his soon-to-be reporting partner Carl Bernstein. The two collaborated on a series of stories that changed their careers, yes, but also altered the course of their country. Through their reporting it was discovered that the burglars of the Watergate were connected to the reelection campaign of Richard Nixon, who had been in office since 1969.

When news of the Watergate story broke, however, it was unclear how far the conspiracy plunged. Who was behind it? How far into the Nixon administration did it go? These were questions that needed to be answered for the democratic safety of the country.

Thanks to the doggedness of Woodward and Bernstein and reporters from other news organizations, as well as their pugnacious editors and publishers, the truth—or at least more of it—would eventually be brought to light. While the administration tried to cover the crimes, the reporters uncovered them, tearing the blankets off the scandal and revealing that the conspiracy reached to the top levels of government, even to President Nixon himself.

What's more, Nixon had bugged his own office and secretly recorded his meetings and conversations that revealed his shenanigans, basically an act of self-incrimination. The court ruled that Nixon must release the tapes—a move that wouldn't have gone that far if not for the testimony of presidential assistant Alexander Butterfield and the journalism that followed.

Woodward and Bernstein's reporting helped bring an end to Nixon's presidency, an administration fraught with lies and scandal, causing him to resign from office on August 9, 1974—the first and only president ever to resign from office. It was, indeed, one of the greatest reporting ventures in American history.

This daring duo of reporters, of course, were not the only journalists on the Watergate beat. *The New York Times*, *The Los Angeles Times*, CBS News, and other news organizations aggressively covered the Watergate story, but it was the *Washington Post* reporters who persistently dug into the conspiracy, with Woodward finding a top FBI official who fed information to him in the dark recesses of a parking garage late at night. Known only as Deep Throat to hide his identity, Mark Felt in 2005 revealed it was he who was Woodward's secret source.[13] The *Post* won the Pulitzer Prize for public service and won the reporters a book contract. That book, titled *All the President's Men*, is a fine addition to the literature of modern journalism and reveals in great detail the reporter's journey from Woodward's morning phone call to Nixon's resignation. In an afterward to the book's 40th anniversary edition, the authors write, hinting at the shadow that has befallen other White House occupants:

> In the summer of 1974, it was neither the press nor the Democrats who rose up against Nixon, but the president's own Republican Party. On July 24, the supreme Court ruled 8–0 that Nixon would have to turn over the secret tapes demanded by the Watergate special prosecutor. ... Nixon had lost his moral authority as president. His secret tapes—and what they reveal—will probably be his most lasting legacy. On them, he is heard talking almost endlessly about what would be good for him, his place in history, and, above all, his grudges,

animosities, and schemes for revenge. The dog that never seems to bark is any discussion of what is good and necessary for the well-being of the nation. The Watergate that we wrote about in the *Washington Post* from 1972 to 1974 is not Watergate as we know it today. It was only a glimpse into something far worse. By the time he was forced to resign, Nixon had turned his White House, to a remarkable extent, into a criminal enterprise.[14]

In 1999 Woodward published a book, properly titled *Shadow*, that discusses how the legacy of Watergate continued to haunt succeeding administrations after Nixon. Perhaps it still does. The book *All the President's Men* also was made into a legacy movie by the same title.

Among the things that Watergate had taught the public at the time was to think more critically of their leaders, even if they are leaders they voted for and supported, and to not take everything at face value. Like any public relations firm, the presidency, no matter who occupies the White House, will put on its happy face and hide that which it doesn't want the people to know. The Supreme Court's ruling that Nixon must release his secret tapes, however, was another win for the public's right to know. If Woodward and Bernstein, and the other reporters who covered the scandal, had been hampered in their reporting, if the court had ruled against the press, the many truths we now know about Watergate might never have been known.

Spotlighting Sexual Abuse in the Catholic Church

Another example of strong journalism that exemplifies the public's right to know is the Spotlight series about sexual abuse in the Catholic Church. On January 6, 2002, the *Boston Globe* published a breakout article that told of sexual abuse in a Chicago parish.

"Since the mid–1990s, more than 130 people have come forward with horrific childhood tales about how former priest John J. Geoghan allegedly fondled or raped them during a three-decade spree through a half-dozen Greater Boston parishes."[15] The initial two-part series was followed by dozens more over the course of the next several months, each shedding further light on the abuse and the church's efforts to conceal the crimes, digging itself further into the shadow of sin.

The articles—a deep dive into the alleged abuses and biases—were the basis for the award-winning movie, *Spotlight*, released in theaters in late 2015 and which won that year's best motion picture award. While the movie brought to light on the big screen the unfolding drama that had impacted hundreds of lives, it was the journalistic investigations and articles that initially prompted change and more scrutiny of the parishes.

Exemplary Community Journalism

There's a dialogue exchange I like toward the end of the 2009 movie *State of Play*. The movie, which stars Russell Crowe, Ben Affleck, and Rachel McAdams, the latter who also played a reporter in the movie *Spotlight*, tells about a seasoned journalist and young digital reporter who investigate a suspicious murder whose victim was connected to a high-profile U.S. senator. Near the end of the movie, Affleck's character as the senator tells Crowe's character, the seasoned journalist, that he was dumbfounded at the reporter's smug attitude.

"You know, it's laughable," he tells Crowe, "your sense of your own self-worth."

Crowe's character responds: "Why is that, 'cause nobody reads the papers anymore, is that it? It's just another story, a couple of days ... and it's wrapping paper? You know, in the middle of all this gossip and speculation that permeates people's lives, I still think they know the difference between real news" and fake news. "And they're glad that someone cares enough to get things on the record and print the truth."

And so it is. The American news consumer, by and large, is not stupid. They know what is important and what is not. But there are a lot of voices out there right now, lots of information to absorb and a lot of different ways to access it. One of the best ways is through your community news organization, which people may generally trust more than the big media companies.

Not all news with impact reporting is known nationally. In fact, most of the journalism that impacts lives and livelihoods, and other aspects of life and community, is reported by the community newspaper or covered by the local TV station.

In December 2020, for instance, the *Grand Forks Herald* in Grand Forks, North Dakota, published a three-part video documentary that discussed the Canada border closure during the COVID-19 pandemic and how the restriction affected residents and the economy in northern Minnesota. During normal years the border state receives an economic boost by Canadians who travel to the North Star State, spending money on entrainment, food, and hotels. "People talk about the economic impact of being locked down for six weeks, whatever it was, a month," one source told the newspaper. "We have been locked down since March and here we are coming into November. There is no place like this that has been hit this hard."[16]

On March 8, 2021, *The Orange County Register* published an investigation about an 800 percent increase in fentanyl-related deaths over a four-year span in Riverside County, California, and how the county was pursuing murder charges against those believed responsible for the fatal overdoses. According to the report, a staggering increase in deaths was driving the aggressive crackdown on alleged drug distributors. Apparently, the trend was not only local; national trends showed how prosecutors nationwide were partnering with law enforcement to launch a frontline assault on drug suppliers.[17]

On May 2, 2021, *The Salt Lake Tribune* published a story about how the coronavirus pandemic had put a wedge in many people's religious faith because of the way some members of one church were treating those of differing political beliefs.[18] The article highlighted one individual who had lost his grandmother due to COVID-19, but some of his fellow members of The Church of Jesus Christ of Latter-day Saints, instead of comforting him, debated mask-wearing and the reality of the pandemic. Was it really COVID that killed his grandmother? some had contended with him. The man discerned that the people of his congregation who made such judgment calls were self-righteous folk who seemed to wear two faces, even if they didn't wear a mask. They talked Christlike service but didn't seem to exemplify it at such a dire time for him and the country. Unfortunately, such actions had impacted his own faith in his congregation's humanity.[19]

And there are many, many more instances of impactful community reporting. In fact, it happens every day.

There also are papers such as *The Laconia Daily Sun* in Laconia, New Hampshire, which publishes The Sunshine Project on its website, a project in which stories are compiled that "report on issues of civic discourse and social determinants of community health—and not just health in a medical sense," reads a description of the project. These types of projects are gems at news organizations, and kudos to those who do them, because it not only compiles important topics under one section, but they aim to promote community discussion.

As the description of The Sunshine Project further explains, it examines "medical issues as well as broad indicators of health, looking at data that may shed light on which communities and subgroups are doing well, and which are facing unique challenges, why, and what can be done."[20]

Of note, it is interesting to peruse reports from newspapers and other news organizations across the country to not only see what types of journalism are impacting communities but to gain a broader view, a larger snapshot, of society and news reporting taking place throughout the nation.

My suggestion: go outside your usual routine; take a few minutes from time to time to scan the stories from the various news outlets in different states. Now and then take a few minutes to find those special nuggets, those deeper dives of investigative journalism and not just today's headlines. Taken as a whole, it paints the country's picture and that of community journalism in new strokes of color.

Gotcha Journalism or Public Service

Every reporter, a new entrant into the newsroom or a seasoned pro, wants the big story. It would be a lie to say they want the big scoop only as a means to serve the public. Truth be told, there is a little self-aggrandizement in the work of a journalist. But in the face of gotcha journalism, the public is served.

The public has a right to know about the above grievances, and it is one of the main responsibilities and obligations of journalists to make sure that such disgraces, done in darkness and away from public view, are brought to light so the public is aware and informed. Such bringing to light may be of a safety or health concern; sometimes it might be so citizens know better about the shenanigans of business and government or about the dangers of sexual predators that lurk in churches.

What do you believe? Do you believe the public had a right to know the criminality of the U.S. government and its ties to Vietnam? Do you believe the public had a right to know about the Watergate cover-up and the deepening scandal by President Nixon? Do you believe the public had a right to know about the sex crimes of priests in Catholic parishes in the Greater Chicago area and in other affected regions across the country and around the globe? If you answered yes to the above questions, you answered in defense of journalism and its prime objective: defending the public's right to know. Your right to know!

Dona St. Plite, 1993
WKAT Radio

Two radio commentators, both Haitian-born but working in the United States, were gunned down in the early months of 1991. Their names were Jean Claude Olivier and Fritz Dor. Olivier was shot three times in the early morning hours of February 19 while leaving a nightclub that hosted a band he had promoted on the air. Dor was shot a month later, on March 15, outside the office where he worked. Both of the killings happened in Miami's Little Haiti community—two in a string of politically motivated killings in the early 1990s.

But Olivier and Dor were not the only media workers on the killers' hit list. More than two years later, on an October evening in 1993, another Haitian-born journalist and radio commentator in the U.S. named Dona St.

Plite would meet the same fate while attending a fundraiser for the family of his slain colleague Fritz Dor.

The shootings remain a strong testament to the dangers of political journalism and public commentating.

Taking Opinion to the Airwaves

The radio waves today are filled with political commentators and opinion heads. From my experience in radio, often the people behind the microphone act differently than they do when their audience is in-person with a close friend or family member. For some people, sitting behind a microphone (or when recording a podcast or video, perhaps) allows them to create a new persona, one they use as their public image. I always thought it a bit pretentious, and as a news reporter I had a tough time trying to grasp this reality of radio; the studio is not always what it seems to be portrayed on the airwaves. I have good friends in radio, including one who manages a conservative talk show. Hearing him on the AM band, listeners would think he is the strictest of conservatives, but off the air he lets down his guard and isn't quite the fanatic he seems to be on a certain radio dial. He and others who work the radio bands have even gone so far as to tell me that the persona on the air is part of their "show"—which brings more meaning to my mind about what the word "talk show" really means. A good host knows his audience, and my friend knows his audience well. He knows what triggers them, what topics get them fired up and make them want to call in to spout their own opinions or debate about an issue. This kind of dramatis personae makes people tune in, which in turn bumps up the ratings. It is, after all, a "show."

I don't believe I am giving any secrets away here, nor am I casting a bad light on my radio friends. They are remarkable individuals who have always treated me well and will do about anything to help someone in need, and through their kindness and professionalism I understand better today what it means to be on that side of media.

But it takes a certain type of person to be able to draw in large numbers of listeners—and keep them tuning in for more the next day. People do not necessarily tune in to radio for news, not like they did in the time before television, but they do turn to it for commentary and opinion. In doing so listeners hope to affirm their own political or social beliefs, for it is much easier to believe a certain ideology if a media celebrity is showboating the same opinion. It helps validate their own beliefs. My talk show friend does an exceptional job at this. He knows his audience, knows what they tune in for, which is not to hear an objective political stance. They want to hear the things they agree with—conservative philosophies that trash talk the other side of the political aisle.

This is not to say that all broadcasters put on a face or don the show robes to attract a listening audience, and I do not mean to imply that my talk-show friend is fake. He just understands the nature of the "show" in his line of work. Some commentators are very much themselves when they go on the air, deeply committed to what they share on a daily basis over the airwaves and streaming devices.

Dona St. Plite and his slain colleagues were a few of them.

Stirring the Ire of the Beast

The killing of St. Plite and his colleagues was another effort to silence free speech. The three had supported bringing a democratic leader back into power in their native Haiti, and the thugs who did not agree with them took extreme retribution measures.

At the time of his death, St. Plite worked for the radio station WKAT-AM in Miami, where he hosted a weekly program that aired from midnight to 6 a.m. on Fridays.[21] Among the topics he covered was promoting the return of Haiti's ousted president, the Rev. Jean-Bertrand Aristide, who was by then living in exile in the United States. Aristide had been Haiti's first democratically elected president in 1990, but his initial tenure didn't last long. At the time, he was in office only from February 1991 until he was ousted by Lt. Gen. Raoul Cedras, who led the country's de facto military government that September. The United States, in an attempt at defending democracy abroad, urged the Haitian government to reinstate Aristide, but it wasn't until 1994 that Cedras left the coup d'état and his country after being warned by the United Nations that force would be used if Aristide was not returned to power. Aristide returned that same year, but not before a number of people, including three on-air journalists, St. Plite among them, were killed in efforts that supported his election and return to power.[22]

"The day he was killed, St. Plite was on the air discussing the mounting political tension in Haiti," according to a report by the *Sun-Sentinel*. "He criticized the military for not rescinding power, as Haitian military leader Cedras and Aristide had agreed in a July 2 accord."[23] While outside the school where a fundraiser was being held for the family of Fritz Dor on the night of October 24, 1993, a man approached the radio journalist and shot him several times in the chest. Police at first didn't know what to make of the crime, thinking perhaps it had been a robbery gone bad.[24] But those who knew St. Plite and the other Haitian-born broadcasters suspected something more sinister. They said because of the journalists' high-profile support of Aristide that they were likely deliberately targeted by those who opposed the exiled president's return to power. "Some Haitian-American leaders warned that the Sunday night slaying was another sign that political violence in their homeland could be spreading to U.S. shores."[25]

Olivier, whose radio program for WLQY-AM was more music than talk, was the first of the three journalists to be assassinated on February 18, 1991. Among the discussions he broadcast on the air was calling for the boycott of Little Haiti businesses that did not support Aristide, who by this time had already been elected. While leaving a nightclub, a man approached and pointed a gun at the broadcaster, pulling the trigger several times.

Fritz Dor, the second journalist to be killed and who also worked for WLQY-AM, was shot outside his office on the night of March 15, 1991. Like Olivier, Dor shared his views on the airwaves, supporting the election of Aristide. Both radio personalities had received threats before their killings, according to press reports about the broadcasters.

In short order, Olivier and Dor supported the election of Aristide, who was overthrown in September 1991, several months after the radio personalities were killed, while St. Plite vied for his return to power. It was discovered that all three broadcasters appeared on a hit list with the names of 34 others who supported Aristide and his return to office.

Initially three men were arrested for the killing of St. Plite, but two were released after prosecutors said there was not enough evidence to convict them. Police found that the gun used to kill St. Plite was the same firearm used to kill the other two broadcasters in 1991. The gun was linked to a man by the name of Billy Alexander, 24, who was arrested and charged for both murders. A man named Moses Durosier was in the getaway cars used during those shootings, according to a report by the Associated Press. Durosier identified Alexander as the gunman and said he was paid $2,000 to kill Olivier.

Dangers of Gotcha Journalism

No journalist is safe from harassment and threats, but the severity of such pernicious acts may depend on the journalist's beat, story coverage, and whether he or she is perceived as taking sides. Or, in the case of radio journalist Bill Mason, it may depend on who you call out.

In 1949 Mason, who worked for KBKI in Alice, Texas, was getting out of his car when a bullet ended his life. The shooter was not your typical thug; it came from the gun of a deputy sheriff named Sam Smithwick, whom Mason had accused of owning a strip bar that fronted as a prostitution ring. "Smithwick jailed himself after the shooting Friday," according to a July 31, 1949, report by the *Sarasota Herald-Tribune*.[26]

A decade before St. Plite was killed, another radio host was gunned down for speaking out against white supremacists. Chicago-born Alan Berg came from Jewish stock and in the early 1980s lived and worked in Denver, Colorado, where he hosted a talk radio show. His liberal and sometimes combative style made him a popular radio icon in the area, but it also caught the attention of a fringe radical group who hated Blacks and Jews. It is reported that Berg had the knack of offending just about anyone, Christian and Jew, Black and white, gay and straight. He also had received a number of pernicious threats, including one from a Ku Klux Klan member who once came into his studio and threatened his life.[27]

Berg, not a trained journalist, was instead a lawyer who had harnessed the microphone, where he lambasted his enemies over the airwaves, much like some of today's commentators who also do not have a journalism background. However, he became a member of the media once he secured his spot at the radio station.

On June 18, 1984, Berg was shot 12 times when he stepped out of his car at his apartment after returning from having dinner with his ex-wife. Two men were arrested, but no one was ever convicted for the killing. In an interview with the *New York Times*, one person said the shooting of Berg was "an early signpost on the road that led to the 1995 Oklahoma City bombing," the shooting having served as "the opening shots of a truly revolutionary radical right."[28]

5

The Uncomfortable Press

Our liberty depends on the freedom of the press, and that cannot be limited without being lost. —THOMAS JEFFERSON

The Fourth Estate is one of the pillars of American democracy, but that doesn't mean it doesn't make mistakes. It is not a perfect press. If anything, it is an uncomfortable press—a term I use to describe an industry trying to rediscover its place in the modern world. While it has never been perfect, there have been fits and starts where it has stumbled over the past few years.

Journalists and the public must recognize both the strengths and weakness of the press, and then work together to help them become better. We must start with the mistakes so we may know where to improve.

This chapter discusses some of the common mistakes by journalists and newsrooms from my own perspective working in the field. This is not all of the press' mistakes, and perhaps you may think of others. Other chapters offer suggestions on what journalists and newsrooms may do to improve relationships with the public, as well as what the public's role and obligation is to the free press.

Recognizing the Uncomfortable

The word "uncomfortable," according to *Merriam-Webster*, means "causing discomfort or annoyance" or "feeling discomfort: uneasy." We perhaps all have felt discomfort at times, annoyed by certain situations or even have felt uneasy. Such feelings could be physical in nature, such as sitting in a chair that aggravates the back or lying on a sagging mattress, but they can also tickle the emotions. You may have felt uncomfortable being in a certain place or situation or at one time or another felt uneasiness about a request or new responsibility, wondering if you'd measure up to the tasks at hand, or maybe you have even been annoyed by a colleague's irritating habits.

It is part of the human experience to feel uncomfortable at times. I know I certainly have felt all of the above emotions during the course of my career—uncomfortable, annoyed, and uneasy while working as a journalist. One example, though embarrassing to me even now, is when I unintentionally used the wrong word in a story I wrote about off-road vehicles while working as the Outdoors editor of a daily newspaper. In describing the pulley that attaches to the front- or backend of a vehicle, I wrote the word "wench"—a loose woman or prostitute—instead of "winch," a hauling or lifting device.

It was a simple typo, but one I and/or my own editors nonetheless should have caught; instead, it escaped all of our eyes and caused me great embarrassment as I became the butt of community jokes for several days. It only grew worse when a local radio host read the mistake over the airwaves and jested about it on his program. I never heard the broadcast myself (I never knew my mistake and I were talked about on the airwaves until after the fact), but a week or so later I remember talking with a friend at church who said he had heard my name on the radio and that, yes, I was being pegged in tones I probably wouldn't appreciate. He even admitted to laughing about it.

That was my introduction to radio, but it wasn't one I have forgotten. I tried to take it in stride, but as reader comments kept flooding into my inbox, I began to get more annoyed. One reader mentioned how he wouldn't mind taking a wench with him on his outdoor excursions. I felt uneasy and uncomfortable and ashamed that I and my editors had failed to catch the error before the article went to press. If it had been caught, the jokes and embarrassment could have been prevented, my pride not so bruised. I chuckled about the misspelling whenever it was brought up by others, but inside I felt irritated and wanted to verbally express to the hecklers: "I take it you have never made a mistake, ever, while doing your job? How would you like it if something you did wrong, just a simple mistake that you later caught, became the butt of the community joke?" I never did express such sentiments, of course, but I wanted to say *something*. We ran a correction in the newspaper, but other than that I remained silent except for letting readers know it was just a typo, that I really did know the difference between winch and wench.

I learned something from the blunder, besides redoubling my efforts on my copyediting skills. I learned that people can be unforgiving of the news media; even the smallest mistakes can cause unintended consequences. I guess it shouldn't have surprised me, because the press has always been attacked for both real and alleged mistakes, simple misspellings of names to more egregious errors of fact. It makes no difference to a great many people what the mistake is, to them the news media should never get the story wrong.

They are right, of course. But there's only one problem with that idealistic assumption: journalists are human, too. What can and should we do, then? Answer: use our humanity. "It is time for journalists to trade in our hubris," Jeff Jarvis writes in the foreword to Craig Silverman's excellent book, *Regret the Error*, "and recapture our humanity and humility. And the best way to do that is simply to admit: We make mistakes."[1]

Learning Lessons

One of the aforementioned stumbles of the press in recent years happened in 2016. A number of news organizations made a big blunder during the presidential election that year, which caused many journalists and news outlets afterward to conduct some self-evaluation. The sensitive ones, those who learned something from their introspection, asked what could they have done different? Where could they improve so such a mistake doesn't happen again? It was a lesson in humility.

You know the story: Many news agencies predicted that Secretary of State Hillary Clinton would win the presidential election handily, defeating businessman Donald Trump at the polls. It would be a landslide, some of them said. By the end of election night, however, these same media enthusiasts were shaking their heads, wondering how they got the story wrong. It wasn't Hillary Clinton who had won the presidency but Donald Trump.

Kyle Pope, editor in chief and publisher of the *Columbia Journalism Review*, lamented the industry's oversight, noting, "it has done reporters no good to think of themselves as part of the establishment or a megaphone for the conventional wisdom," he surmised in an article published in the magazine the day after the election, November 9, 2016. "We need to embrace, even relish, our legacy as malcontents and troublemakers, people who are willing to say the thing that makes everyone else uncomfortable." Could that have meant in 2016 the media shouldn't have focused solely on the polls that Clinton would win but broaden their scope to include the conservative base who likely would vote for Trump? He stressed the importance of journalists interviewing people outside of the public relations circle, talking with people in rural communities and beyond. He also suggested the importance of diversifying newsrooms, not relying so much on public relations professionals' official agency comment but instead tapping a wider range of sources, and "de-emphasizing social media."[2]

Pope struck at the core of the problem and said journalists and newsrooms needed to shoulder responsibility and rethink how they do business. In a similar vein, it was something the *Boston Globe*'s Spotlight reporters learned during their investigations into the sexual abuse crimes of the Catholic Church.

One of the great things about the movie *Spotlight* is that it depicted the journalists' humility and humanity. Toward the end of the movie, it was revealed that a news tip about the sex crimes was passed to the city editor several years previously, when he was fairly new on the desk. The editor buried the story inside the paper and never demanded any follow-up until the investigative team, Spotlight, dove into the topic under the urging of a new managing editor. Without pushing blame, the editor who had goofed assumed responsibility for the oversight, letting the weight of the moment and the years past settle on his shoulders. It is what good journalists and news organizations do as part of humanity's schooling; they recognize and regret the error.

Whether the press learned much in four years' time, from the presidential election of 2016 to the election in 2020, is debatable. Many news outlets predicted, based upon nationwide polls, that Joe Biden would likely win the presidency in 2020, which he did. But it was no landslide, like many of them predicted. And what about the local community papers and stations? How did they fare in their election reporting? You know your community news organization better than I do, and so I'll let you answer that question.

The job of a journalist is to mitigate error as much as possible, not create it, and that, as Pope suggested, starts and ends with basic journalism tenets and, sometimes, thinking outside our cozy little boxes. Otherwise, the journalist—reporter, editor or publisher—puts him- or herself in a compromising and uncomfortable position. Let the press be uncomfortable for the right reasons, not the wrong ones.

Pride Precedes the Fall

I like movies that are impactful, because they are visual means to tell a good story but also teach valuable lessons. Movies too many to count have been made about journalists and their craft; some of the movies are wholly fictional, and others are based on real-life experiences. One of the classics is a film called *Ace in the Hole*, a 1951 noir drama starring Kirk Douglas. The protagonist in the film, played by Douglas, is cocky reporter Chuck Tatum, who has been fired from a number of newsrooms because he has a problem with telling the truth—never a good sign for someone working in a profession whose ethics revolve around truth-telling. We also learn that he was fired from one newsroom position because while working at that publication he was caught to have slept with the publisher's wife. (Also not a good thing for a reporter to do.)

It sounds a bit melodramatic, as many old movies are, but the film, directed by Billy Wilder, is a classic. Besides its entertainment appeal, it also is one that teaches a couple of valuable lessons about the role of journalists and the dire consequences when they fail to live up to the ethics of their profession.

Be warned, there are a few spoilers here:

Tatum, after convincing the publisher and editor of the *Albuquerque Sun-Bulletin* paper to hire him, is assigned to cover a fluff feature about a rattlesnake hunt in a distant town. He and the paper's photographer set off to cover the event, but Tatum is disappointed. He expresses his misgivings while on their journey. In short, he's stuck on himself, thinking if he finds a big story to cover instead of the rattlesnake shoot, he could get out of the rut—and the small town—in which he landed and make it back to a big city paper.

"You know this could be a pretty good story, Chuck," his photographer says. "Don't sell it short."

Tatum, a hat drawn over his eyes as he sits in the passenger seat in the convertible, responds: "Big deal. A thousand rattlers in the underbrush." And then he opens his eyes and shares a flamboyant idea. "Give me just fifty of them loose in Albuquerque. Like that leopard in Oklahoma City. The whole town in panic. Deserted streets. Barricaded houses. They're evacuating the children. Every man is armed. Fifty killers on the prowl. Fifty. One by one they start hunting them down. They get ten, twenty. It's building, they get forty; forty-five. They get forty-nine. Where's the last rattler? In the kindergarten? A church? In a crowded elevator? Where?"

To which Harvey replies: "I give up, where?"

"In my desk drawer, fan," Tatum says. "Stashed away, only nobody knows it, see? The story is good for another three days and when I'm big and ready we come out with a big extra: *Sun-Bulletin* snags number fifty!"

"Where do you get those ideas?" Harvey asks.

"Herbie, boy, how long'd you go to that school of journalism?"

"Three years."

"Three years down the drain," Tatum says. "Me, I didn't go to any college, but I know what makes a good story because before I ever worked on a paper I sold them on a street corner. You know the first thing I found out? Bad news sells best, because good news is no news."

While they continue on their way to their assignment, they stop for gas in a town called Escudero, so small that if a person blinked, they'd miss it. While there, they see emergency vehicles and others heading to a cliffside cave. A sign says it is 450-year-old cliff dwellings, and there is no admittance fee to see the centuries-old wonder. The two journalists, one with a camera and the other with a chip on his shoulder as big as Mount

Everest, decide to see what the commotion is all about. When they arrive at the scene, they find that a man has been trapped inside a collapsed cave, some 26 hours by then, where he was digging for artifacts. Tatum, playing the hero, berates a deputy, who is too afraid to enter the mine, and ventures into the cave himself. Inside, he talks with the trapped man, whose leg is stuck and injured, preventing him from freeing himself. Tatum takes a photograph of the man and tells him help is on the way. He returns from the mine and to a waiting crowd with news that the man will be able to be retrieved, but it would likely take several days. As the story unravels, he then forms a deal with the unscrupulous sheriff.

Later, while meeting in a diner, Tatum reassures the sheriff that if he plays along with his plan, he will help the lawman get reelected by making him out to be the hero of his stories; he promises to tell readers he, the sheriff, directed the rescue operation. "Here we have an ace in the hole," he tells the sheriff, but with one caveat: "Now here's the deal. The way things look there's going to be other newspapermen trying to horn in on this story; a lot of them. Maybe all the way from New York. This is my story, and I want to keep it mine. You're gonna hep me."

As the rescue operation drags on, and Tatum publishes his articles, more and more people flood to the town to see the drama unfold, spending money on all sorts of offerings, including an admittance fee to access what has turned into a public venue outside the cave and putting money in the town's coffers—or in the pocketbooks of the rascals running it.

The sad tale plays out: Tatum feeds hope and water to the trapped man, but while outside the collapsed mine, he feeds another story to the public. He instigates rescue efforts that take several days instead of a quicker, more efficient route into the mine. Tatum is using the man's tragedy—and prolonging his agony—to promote himself and his career ambitions, this while a distraught father prays for his son's speedy rescue. The public doesn't know Tatum's ill-conceived plan. He only hopes the trapped man will survive long enough for the planned rescue, days hence, giving him more time to capitalize on the story. The longer the exclusive story stays in his hands, the more fame and status he attains. Every newspaper worth its salt, he reasoned, will want him, and to get him they'd be willing to pay the big bucks.

As the story becomes more sensationalized, the crowd at the scene grows bigger. As such, the price of admission has bumped up incrementally from .25 cents to $1. A Ferris wheel has even been set up for the paying crowd. The showboating rescue operation has turned into a carnival.

Movie viewers know where the story is leading, and we often see moments of self-evaluation and compassion from Tatum, but these are fleeting moments until the irony of the story is played out to its raw conclusion. The trapped man dies, and the reporter loses his credibility and any possibility of working in the news business again. What to him could have been a glorious rebirth turns out to be a tale of woe and his own personal tragedy.

The movie didn't do well at the box office when it was first released, but *Ace in the Hole* has since been classified as one of the all-time greats. The film, sometimes overly melodramatized, is a nice journey back in time when movies had a different kind of atmosphere and mystique about them that is often lacking in today's theater films and streaming stories. Whether he meant to or not, Wilder, who produced several other movies involving journalists and newspapers, including *His Girl Friday*, allowed *Ace in the Hole* to become a teachable film about journalism and the public's response to it. One of the takeaways of the movie is that it exemplifies how the public can be manipulated by an unethical press. Is the public implicit in the sensationalism by feeding into the frenzy? Also, a question brought up for modern-day viewers is, if the press checks the facts of presidents and politicians, among others, who is fact-checking the press?

But the film also teaches by way of an extreme example the pitfalls of journalists who put themselves above the story, warns of the dangers of sensationalizing news at the expense of others' well-being, and, perhaps on a lesser scale, reveals that being too cocky is not one of the traits a journalist should have in his or her toolbox. It teaches that pride in all of its forms—exaggerated ego and cockiness—precedes the fall.

Did the American press come close to this during the 2016 election when they got the big story wrong? How did it fare during the 2020 election?

Common Mistakes

What are some media mistakes that you notice? Among the more common errors I have noticed in my profession—and some which I have made myself—include not having enough sources in stories, rushing too quickly to publish or broadcast, not verifying facts, and having short attention spans. Among the causes of error include shrinking newsrooms, placing more responsibility and demands on fewer journalists, and simple laziness.

Too few sources: I learned early in my career that a good, well-balanced story has multiple sources. At least three, one editor told me, and it's a good rule of thumb for the most basic of news stories. There are, of course, some exceptions when this rule doesn't seem to work at first glance. Some stories, such as business profiles, might seem to work with only one source, or a breaking or developing news story, when information is still being gathered but the news desk broadcasts or publishes basic information to alert the public. Often only one source is available at the time. The reporter can add to the story later with additional sources of information, when applicable, but in the 24-hour news cycle of our times it is important to get pertinent information to the public as quickly as possible. That doesn't leave a lot of room to get multiple sources in the first draft.

Reporting the basic five Ws—who, what, when, where and why—is always a good beginning, but follow-up can lead to additional sources and information. Outside of breaking news, all too often I have seen important stories with few instances of attribution. It is a mistake to not attribute a story, of course, but it also is unwise to not have enough attribution.

For a period of my career, I worked as a digital reporter for a radio group (yes, this was in spite of my previous and unwelcome introduction to radio as mentioned earlier) in which I posted a lot of breaking news items, such as pileups on the interstate, new guidelines or health warnings from the local health district, criminal and police activity or manhunts, et cetera. Often these stories were based on police scanner traffic or news releases sent by the agencies, and in an effort to get the word out as quickly as possible I would make brief phone calls or quickly edit the news release for style and post the developing story to the website. Depending on the type of news, these stories also would be shared over the airwaves as breaking news alerts. On later follow-up, however, there was almost always the means to come up with something deeper, to get additional sources, and to tell a fuller more complete story. That didn't always happen, of course. Sometimes there was no new information available, or law enforcement agencies were not releasing additional details, but when other sources could be tracked, it was a way to get a more rounded story without compromising a police investigation or journalistic integrity.

A story about a pileup on the interstate, for instance, when first reported had only the immediate details of what happened, where it happened and when it happened, plus any additional information about lane closures or emergency crews at the scene. Sometimes that was all we could get, but when follow-up and digging deeper were warranted, the story flushed out further details that drivers should know to lessen the same thing from happening again. A follow-up story on a health topic could involve interviews not only with the local district officials but, depending on the nature of the news, epidemiologists, local citizens, the police department or sheriff's office to see what role, if any, they play in the current crisis.

These are very basic examples, but they serve to highlight the importance of getting more sources into stories in an effort to deepen the perspective and news. Doing so not only makes better stories, but it provides better information to the public. I have seen too many one- and two-source news stories (and lamentably have contributed a fair number myself) that could have been better fleshed out with more attribution and, as such, have a greater impact on the audience. But then again, even two sources are better than only one.

Too quick to publish or broadcast: Police tried to detain a young man who allegedly had been outside of a local business brandishing a firearm on a day in June 2020 in St. Cloud, Minnesota. Law officers never fired their weapons, but during their effort to detain the man, the gun in the suspect's possession apparently went off and shot one of the law officers in the hand. If you were to read the report on social media, however, which many did after the incident, you would have thought that police had shot at least one Black man but maybe even two. In response to this false information, a crowd had formed outside the police station to protest.

"Properties nearby were damaged, as well as the police station, according to an editorial in the *Grand Forks Herald*. The next morning, the town's police chief was frustrated by the spread of misinformation, which he said was reckless and dangerous. 'This place could have been on fire because of a lie,' he said."[3]

This is a perfect example of real "fake news," misinformation that is spread by rumor, innuendo, misinterpretation, and downright lies. Social media was the culprit, which spread the disinformation that caused anger to flood the streets in front of the police station. Unfortunately, it was a scenario of being too quick to jump on what seemed like another sensational story in a summer of many; people used the social posts as their source instead of doing due diligence to vet the facts.

I have known journalists who also have jumped on alleged news rumors only to find out later they had been duped by their own quick response. Those kinds of mistakes make for an interesting hustle to get the story published, only to find out later it wasn't much of a story at all. As the editorial board of the *Grand Forks Herald* suggested after the St. Cloud incident: "Slow down, get important information from professional news sites and do what trained reporters do: Verify information before spreading it."[4] Good advice to journalists, too—do the work of a journalist and verify!

Sharing news without verifying first: In the push to be first, or not be left behind, news outlets sometimes share breaking news from other outlets, such as one news organization attributing another, saying in essence, "{name of TV station} is reporting that police are looking for a suspect in a hit and run that happened at noon today at the corner of." This seems to be a common practice among some organizations, not all, but the problem is if the attributed outlet winds up being wrong, the one who used that story as the basis for their own is doubly wrong. Depending on the nature and sensitivity of the story, this can cause extreme problems.

I remember at least a couple of instances while working in radio that the local television station had produced a story quicker than we got to it. One day, the general manager came to my office and asked if I had heard the news the local TV station had published on its website and if I had planned to post anything on it. I told her I was looking into it but would not post anything until I could verify some basic facts of the story. Even though the TV station and radio station had a relationship in which we could share each other's stories, we still operated independently and, depending on the story, I felt better if we could verify the facts of a breaking news story ourselves before posting.

Sometimes it caused us to be a little late but not always—often we were first, but it paid big dividends in the end. My decision to wait on the story the GM had asked me about was the right move: the TV story wound up having discrepancies in it. I couldn't help but feel a dash of pride that I had waited and gotten the facts straight instead of rushing to publish and broadcast. Independent verification is best, whenever possible—which, with few exceptions, is most of the time.

Media's short attention span: In the fast and frenzied profession of journalism, it is true that most of today's news will be forgotten by tomorrow's headlines. We see it happen all of the time; one day a big story tops the headlines, but by the next day the reports are flashing the next big story. This is not necessarily sensationalism; it is the business of news. Because news varies from day-to-day, so do the headlines and the topics of discussion. This is not a bad thing—it is what keeps journalists employed—but where the news might fall short is when important stories have been dropped and forgotten or paid little attention to after the next breaking news alert happens.

"With the rapid-fire changes in internet technology and social media, our society is barely coming to terms with the cataclysmic changes these phenomena are having on us," according to an article by *Psychology Today.* "It has affected our elections, our human interactions, and our societies dramatically—and, by its own nature, at such a pace that we have had no real time to reflect or analyze sufficiently on what is happening."[5] Something similar could be said of journalists, especially those in smaller organizations who have multiple stories to juggle and sometimes multiple beats. They jump from one news story to the next, each seemingly important as the first—until the next story breaks.

When possible, and depending on the story, it is good practice to follow up on or revisit stories to see their conclusion. These ventures can turn into more enterprising pieces and, at times, create leads to additional topics of reporting and discussion. In the same vein, it is sometimes a good idea to visit the news organization's archives to find stories from previous months or even years that might have value to revisit in the present. I have found a few good story leads this way.

Tunnel Vision: On the flip side of their short attention span is the media's tunnel vision when journalists find a story that attracts audiences, focusing on a certain topic while neglecting other topics that could make important headlines. The mainstream media is very good at this. One example is election night 2020—and every other election night. When it was determined that the race between Trump and Biden would be close and some states had not yet counted all of their ballots, instead of discussing what each candidate might do over the next four years or report on other news of the day, some of them kept repeating over and over again the path to victory for each candidate. This was nothing new, as it seems to happen every election night. What doesn't happen every election is the ballot count dragging on for consecutive days without declaring an official winner. What that meant for news viewers was they saw these same discussions on the networks and cable channels—over and over and over again until victory was declared by the Biden camp. The repetition was nauseating.

"Instead of analyzing results and discussing what a presidential victor might do in the next four years, the networks mostly kept to the same, vague formula: Numbers crunching, 'what ifs' and calls to relax and be patient."[6] Sometimes, in similar fashion, our local outlets do much the same thing. They stay on a story and hound its audiences to boredom with it.

Tunnel vision is merited at times, and election night is the big news of the day every fourth year in November, and so maybe it's not an egregious sin for the networks and cable channels to focus on it the way they do. But I have heard people complain about the front pages of some newspapers, wondering why they focus so much on certain topics or themes while neglecting other weightier matters in their community. Obviously, these decisions are part of an editor's or news producer's news judgment, but having audience engagement (discussed further in the next chapter) could help newsrooms to rethink and hone their news judgment so that tunnel vision, when appropriate, can be a boon and not a burden.

Not being the voice of the voiceless: "Giving voice to the voiceless is sometimes more a cliché than an ethical cornerstone of journalism," writes Steve Buttry in a 2016 article in the *Columbia Journalism Review.* "You can read through whole editions of most newspapers or magazines, or watch a full network or local newscast, without finding anything that would qualify."[7] News outlets of all varieties—not just newspapers—need to be better at getting varied community voices in their stories. We need to find those unique stories, often from minority groups or overlooked populations. When one starts looking at what those groups might be in one's own community, thinking outside the general box, it becomes quite the eye-opener. For instance, one might think of ethnic or gender groups, but what about religious groups and nonprofits' efforts in the community? What about senior populations and the medically compromised? The door of story opportunity swings much wider when one thinks outside the box.

The problem with bias: One of the more common complaints about journalists and the news is that they are biased, not objective, that they slant stories and share only the facts they want the public to know. Bias— the elephant in the room—is a heavy, oft-repeated topic and one that will be discussed more fully in the next chapter, but suffice now that there are different types of bias in the news media. Not all bias is bad, but some biases are egregious sins, such as the belligerent take-sides political biases that seem to haunt some newsrooms.[8]

Causes of Media Mistakes

There may be more mistakes made by the news media than there are *causes* for media mistakes, but for clarity and perspective I offer four causes here, though you may recognize others:

1. *Too many cooks in the kitchen:* When the internet was new, we heard time and again how it would change the news industry, affect newspapers, and revolutionize the market. It has done all of that and more. Today not only have newspapers and television stations adapted to the age of the internet, but the information landscape is now dotted with blogs, e-zines, newsletters, podcasts and websites that spread information in milliseconds. Even companies and municipalities have their own news sections, sometimes offering more than just the latest press release. And we have several brands of social media that give everyone a platform to share their opinions, their rants and raves, and to pass on links from their own favorite internet sources. On top of all of this we have the never-ending cycle of television and radio, cable news, and our long-standing community and national printed newspapers and magazines. There is so much information provided constantly to make any head spin in frenzy. This makes it tough for the consumer to decipher what news is most important and beneficial to them and adds confusion on what news to trust when there might be contrary reports from different sources. "The single biggest change in our public sphere

is that we now have an unimaginable excess of news and content, where once we had scarcity." And yet, William Davies in *The Guardian* writes, "the explosion of information available to us is making it harder, not easier, to achieve consensus on truth."[9] It also places additional stress on the journalist and their outlets. Not only are they trying to be first to get the news to their audiences, but they have a lot more news groups and alleged news groups to compete with, often fighting against many sources of disinformation. In the process, and in the big picture of this ceaseless battle, there are undoubtedly some casualties, mainly facts that fall by the wayside. Errors occur in this fast-paced world of the 24-hour news cycle that spins not only on broadcast reports but anymore at the daily newspaper office.

2. *Shrinking newsrooms:* Another problem with today's news media is that too many outlets continue to shrink. As they do, and more responsibilities are placed on fewer journalists' shoulders, the more likelihood there will be for mistakes to happen. Like news consumers, reporters can experience news fatigue, especially if they are the ones doing double-duty, sometimes off the clock, to keep up with stories and meet their ever-demanding deadlines. I have experienced this myself, at one time venting my frustration on social media, writing: "I've been feeling a bit overwhelmed with all of the projects on my plate. Been trying to sift through lots of notes and research and still have a number of interviews coming up. It's a good thing I like what I do, but I'm looking forward to a breather this weekend. Maybe." A colleague responded, "Me too. … We'll weather this storm and finally go out to dinner." I followed up with my progress a few days later, expressing on the same news feed: "Whew! Finished the last of my interviews for this week and so I am hoping to spend Friday writing. I have a couple of big projects partially done and several smaller ones I still need to work on." Some journalists, of course, thrive off the work overload and deadlines. It's always a rush, a natural high, working on a big project and finally seeing it get to print, or tackling a breaking news story, trying to beat the competition and sharing it with your audience. But it is not always an easy journey, and sometimes mistakes happen along the way, especially on tight deadlines as the journalist juggles multiple hats. As newsrooms continue to shrink, the hats that journalists wear will continue to increase, and, if safeguards are not put in place, so will the mistakes. Of course, there is a ceiling on how much a journalist can juggle, just as there is a ceiling on how much a newsroom can shrink before it becomes unproductive. At what point does producing content become irrelevant? There must be checks and balances in the newsroom that, among other things, help prevent journalists' news fatigue.

3. *Lack of training*: In today's media landscape, and with an industry that is being stretched and tried financially, as it has been for a long time, newsrooms often don't want to spend the money on hiring experienced reporters, especially for general assignment or beat coverage. These types of jobs often go to newbies in the field, recent graduates whose only newsroom experience may have been at the campus newspaper. These talented, young journalists need to break into the field somehow, and the crime beat or GA positions are good introductions for them into the real world of journalism—a world that is often much different than what is discussed or experienced in school. However, a problem is that often these young reporters go afield learning to navigate their own way in the real world, trying to apply principles they have learned in college to their chosen profession but finding that sometimes those items don't translate well in full-fledged newsrooms. For instance, something schools often do not teach aspiring journalists is that journalism is a business, and once in the newsroom there often are decisions made by the publisher or advertising director that, unfortunately, affect the approach of some news topics. Eager young journalists wanting to become the next Bob Woodward or Carl Bernstein sometimes are too ambitious for their own positions and fumble as they story-gather, sometimes appearing inexperienced instead of ambitious. Newsrooms need young journalists with fresh ideas and ambition, but they also need to make sure they train their news reporters in the ways of real-world journalism while encouraging the ethics these young reporters were taught in school. Nothing can replace experience. Offering a higher salary where appropriate to seasoned journalists is not only good business but has dividends for both journalists and news organizations. Also, we media types do a lot of talking about how important journalism is, but the pay scale doesn't often reflect those idealistic notions.

4. *Laziness:* Sad to say, but I have worked with lazy journalists over the course of my career, and there have been times when I have found myself not very motivated in the newsroom. News fatigue, the constant demands and deadlines, having your work constantly scrutinized by the public, and juggling multiple assignments and responsibilities have their impact. Not only can a journalist become physically exhausted, but, as previously mentioned, also mentally fatigued. At those times when I have felt that type of fatigue, the motivation doesn't just bounce back the next morning. Sometimes it does but not always. The more culpable laziness is when a reporter is careless in his or her duties, in their interviews, in their note-taking, on their research and writing, or just not being willing to go the extra mile to get the pertinent information

that would tell a better, more complete story. Laziness, I fear, is a transgression that haunts many newsrooms, for whatever reason, another one of which is not feeling appreciated. If a reporter doesn't feel like part of a team or that her or his editor doesn't care enough about them while noticing that other reporters get more attention, it could be a case of the first reporter feeling neglected and unappreciated. Such feelings, as with any job, can cause employees to hold back and not put their best effort forward. In the end, it amounts to the same thing: laziness.

Media as Business and the Loss of Credibility

A newsroom in which I once worked had a wall that divided the advertising department from the editorial department. It not only provided a conducive working environment, where ad reps could focus on sales and journalists could concentrate on what they do best, but also served as a very real reminder that advertising and the news should be separated. That doesn't lessen another reality—that the business of news is just that, a business. Sometimes ad revenue does affect story coverage—though the journalist will tell you it never should.

Aspiring journalists learn about the great exposés in American history by stunt journalists or the in-depth, dogged reporting of yesterday's great investigative reporters, and they want to make the same impact in their own professions. They learn about journalism's ideals and virtues and what it means to be an objective and ethical reporter, not being influenced by bribes or businesses or the bias of public relations. But when they get into the real world of news reporting, they learn something else not always mentioned in school, and decisions by the executives often reflect this reality, causing the new reporter to finally see the real world of the news business—that it is indeed a business, like any other. But *unlike* any other.

Mistakes, especially those that are not acknowledged and corrected, can cause a news organization and its journalists to lose credibility with the public. Being perceived as biased and repeating the same mistakes time and again will do the same. It is human nature to make mistakes, to err, to have an opinion, but it also shows journalism's humanity when those mistakes are acknowledged and corrected and efforts are made to improve so that the possibility of making the same mistakes again is lessened. Journalists and their organizations—because journalism is a business that relies on advertising—cannot afford to make mistakes without regretting the error, a topic that will be further discussed in the next chapter.

James Edwin Richards, 2000
Neighborhood News

James Edwin Richards, a community anti-crime activist and reporter, sought to better his community by publishing a weekly online newsletter called the *Neighborhood News*. In the weekly newsletter, which he sent to subscribers via email, he shared information about community events and projects of the Oakwood section of Venice, California, where he lived and worked. He also published stories about local crime. It was the latter that targeted him for assassination.

His journey to journalism didn't take the usual steps, coming to the profession in a self-proclaimed fashion. And yet once he was there, he put his whole heart and mind into the effort and, as is seen at the end of his life, impacted the community in which he lived and worked.

Richards was born in 1945 in Dayton, Ohio, and attended Ohio State University but later migrated to California where he earned a master's degree in business from the University of California–Berkeley.[10] He was a businessman for much of his career, dabbling in work as a house painter, property manager and real estate agent before turning to citizen journalism.[11] Why he made the switch is anyone's guess—a new business opportunity, perhaps, but most likely it also was because he wanted to effect change. Whatever the reason, he took to his new vocation seriously, diving into journalism with a no-holds-barred attitude of reporting the events and issues of his community, a 12-square block of the Oakwood section of Venice. Like a good community reporter, he published the positive happenings of the neighborhood, such as beautification projects and fundraisers, but he also published stories about the darker side of the community.

Oakwood was known for its high crime rate, and Richards published the local police blotter, everything from petty theft to hard crime. He listened to the police scanner, sometimes sleeping with it near him, and because he lived in the same community, he was often the first to arrive at local crime scenes.[12] Besides publishing his weekly newsletter, Richards also served on the local community police advisory board and was the block captain for the Model Neighborhood Program.[13] Because of his activism, Richards was deemed a controversial figure in his neighborhood, someone who video-recorded criminals and their drug dealings. He'd listened to the police scanner faithfully and was often at crime scenes before authorities showed up.[14]

His work brought darkness to light, but it also brought something else out of the darkness: the ire of those whom he wrote about and exposed. The risks didn't seem to deter his ambition or his cause. "Mr. Richards had received threats from local gang members and his property was often vandalized prior to his murder," according to a news statement by the Los Angeles Police Department. "However, these threats never dissuaded Richards in his efforts to improve the Venice neighborhood."[15]

Ultimately, his work cost him his life. In the early morning hours of October 18, 2000, at least a couple of hours before the sun arose on the West Coast, Richards was already tackling the day with a workout at an all-night gym. When he returned to his home at a little after 4 a.m., two men were waiting for him outside. One of them pulled a gun on Richards—and then the man pulled the trigger, shooting the journalist several times in the very community he sought to improve through his reporting and publishing efforts. Richards died at the age of 55 from multiple gunshot wounds.

Investigations

After his death it was apparent to many community members that Richards had deliberately been targeted for his reporting efforts. It seemed to be a "straightforward assassination," City Councilwoman Ruth Galanter alleged in an ABC News report, noting that for some time it had been "a morbid joke in the neighborhood that Jim had better be careful or he was going to get shot."[16] She said the killing was "a heinous act meant to intimidate the community and threaten residents into staying quiet in the face of a criminal takeover of their community by gang members and drug dealers."[17]

Not having any leads, the Los Angeles City Council proposed a $25,000 reward for information that led to the arrest of those who committed the murder. During the course of the nine-month investigation, detectives found that a number of individuals were involved in what police described as "a violent pattern of cocaine distribution in Oakwood and other parts of the United States."[18] The investigation culminated in the U.S. Attorney's Office indictment of 24 individuals for conspiracy to distribute cocaine. "The indictment specified the murder of James Richards and the attempted murder of a male black resident of Oakwood, as overt acts in their continuing criminal enterprise," police said.

The Journalist as Activist

Richards's story brings up important questions about what role journalists should play in their communities. Should they be activists or be objective bystanders, even when recognizing wrongdoing in their neighborhoods? Should they speak up or remain silent? Should they pass information to colleagues so there doesn't appear a conflict of interest, or should they confront the issues themselves?

Richards obviously didn't harbor any qualms with being both activist and reporter, even when his life and property were threatened. In hindsight, should he have backed off when the threats started? Or did he do the right thing, even though it cost him his life, by continuing to publish the discrepancies and transgressions of his community so that other people became aware of their neighborhood happenings? Was he wrong for holding criminals accountable, even bringing their names to light by his published articles and photos? Should journalists be activists or merely serve as eyewitnesses?

These are questions that may find pat answers among some, but the deeper answers are harder to assimilate. Are the life and safety of the journalist paramount, for instance, or is there a larger purpose to be served by doing journalism in the face of life-threatening situations? The obvious answer is yes, the life and safety of the journalist are paramount. But much like others who put themselves in harm's way, many journalists risk life and limb to tell the stories they hope will impact their communities and country. They know the risks, sometimes receiving threats like Richards did. Sometimes the impact of their reporting, unfortunately, isn't recognized until the journalist has paid the ultimate sacrifice.

While many might say they want journalists to report only the facts, basically to be scribblers and not news analysts, it's more of an "appealing idea … that doesn't always work," writes Margaret Sullivan, media columnist for the *Washington Post*. "Every piece of reporting—written or spoken, told in text or in images—is the product of choices."[19] In Richards's case, he purposefully chose to focus his beat on crime and publishing reports and opinions about it in an effort to bring awareness. Awareness, if acted upon, makes change possible—and change can turn the tide of history.

Most journalists likely do not set out to be activists. Even beat reporters, by and large, try to bring balance to their reports. As such, it reposes the question: What is a journalist supposed to be? It is a question perhaps best answered by the reporter.

Richards was reporter and activist—a role that some onlookers at the scene of the crime apparently didn't like. Some were overheard to allegedly have said they were glad he was dead because they felt he had overstepped his bounds.[20] And what bounds, exactly, did he overstep?

Activist, reporter—in the end, he also became martyr.

"The assassination of Jim Richards was a brutal, cold-blooded act that terrorized our community," Councilwoman Ruth Galanter said in the

LAPD news release. "His murder was meant to silence those who defend their neighborhoods and stand up against gangs, drugs and crime. These arrests demonstrate that we will go to any lengths to see justice served and to remove the scourge of violent crime."

In 2008 the Venice Neighborhood Council voted unanimously to name October 18 as Jim Richards Day in Venice.[21] "By creating a day of remembrance, residents of both Venice and Los Angeles could be spurred on to join people who work for the good of their communities," Council President Mike Newhouse wrote in a letter to a councilmember dated November 2, 2008. "As Ruth Galanter said at the time, 'Jim was a brave and dedicated man. The City and the community owe a debt of gratitude to him. Those who believe they can intimidate this community have sorely underestimated the good people of Oakwood.'"[22]

6

Disinformation,
the Public and the News

In a world where everyone is a publisher, no one is an editor.
And that is the danger that we face today.—SCOTT PELLEY

A question asked by contemplative and observable minds for centuries has been, what is truth? It was this very question that Pontius Pilate asked of Jesus, when the Messiah stood before him donned in purple robes.[1] The answer to the age-old question isn't always an easy one to find, apparently even for some when the embodiment of truth stands before them. The challenge of the quest hasn't changed much over the centuries. Finding truth in our day also is not always an easy task, either in most disciplines or in many aspects of life and existence. The journey to uncover truth is sometimes a long and arduous one, but if the person is persistent and sincere enough in the quest, it is only a matter of time before truth prevails. Often it is the journey that provides the great teaching moments of this worthwhile pursuit; often, the discovery of truth is found in the journey itself.

Journalism, the act of gathering and disseminating news, is a quest to find truth. That journey seems longer these days, the obstacles more challenging. Those challenges to truth-finding are faced not only by the journalist but the consumer of news.

Let's be honest. It is tough to be a news consumer these days. There is so much information at our disposal instantaneously—24 hours a day, seven days a week, month after month—from a variety of mediums and sources that if our brains had a ceiling on the amount of data they could hold they would have maxed out long ago. There are times when we might literally feel as if we're in a state of information overload. Not only is there a hyper-massive amount of information that we're consuming on a daily basis, but, conscientiously or not, our instincts are trying to sift through what is important and what is not.

One of the drives of our inner news-gathering center, again

conscientiously or not, is that we want information to commove. It is one of the reasons there is "news" in the first place and why we seek it. If it does not appeal to our senses, we might toss those items aside or scroll past them on our social media feeds. Once we have gone through the sifting process and found those items that have either agitated or stimulated us, we're then often confronted with various angles or opinions about the topic.

Whom do we believe? Which report or analysis is correct? The problem is compounded in the no-holds-barred world of digital and social media, in which everyone with a cellphone is now their own reporter and columnist, each spewing their own assumptions and values.

And yet the challenge still goes deeper.

Today there is a pernicious battle to dissuade and belittle truth, to make facts seem irrelevant. Facts, the journalist's bread and butter, have been attacked with the illicit notion that there are "alternative facts," which are not facts at all but falsehoods.[2] The pursuit of truth does not deal in an alternative reality. Truth, including facts, exists in the real world.

Alternative facts are disinformation labeled in a politicized way to seem less culpable. It is but only one tool of the disinformation campaign meant, at least in part, to discredit legitimate news stories and journalists. Unfortunately, the spread of alternative facts—falsehoods disguised as facts—has caused many casualties, but the martyr most mourned is truth itself. Sadly, even some who work in the news media have stained their own hands with the sin of false or misleading information.

Where does this leave the honest truth seeker, which is, I believe, the majority of news consumers? We all want to get to the bottom of stories and know what really happened. We all want to know the facts—and in a larger context, the truth—of what is being reported. But how can someone know what report to believe and what they should be weary of?

It's a good question but one without an easy answer. There are, however, a few things that might help that I have learned over the course of my career in the news business and being a lifelong consumer of news.

One: Is the news report coming from a legitimate and reputable news organization? It is much easier to believe reporting if it is done by a news outlet with a history of fair and reputable reporting. When judging what is reputable, some things to consider are: What is the track record of the organization, be that broadcast, digital or publication? Do they tend to sensationalize stories and headlines or keep reporting fair to the news consumer? What kind of images do they use to accompany the stories? Do the images complement the story or do they sensationalize it? Does the outlet offer audience engagement? Also, since no news organization is infallible, no matter how reputable, something else to consider is does it have a history of admitting and correcting errors when they have been found? "Regret the error" is a reputable effort on any news organization's part.

Two: Is the report from a journalist in the field or from an opinion editor or columnist? There is a difference between a news article and a column, and yet it seems there are plenty of consumers who seem to get the two confused. Also, once again, consider the author's reputation and track record. The same is true from your social sites. Who is sharing the link? Where is it coming from, and what is the perceived effort in sharing it? Is it meant to sway or only to inform?

Three: Can the article or broadcast be weighed by reports from other legitimate and reputable sources? Official news agencies that have the same or similar story help validate what is being reported. In other words, what is the consensus from other reporting done on the same topic? Journalists are always trying to beat the competition by being first on a story or having an exclusive, but usually if the news is important enough for an exclusive, there will be follow up from other organizations who do their own vetting and reporting. If not, again look at the reputation and legacy of the journalist and news organization doing the reporting. Be wary of those that seem not to do their due diligence to vet the facts.

Four: Use your own inner editor to determine which report is likely to be more accurate, taking into account the other reporting done on the topic. And, as you want from your reporter, be objective yourself, willing to accept the revealed facts even if they lie outside of your own first assumptions or beliefs. That doesn't man your beliefs automatically change, but it means the news consumer should be open to accepting other possibilities as reported from reputable and verified sources.

The latter is perhaps the most difficult because we all want to be right and stay true to our long-standing impressions and convictions. But if we're not willing to allow ourselves an open mind, and to engage open and fair dialogue, it closes opportunities for us to show empathy for those who share differing points of view. Everyone believes the way they do, be that religious, political or how they view the news media, for a reason. Your view may very well be the closest inclination to truth about a given topic, but if it's not, wouldn't you want to know? We don't want to nail truth to the cross because we were overly confident in our stance that we failed to open our minds to the revealed facts.

A Conversation About Bias

The disinformation campaign is a real and direct attack on truth. The battle against disinformation is being waged by both the press and the public. On one hand is the never-ending flow of news reports and on the other a weary public that at least partially believes whatever they are told by the press is inaccurate, that it is "fake news." That makes the journalist's job tougher and the truth harder to recognize. On those same hands is a press trying to combat disinformation spewed from many corners, including some instances from the White House, and there is the public that seems to believe only what it wants to believe as long as it conforms and strengthens their own social and political beliefs. Saddest of all, perhaps, is that some media, instead of trying to combat falsehood, add to it by their own biased reporting and analysis. This is more prevalently seen among on-air commentators—commonly referred to as "talking heads"—and opinion writers.[3]

We've already discussed some of the faults of the press in a previous chapter, but what about the public's biases and its disinterest to be fair and balanced? Don't news consumers have an obligation to stop criticizing everything from legitimate news organizations and start questioning their own biases? News consumers share some of the blame for the predicament we are in today. There are problems in the press—highlighted by their critics and media analysts ad infinitum—but there perhaps are even bigger problems with the public and its "perceptions" of the press.

Often those who distrust the news media believe journalistic institutions are controlled by liberals with nefarious schemes to promote their own agenda. A conversation with a reporter and a conservative news consumer might go something like this, with no end to the debate in sight:

JOURNALIST: You should put a little more trust in the news media.

PUBLIC: Why? The media is biased and cannot be trusted.

JOURNALIST: Because journalists vet stories, uncover the facts, and report the truth. We are the messenger, not the message.

PUBLIC: There might have been instances of truth-telling in the past, but today's journalism is left-wing propaganda. It only reports what it wants the public to know.

JOURNALIST: No, that's not correct. It is true that journalists are trained to be open-minded, to look at stories from both sides of the aisle. A lot of journalists have conservative values, but we have to be open-minded and fair. A good journalist doesn't let his or her bias show.[4]

PUBLIC: That's funny. Because from what I see and read, it seems to me there is plenty of bias in today's news media. Just turn on the TV or pick up one of the big papers. It's pretty easy to notice. What happened to objective news reporting?

JOURNALIST: You're right, there is some bias in media, especially from the talking heads and opinion writers. But that's their job. An opinion writer is not the same as a reporter, just like a column is not the same as a news article. A reporter's job, those in the field and doing the legwork, are, for the most part from my experience working with these journalists, objective in their reporting.

Public: I doubt that. I've seen correspondents during televised news conferences at the White House when Trump was in office who seemed very much intent on attacking the president, setting him up with a trick question.

Journalist: A reporter's job has always been to question those in power and hold them accountable. It's one of the fundamental privileges and obligations of the Fourth Estate. Don't you believe the president should be held accountable? Is it not you being biased for not wanting the questions asked?

Public: What do you mean? I'm not biased. It's pretty easy to see how the press attacks one president but not another. They've been very lenient on Biden compared to how they were with Trump. Everything he seemed to do was scrutinized and assaulted. And besides, I'm not a journalist. I have the right to be biased if I want. You, as a journalist, should be objective and fair. Journalists should not be biased.

Journalist: We all are human, and that means we all have our biases. But I agree with you; a good journalist doesn't let her or his bias show. I know plenty of good journalists, and I try to be one of them. But let me ask you this: If a newspaper published an article based on records it obtained and eyewitness sources about a president's misdeeds, even if it were a president you supported and there was little to nothing to discredit the report, would you believe it?

Public: It depends.

Journalist: On what?

Public: On which newspaper it came from.

Journalist: Let's say the *New York Times* or *Washington Post*?

Public: Probably not. They are two of the most liberal papers out there. They are not balanced or fair.

Journalist: But you're not being objective if you're not even willing to consider the report might be true.

Public: I don't have to be objective. If the president denied the report, I'd believe him over one of those liberal newspapers.

Journalist: Why is that? The president, summoning his defense, would just be trying to cover his misdeeds by in turn verbally attacking the press, saying the report was fake news to make the real news seem less relevant than what it is.

Public: But he's the president of the United States, and I'd believe him over the liberal news media.

Journalist: What if the same report was made about a president who sat on the opposite side of the political aisle, one you did not support?

Public: Well, I guess I'd have to look at the report. If the misdeed happened from a liberal president, I wouldn't be surprised. It probably really did happen. But why would journalists report that? They're in bed with the liberals.

Though fictional, the above conversation is not hyperbole. It is a composite of conversations I have had with news consumers, some of them with friends and acquaintances. It seems to be a no-win situation: the legitimate press informing the public about pertinent facts and much of the public believing that what is reported is fake and made up or at the very least that they are provided only selected facts by the news media and not the big picture facts. Is this true? Yes, to some extent, but not all of the time and not by all media organizations. An investigative news report by the *New York Times*, for instance, told how President Donald Trump paid only $750 in U.S. income tax for the years 2016 and 2017, used questionable tactics to lower his tax bill, and paid no income taxes in ten of the then past 15 years.[5] It revealed that Trump also had encountered a series of financial loses, including $47.4 million in 2018.

The president quickly came out to discredit the report, calling it fake by the "failing *New York Times*." In later interviews with media outlets, the president did not deny the facts of the report, only said that he, as a businessman, had a large portfolio that made him "under leveraged."

"The Fake News Media, just like Election time 2016, is bringing up my Taxes & all sorts of other nonsense with illegally obtained information & only bad intent," Trump tweeted after the bombshell reporting by the *Times*. "I paid many millions of dollars in taxes but was entitled, like everyone else, to depreciation & tax credits. Also, if you look at the extraordinary assets owned by me, which the Fake News hasn't, I am extremely under leveraged—I have very little debt compared to the value of assets."

The facts stood on their own merit and, as uncovered by the *Times*, revealed that Trump paid much less than the average citizen. "Roughly half of Americans pay no income taxes, primarily because of how low their incomes are," the Associated Press reported in a follow-up piece. "But IRS figures indicate that the average tax filer paid roughly $12,200 in 2017, about 16 times more than what the president paid."[6] The *Times* said it obtained the tax return data over a period of two decades.

And yet many of Trump's supporters, instead of it being an eye-opener for them about the shrouded shenanigans of the president, jumped on his bandwagon, taking to social media in his defense and calling absurdity to the "fake news media."

The great Bob Woodward said journalism is about gleaning the "best obtainable version of the truth." We start by obtaining facts. But in today's politically and socially volatile world, the journalistic end result of that task—the published and broadcast news reports—has become, to a great many people, irrelevant or murky at best. Truth is the martyr, disinformation the slayer.

For those who seek facts—which will lead to a bigger picture of the truth—how does the news consumer know what one is reading and hearing and watching is correct? It is not as complicated as it seems (see suggestions early in this chapter). What is the bigger challenge is changing the mind-set, developing a little more trust in our institutions, and becoming more objective news consumers. But first there are two things we must better understand: the proper and fundamental role of journalism and the attack on journalism through a deliberate and divisive disinformation campaign. The latter will be discussed first.

Fake News and the Disinformation Campaign

"The lowest form of popular culture—lack of information, misinformation, disinformation, and a contempt for the truth or the reality of most people's lives—has overrun real journalism," said one of the country's great reporters, Carl Bernstein. "Today, ordinary Americans are being stuffed with garbage."[7]

That's tough for anyone to hear, journalist and news consumer alike. The honest journalist views the disinformation campaign as an assault on the profession, while the news consumer views it as an attack on their own senses and sensibilities. News consumers—of which journalists also are a part—are not stupid. But it's tough these days with so many contrary voices and viewpoints to sometimes tell the difference between real news and fake news, especially when that which is real is called fake.

The challenge is perhaps not new, but it has become more challenging with that now-popular chant—"fake news"—ringing out whenever someone doesn't like a legitimate news report about a person or issue the consumer supports. This and the fact that, on the opposite side of legitimate news, lies are often packed in bundles and adorned with the most appealing ribbons to look real. Sadly, some of journalism's own history has some dark spots.

On August 25, 1835, for instance, the first of six articles was published in the *New York Sun* telling about the discovery of life on the moon. This and the subsequent articles purported to be reprinted from the *Edinburgh Journals of Science* and bylined by Dr. Andrew Grant, highlighting the supposed credibility of the series. The articles laid out the alleged discovery thus: Sir John Herschel, a famous astronomer of the day, looked through his telescope and detected fury and winged human-like creatures, unicorns and two-legged beavers. The articles, to further give it the flair of reality, went on to describe in great detail the geology of the lunar landscape, noting it had an ample supply of vegetation and flowing rivers.

The articles ran for several weeks and caused a stir among readers, believing that the big night globe in the sky held life beyond anything found on earth, until the newspaper admitted on September 16 that the stories were made up and meant as satire. It has gone down in history as the "Great Moon Hoax of 1835."

The medium of radio did much the same thing when 23-year-old Orson Welles and Mercury Radio broadcast an hour-long program depicting the alleged attack of space aliens on October 30, 1938. The broadcast, known simply as "The War of the Worlds Broadcast," was based on novelist H.G. Wells's science fiction thriller by the same name, in which Martians come to earth to wreak havoc and take over the third planet. Welles, who later became a famous Shakespearean actor and played a newspaperman in the classic movie *Citizen Kane*, set his fictional Martian attack on a small town in New Jersey, before allowing the alleged creatures to land in other locations across the states and, eventually, around the globe.

Welles later said the broadcast was meant as a Halloween scare, and with its seemingly real-life depictions of broadcast interruptions, interviews with supposed scientists and law enforcement, people hallooing, and alleged news reports to alert listeners to the growing threat, the broadcast did just that: scare many of its listeners. Many believed the world was actually being invaded and attacked by creatures from Mars. Lucky for them—and us—it was, like the book on which it was based, only fiction.

These are extreme examples of alleged news packaged to look and sound real. But just because we live in what is supposed to be an enlightened time with our 24-hour access to information and the handy disposal of internet tools, the threat of being deceived is no less palpable. These same modern tools only increase our chances of being duped. It may be tougher to discern what is true these days, especially when today's fake news is not meant for entertainment or satire but to dissuade and misinform the public about crucial issues, some relating to their very well-being. The real danger we face today is not from hoaxes but from a deliberate disinformation campaign sparked by a number of people and organizations, in part, to discredit legitimate news outlets and/or to promote the fakers' own agenda.

You don't have to look far to see the disinformation and lies which, unfortunately, have caused a high number of casualties in their illegitimate news streak. The biggest casualty, of course, is that fact and truth have been labeled the bad guys. The coronavirus pandemic is a prime example, which has spawned a "vast and complicated mix of information, misinformation and disinformation."[8] For instance, there has been bogus information that the virus was planned or that symptoms are caused by 5G wireless communications technology among other absurdities. "The notion of disinformation often brings to mind easy-to-spot propaganda peddled by totalitarian states, but the reality is much more complex. Though disinformation does serve an agenda, it is often camouflaged in facts and advanced by innocent and often well-meaning individuals."[9]

"Think of it," James Warren writes in an article published on Poynter. "The goofy stories, the lies, the conspiracy theories that now routinely gain credibility among millions who can't be bothered to read a newspaper or decent digital site and can't differentiate between Breitbart and *The New York Times*."[10]

The "fight against misinformation won't go away," according to a report by the BBC and noting that even though fact checkers are helping, visual images are tougher to fact-check, and doctored images are "very powerful vehicles of disinformation."[11] On the brighter side, the same report said that according to researchers at Princeton, Dartmouth and the University of Exeter, only about 25 percent of U.S. citizens visited a fake news website during a six-week period around election time in 2016. "But the researchers also found that the visits were highly concentrated—10% of readers made 60% of the visits. And crucially, the researchers concluded 'fake news does not crowd out hard news consumption.'"

Sadly, and most likely unintentionally in a competitive market, in some instances news organizations have contributed to the disinformation campaign. At least that is the perception from much of the public. A survey done by the Pew Research Center found that 59 percent of Americans said "made-up information" intended to mislead caused "a 'great deal' of confusion" in the lead-up to the 2020 presidential election. "Many say the same about breaking news that is not fully verified (47%) or factual information presented to favor one side of an issue (42%)."[12]

The Biased News Consumer

Truth in journalism shouldn't be a convoluted or complicated ideology. The quest of journalism is about uncovering and heralding truth. While some people claim every person has her or his own perception of truth, which may vary from one another, the simple fact is there is only one truth in a news story. The mayor either did launder money, for instance, or he did not; the board of education either did propose a new middle school, or it did not; the president did pay only $750 in taxes, or he did not. There are no gray or shaded areas when it comes to facts, which gets us closer to the bigger picture of truth.

The problem is how truth is reported (by the news media) and how it is received (by the consumer of news). It is the job of a journalist to report the best obtainable version of the truth, and it is the responsibility of the media recipient to discern and accept truth, even if it contradicts one's own personal biases. That doesn't mean the consumer should take everything at face value, but it means the consumer should be a little more forgiving and open-minded, the same traits they say journalists should practice. And it means they can do their own digging against verified news reports to come to their own understanding of the facts presented.

The shouts have gone out—we've all heard them ad infinitum—that too many news media are biased, but there's another problem which compounds the controversy: the public is biased against news reports if they don't align with their preconceived beliefs and notions.

When *The New York Times* did its story about Trump's taxes, many labeled the report as fake. Where was the trust from the public? Where was its objectivity, allowing for even the consideration that maybe it was the president who wasn't being honest with them instead of one of America's legendary newspapers?

Something similar happened during the 2020 presidential election when former Vice President and Democratic contender Joe Biden won the White House over Republican incumbent Trump; the hate held for the media by the right had reached its tipping point. Many people, again following Trump's example, shouted in their social media voices that the election was rigged or that it was stolen and that the media does not declare the winner in a presidential election, the people do.

Yes, of course it is the people who elect the next president. This is a democracy, not a dictatorship. The news media only project the winner, but even then, the projection is not foolproof. The results still have to be canvassed by the electoral board. Take, for example, the presidential election of 1948. There's a famous photo of Harry S. Truman holding up a newspaper from November 3 with the bold headline from the *Chicago Daily Tribune*: "Dewey Defeats Truman!" Just the opposite had happened; Truman won the presidency in an upset victory over Republican challenger Thomas E. Dewey, but so sure was the *Tribune* of Dewey's victory that it had run the wrong version of the paper.

On the flipside, there was this: The Trump campaign tweeted an alleged issue of the *Washington Times* from the 2000 election, whose headline read: "PRESIDENT GORE: Gore over the top with bare majority," above a large photo of Al Gore. The social media rant by Tim Murtaugh from Team Trump said: "Greeting staff at @TeamTrump HQ this morning, a reminder the media doesn't select the President." The newspaper responded to Murtaugh, writing: "Those photos have been doctored. The *Washington Times* never ran a 'President Gore' headline." According to the Associated Press, the doctored photo had been circulating for the past decade.[13]

The public, and that includes any president's supporters, should be objective too and not hold so many biases if they want to find the truth behind the facts. Otherwise, they are pandering to the dangerous philosophy of propaganda, a dish they hand cold to the news media often.

Even Good News Can Deceive

Another criticism of the news media is that it is too negative and, sometimes, sensationalist because of its reporting of the bad happenings in the world instead of the good. I have heard this attack time and again when a reader calls up or writes in saying there is too much negativity in the paper and why cannot we report anything good? My first thought is always that the person doesn't know the newspaper very well and must not have read past the front page. She or he must not be familiar with the feature sections, which are more often than not devoted to the more positive news in the community: lifestyle and religion sections, entertainment and outdoors, community and sports. These are, in my opinion, the good news sections and comprise most of the newspaper.

Still, an old saying in the newsroom is, "If it bleeds it leads." There are two connotations to this: One, if a story has blood in it, so to speak, such as a murder, it will likely get front-page treatment or lead that day's news broadcast. The reason being is because it is such a drastic story and people should be aware of the criminal and cop activity in their community. Second, and perhaps this does verge a bit more on the sensationalist aspect of journalism, when stories like that are placed on the front page or are the first broadcast on the nightly news, it does help increase readership and viewership numbers. People who complain about the bad news of the day being prevalent in the media are likely also in the mix of those reading and watching those very news items. They wouldn't be popular if people didn't read or watch them. Analytics that track stories online in newsrooms where I have worked have been consistent to show that those stories that people complain the most about are also the ones that seem to get the most clicks from audiences.

There have been attempts at "good news" publications and online sites, but, with few exceptions, they have done poorly in garnering revenue, making such efforts seem unfeasible in a world where bills have to be paid. One of the more successful creations was by John Krasinski, who played Jim Halpert on the hit television series *The Office* (2005–2013).

In April 2020, not long after the coronavirus pandemic was declared and people were already tiring of the daily and depressing news about the increasing death toll and infection rate, he shared on YouTube the "Some Good News" broadcast in which, with his sense of humor and on-screen gimmicks such as ending the broadcast by letting viewers see he had shorts on behind his desk instead of pants, told about the lighthearted stories in communities. It was a refreshing moment that, for many people, seemed to fill a void in the daily coronavirus reports from legitimate news services. Krasinski shared eight episodes, which, over the first two months had reached more than 71,000,000 views and more than 2,500,000 subscribers, according to a report by *USA Today*. It wasn't long before the networks came knocking, and it was announced that ViacomCBS had picked up the segment.[14]

Perhaps some news organizations were jealous: Why didn't we think of that? But there actually have been and are organizations that devote at least part of their effort to "good news." There's the Good News Network, for instance, the DailyGood and Positive News. In 2020 with a pandemic raging, however, people were looking for more positive stories, even those presented in a way that could make them laugh. It was the right time for "Some Good News," not to mention a built-in base of Krasinski fans who have followed the actor in his on-screen roles and directing projects.

I personally believe that such efforts have their place in the modern and frenzied multimedia world. I have spent much of my career in what I like to term the "positive news" segment of journalism. I spent several years being a feature writer and editor, in which the stories I told were on the lighter side of the news aisle—covering outdoor topics and issues, writing lengthy human-interest stories, and going into churches and mosques to dig into faith and lifestyles topics. I have written about people who have interesting hobbies, have done food reviews and cooking profiles, and have produced articles and videos about the positives displayed in community events and businesses.

But we have to be careful when good news—and bad—is published or broadcast willy-nilly and with little regard to news judgment. This is one of the problems with social media. They are platforms for anyone to produce and promote their own news, good and bad. That, of course, is not a negative thing in a country of free speech, but the pitfall is that very little of it is vetted. "Often," a *New York Times* article intones, "the most widely shared good-news items are baseless."[15] And yet such baselessness often becomes "news" by its popularity. Even some prime time news professionals have a hard time staying away from such viral baselessness. CNN's Chris Cuomo, for instance, shared on his broadcast one evening in 2020 a video clip of a man riding a longboard, lip-syncing a song, and drinking a bottle of Ocean Spray while holding onto the back of a pickup truck. It was a funny video that helped refreshen the mood of the season, but there was no news value to it whatsoever—except that it became news once the video had gone viral. It showed a guy having a good time on a longboard, seemingly with not a care in the world during a tumultuous time in history.

If only life was so carefree. If only news was so fluffy.

Perhaps that is why we need these moments in an otherwise heavily depressed world of bad news stories. We have to be careful to put such good news in its proper perspective, however, and realize that in many cases (not necessarily just a video of a guy riding at the back of a truck) even fluff pieces might need to be vetted.

The *Times* credited *National Geographic* for doing its part in being vigilant to correct the record, noting a social media post that had become popular about swans returning to the canals in Venice, Italy.[16] The swan story was hyperbole, however, and "quickly fell apart under scrutiny."[17] The article pointed out other examples, too.

In this rock-a-frilly world, in which even good news can deceive, journalists continued to report the more impactful stories of the day—about COVID-19 numbers, the shortages of equipment at some hospitals, and how the virus was impacting a great many people. And the numbers continued to rise, hitting 300,000 by mid–December.[18] The numbers continued on the upward march as the new year approached and the world entered another year of a new decade.

A decade in which truth and disinformation continued to draw their armaments against each other.

Why We Need Journalism

Some people may question why we need journalism today since information is now available 24/7 via an array of sources. With the phones we hold in our hands and put in our pockets—mini computers, really—we are able to access an insurmountable amount of information instantaneously.

We can look up the best places to eat in an unfamiliar city, find hotel accommodations and a community's entertainment and outdoor recreation venues. We can find auto repair shops, medical providers, and law enforcement agencies. If we have a question about a certain topic, we can look that up too and discover new things we may not have ever thought or heard of before. We also can access local agencies and businesses, many which have their own newsletters and videos on their websites. We can subscribe to newsletters, access our social accounts, and see the latest rants and raves. And, at our inclination, we can click on any news and alleged news site within a matter of milliseconds. Never in the world's history has there been so much information available at our fingertips as there is today.

While easy access to technology has made everyone a virtual reporter, these very tools also are what makes today's legitimate journalists and news outlets even more valuable and needed. We need legitimate journalists to vet stories, clear the noise, and narrow the facts. Often the media hate depicted in the country these days is aimed at its legacy media institutions—the mainstream media—but the drivel and sarcasm have also breached local news agencies and reporters, where even the hometown newspaper or broadcast station is looked upon as fake news. This bias against legitimate news outlets is troubling on many levels, no less than the fact that it is the local outlets that give us the important day-to-day information that helps us become better, more informed citizens. This information helps us, as citizens, make decisions about what causes we will support, both civically and politically; about our taxes and contributions; about our children's education; about places and events to be aware of; about crime and police activity in our communities; about legal matters that affect cities and counties; and a host of other important and pertinent topics. Your neighbor might post a video of police cars speeding down a road, but a news report will flush out the details and tell why there was police activity in the community.

Having a smartphone at our fingertips, with built-in cameras and video-recording capabilities, has turned us all into citizen reporters in one way but in another that is simply silly and is not possible. If you're not a journalist, it is unlikely that you would walk into the city or county building to sift through court records or the latest court docket. With some exceptions, it is unlikely that you're going to attend the weekly school board meeting or city council meeting or county commissioner meeting, or at least regularly. It is unlikely that you're going to interview law enforcement officials about the latest crime, or a health district official about the community's emergency response plans. And even if you were to do these things, how would you make your findings available to the targeted community? Your friends on social media might not be the same ones who'd most benefit from the story. And will you follow up with sources to get further background and details to make the story more comprehensive and relatable as to why it is important for your audience?

We need reporters for these and many other reasons. We need reporters to get to the bottom of stories, unbury the facts, and present the information, whatever the information turns out to be, to the news-consuming public—for the public's benefit. A free press is meant to inform but also cause debate and conversation, where shared opinions are expressed and respected and contended. It is the best way to come together and, despite our differences, help us form a "more perfect union." After all, having correct knowledge is power.

"Journalism exists to keep the people informed," reads a column by Dave Zweifel in the *Times-Republican* in Marshalltown, Iowa. "It exists to spread knowledge and, yes, it exists to provide viewpoints from many different perspectives, to provide the fuel that people in a democracy need to take part in their governments."[19] The Founding Fathers knew this. They knew that a free press, while it does not guarantee a country without its woes, would better position the United States to keep its values and freedoms intact. It is not a debate but a fact: democracy is threatened whenever the free press is thwarted.

William Biggart, 2001
Freelance Photographer

As the first glow of sunlight penetrated the darkness, heralding the promise of a new day, people stirred from their beds and went about their normal morning routines. By all appearances it was going to be a clear, blue-sky day, the perfect kind of weather to enjoy the last few days of official summer. In ten more days autumn would begin, and then it would be a rollercoaster ride to the holidays.

As the sun broke on the horizon, turning the darkness of night into the brightness of day, it sent its rays across the cityscape of America's most populous city, making the tallest buildings in the western hemisphere glisten in the sunlight.

Nicknamed the Twin Towers, or Twins, the World Trade Center's two skyscrapers, each at 110 stories tall, were iconic symbols of New York City and the world of free trade. They were, in fact, the tallest buildings in the world when they opened in 1973. Not quite 30 years later, in September 2001, the world's tallest buildings were the Petronas Towers, some 1,483 feet tall with 84 floors, located in Kuala Lumpur, Malaysia. (As of this writing, the world's tallest building—2,761 feet high—is the Burj Khalifa in Dubai, in the United Arab Emirates. At 94 floors and 1,776 feet tall, the One World Trade Center, completed in 2014, is the sixth tallest.)

Still, the towers never lost their iconic imagery as they towered over Manhattan. In 2001 some 50,000 people worked in the buildings, dubbed the North Tower and the South Tower.

Their windows appeared to shimmer with the adjusting sunlight—the same sun that touched Lady Liberty's eternal flame that, standing across New York Harbor at Liberty Island, was held aloft to the heavens.

Liberty indeed needed heaven's help that day, the second Tuesday of the ninth month in the second year of a new century: September 11, 2001.

On that morning, as the sun climbed higher still, it shortened the shadows of the skyscrapers, and the firmament shifted from its early morning hues of pink and orange to murky gray, purple and then blue. Weather, temperature and air quality all made it a near-perfect day to be outside. Such leisure would have to wait; for now, work needed to be done, and so people dressed, said goodbye to their loved ones, and traveled to their offices in the towers—some to meetings, some to phone calls, some to computer screens at their desks.

Before long, however, the air quality would diminish as it became satiated with dust and debris from the city's collapsing twin icons. The beauty of the day would be shattered by the horror of terrorism. Amid the rubble would be found the body of the only photojournalist killed because of the 9/11 terrorist attacks.

His name was William Biggart.

For the Love of Photography

Some journalists use the pen to tell stories; others use the camera. William Biggart was of the latter mold. He loved the camera and how one picture—as the saying goes—could tell what otherwise would take a thousand words. The camera was, in effect, his means to help right wrong and be an eyewitness through its lens of happenings that shaped the world around him.

Biggart, born in 1947 in Berlin while his U.S. soldier father was stationed in Germany, found his life's calling in New York, where he began as a commercial photographer.[20] Always handy with a camera, he liked to photograph people. He opened his own photography studio but seemed to be more interested in capturing the raw images of people outside the studio.

By 1985 he had his first press card and went freelance. He closed his studio and, with press credentials and camera in tow, began traveling to places near and far to capture images for various news outlets. Among his comprehensive body of work, he photographed for alternative newspapers in New York.[21]

His adventures took him to Brazil, Ireland and Israel where he captured images of civil unrest, military conflicts, religious celebrations, refugee camps, and social and race conflicts.[22] As was his forte, he liked to focus his lens on the people, where whole stories could be told in their expressions and quirks, in every wrinkle or stare, and in their postures and the way they tilted their heads. So much emotion, so many layers of stories are depicted in such images.

It was those types of images he sought to capture when he went to photograph the ensuing chaos at the World Trade Center.

There was no bigger story than what was transpiring on that Black Tuesday in September.

After hearing the news from a taxi driver, Biggart went directly home to grab his gear and quickly headed to the Twin Towers. The scene was pandemonium. Smoke billowed from the buildings. People inside, the fear of being trapped in a burning building oppressing their minds as it would anyone caught in such terrible circumstances, were seen jumping to their deaths. These traumatic images were broadcast and photographed for all to see. It was heartbreaking.

But within a matter of minutes, the scene would get worse.

Ground Zero

As he approached the World Trade Center—later dubbed Ground Zero because of it being the place directly impacted by the attacks—Biggart photographed people reacting to the unfolding catastrophe, as well as the buildings and the activity around him. There were the frenzied first responders, whose dust-coated faces told whole stories in themselves; ambulances, sirens blaring but silent in the still photos, that rushed to the scene over soot-layered roads; civilians working in tandem with first responders to help save lives. And there were the towers—always the lens moved back to the towers, where flames emanated from the buildings as if demons were hosting a party. Smoke billowed into the sky, turning the otherwise blueness of morning into the gray lent of mourning.[23]

Destruction seemed to be all around him, but this wasn't dancing through Armageddon. Biggart focused his camera on as much of the unfolding drama as he could but time and again returning to point his lens ever upward.

He drew nearer the first tower, hoping to get closer images. But then the unthinkable happened. The South Tower, which was the second building to be struck by a plane, started to collapse—110 stories of steel and concrete pounded into the earth, taking hundreds of lives with it.

It was 9:58 a.m.

Biggart had escaped.

He spoke with his wife, telling her he was safe and would meet her at a rendezvous in a few minutes.[24] There were now more images to capture.

But Biggart's luck had run out.

When the next tower collapsed 30 minutes later, at 10:28 a.m., Biggart, who had made his way closer again, was buried in the massive rubble. His body was not found until four days later, his cameras still with him.[25]

Always Remember

A website maintained by Biggart's family showcases his work, some of it retrieved from the cameras found with him at Ground Zero. They are of the images he had captured on that day in America that changed the world. According to a time stamp on the images, the website says that Biggart snapped his last photo at 10:28:24 a.m.[26] The image is of the area near the towers, its scarred and battered buildings looking as if they had been demolished by a succession of bombs and enshrouded with smoke as the sun's rays tried to shine through. In that moment the world had changed.

As with other events that have impacted our view of the world and marked our time and place in it, the terrorist attacks at the World Trade Center have left an indelible imprint on the minds of those who witnessed the tragedy. Obviously, those who witnessed it up close and personal or those who were more directly affected by it ever after will remember best. But even those who saw the tragedy played out on television will likely always remember where they were when they first heard the news.

They will probably remember where they were, what they were doing and, in some instances, even what they were wearing. The memories are even more stark for those who were more closely impacted by the tragedy—the family and friends who lost someone dear, the first responders and others who went to the scene to give assistance, the health care workers who responded to save lives and care for the injured, the journalists who covered the event up close and personal so the world itself could be an eyewitness.

In the end, more than 3,000 people lost their lives in the terrorist attacks on the World Trade Center and Pentagon and on United Flight 93 that crashed in a field in rural Shanksville, Somerset County, Pennsylvania, with 44 souls on board, but the toll is bigger still. The tragedy drastically changed the modern world, and in tones of remorse Americans waved their flags and said they will Never Forget the lives lost on that infamous day in world history.

Every year on September 11 we say prayers and memorialize the victims. But in our political and societal divide for the rest of the year, have we forgotten?

If so, it is yet another reason we need journalists, scribblers and photographers. We need them to help us remember. It is the reason we need journalists like William Biggart.

The Lone Photographer

Of the thousands of people who died in the terrorist attacks of 9/11, William Biggart was the only photographer to have lost his life that day at Ground Zero.[27] But his memory—and his photos—live on, the latter forever retelling the stories he captured through the lens of journalism.

Some may question what a journalist is supposed to do when placed in a situation where others need help. Should they be bystanders and eyewitnesses only, or should they lend a helping hand?

It is a question of ethics, and our humanity has the answer. Journalists at the scene were there to help in another way: document the scenes so that the world, immediately and later, could bear witness. In such work they hold the victims in remembrance and the perpetrators accountable.

Journalism often is a thankless job, especially these days. Not many are given the proverbial pat on the back for their efforts to inform and make aware, but citizens must be willing to stand up for those who put their all on the line to bring information to us. Often it is gathered at great cost.

To Biggart and all of those who have lost their lives in the line of their journalistic duty, and for those who risked all but came out anyway, we owe a hearty thank-you.

As Biggart's wife, Wendy Biggart, said at the time, "Bill was kind of an ornery guy, and luckily, he went out doing what he loved … and, it took two of the world's largest buildings to do it."[28]

7

Activism, Objectivity and Fairness

If you consider the great journalists in history, you don't see too many objective journalists on that list.—Hunter S. Thompson

If asked what traits a journalist or news organization should have, the news-consuming public generally might say they want news presented fairly, objectively, and without bias. They don't want analysis or interpretation, just the facts. This is in line with the hard and fast rules that reporters learn in J-School: be accurate above all else but also report the facts fairly and objectively.

It is an interesting ethical standard, since from journalism's very beginning it has been anything but objective. As we have already seen in Chapter 3, the press during America's revolutionary days were flagrantly partisan. We see the same divide among some of the nation's top news media today, in which the perception is that some lean to the right side of the political spectrum and others lean to the left. And sometimes they don't seem to just lean but to hop, skip and jump into one political aisle or the other.

Their contest with each other—and thus with audiences—is not always so much who has the facts but rather whose opinions and slants do the reading and viewing public want to believe?

And yet there should be only one ideology of news reporting: informing the public about important information.

For the news consumer, belief is part of news consuming—what they believe, whom they believe. We tend to believe those reports that best support our own political, religious, and social stances. It's not much different than what you see on the big-news channels. They present the news packages with their own carefully tied ribbons, and what they do not report or discuss says just as much as what they do report.

Oftentimes what is called bias, however, may not be that at all. For instance, there is a difference between being objective and being fair. I tend to believe that good reporting, even if it seems like it leans one way or another, is a fair treatment of the given issue. If Fox News says that Biden hasn't handled the border crisis well, for instance, and the network digs into the story to present those facts, does that mean it is being biased? No, just as it is not biased if the *New York Times* runs an article about Trump paying only $750 in income tax. When Carl Bernstein and Bob Woodward uncovered the conspiracy at the Watergate, revealing that the criminal deed went all the way to President Nixon, was that biased reporting against the president or was it information the public had a right to know? Were they being fair to the truth of the story?

Bernstein said in an interview about the movie that he and Woodward did not have any agenda to fell the president. Their only agenda was to seek and report the truth, no matter what that revealed itself to be, though because of what their stories revealed it may have looked as if they were out to "get the president."

Our heavily partisan and volatile political climate has made it more difficult for journalists to be seen as objective and fair. But here is an interesting question: Might both CNN and Fox News be fulfilling the fairness rule even with their supposed news slants?

A free press is meant to inform but also cause debate and conversation, where shared opinions are expressed and respected and contended. It is the best way to come together and, despite our differences, help us form a "more perfect union." The Founding Fathers knew this. When they vied for an independent press, they wanted a climate where diverse opinions could be shared. A free press was for both news and opinion, and the discussion they engender is part of the process of truth discovery.

"Journalism exists to keep the people informed," reads a column by Dave Zweifel in the *Times-Republican* in Marshalltown, Iowa. "It exists to spread knowledge and, yes, it exists to provide viewpoints from many different perspectives, to provide the fuel that people in a democracy need to take part in their governments."[1]

And then there is this: do fairness and objectivity mean a journalist should only record events and not analyze and interpret what is presented? Do they mean a news organization should not promote a cause? Perhaps a nontraditional way to view the role of a journalist is best explained from *Washington Post* columnist Margaret Sullivan when she wrote that a journalist is not a scribbler and stenographer. In her column published June 7, 2020, Sullivan writes that the idea of journalists presenting facts without analysis or interpretation is "an appealing idea at first blush," but it "doesn't always work, especially right now."

She discusses what a journalist shares and what the journalist does not are choices. But are not choices a measure of news judgment and, perhaps, bias? "We choose what to focus on, what to amplify, what to investigate and examine. That's why the simplistic 'just the unadorned facts' can be such a canard. And that's why the notion to 'represent all points of view equally' is absurd and sometimes wrongheaded."[2]

During the 2020 presidential election, and when Joe Biden was declared the country's next executive, President Trump had every right to contest the elections. It was his right to investigate alleged voter fraud, and it was proper and obligatory for the press to report truthfully on the process and look into allegations. If investigations into alleged mass voter fraud turn up illegitimate and sterile, however—as they did—the press has the obligation to defend those findings as well; reporters do not need to keep getting both sides of the story when the facts have already been revealed. In this instance, the press had met its obligations to fairness based on their and the courts' findings.

If there are cases of police brutality, the press is not obligated to share the favorable works of those department officers. That's not the news. Bringing awareness to the problem, its causes and effects, is the news and the stories that educate the public why reform might be needed. In such reporting, the public may believe the press is being biased and unbalanced, but the reality is it is being fair to the issue at hand.

Does that mean that journalists are against police officers? Or that there are not departments that deserve more favorable recognition? Of course not. We thank the honorable men and women in blue who do their duty and honor their badge ethically and without bias to skin color or profession. But the journalist's job is to report the news, just as law officers' job is to serve and protect.

The late and great Hunter S. Thompson, who was known for rarely being objective with his gonzo journalism, said: "If you consider the great journalists in history, you don't see too many objective journalists on that list."[3] The kind of journalism and the type of journalists that have the most impact on society are those who take a stand on important issues. Isn't this what any investigative reporter does when he or she sets out to uncover the dirty goings-on of a business that has duped the public. Some might call this crusading journalism, but I call it simply good journalism. Journalist Henry Anatole Grunwald, once the editor of *Time* magazine, said: "Journalism can never be silent: that is its greatest virtue and its greatest fault."[4]

It is easy to give the same amount of time or space to two political candidates and their opinions about an issue, but it is tougher and not conducive to what I call "change journalism." Change journalism may include investigative journalism, but it also may be a community story whose impact is more than just being an objectively balanced story. It is one whose agenda is about fairness to an issue or topic.

"Journalism without a moral position is impossible," said columnist Marguerite Duras. "Every journalist is a moralist. It's absolutely unavoidable. A journalist is someone who looks at the world and the way it works, someone who takes a close look at things every day and reports what she sees, someone who represents the world, the event, for others. She cannot do her work without judging what she sees."[5]

And yet there's that word "bias," which has a negative connotation. People who do not understand the role of journalists might believe a reporter is being biased when in fact she or he is actually living true to journalism's higher ethics of fairness. Let's look at one example:

"I am pleased to inform you that, for the sake of accuracy in reporting, I am considering posting my interview with Lesley Stahl of 60 Minutes PRIOR TO AIRTIME!" President Donald Trump tweeted on social media on October 20, 2020. "This will be done so that everybody can get a glimpse of what a FAKE and BIASED interview is all about."

Trump met with Stahl, a legacy *60 Minutes* reporter, in a broadcast interview on Tuesday, October 20, that was to air the following Sunday, a little more than a week before the presidential election. The popular TV news magazine has a reputation for interviewing presidents and their opponents before elections, and this interview was no different—except that it was different. A lot different. Not because Stahl wasn't doing her due diligence, but because, as seemed to have happened often when reporters would interview Trump, the president took it off the rails. With him in the hot seat, he took the questions as biased, liberal attacks, and after 30 minutes walked out of the interview. Not long afterward, he posted the above rant to social media.

Trump did post the video on Thursday, October 22, 2020, hours before the final presidential debate was to take place between him and Democratic nominee Joe Biden. Before posting the video, the president tweeted: "I will soon be giving a first in television history full, unedited preview of the vicious attempted 'takeout' interview of me by Leslie Stahl of @60Minutes. Watch her constant interruptions & anger. Compare my full, flowing and 'magnificently brilliant' answers to their Q's." A few hours later he posted the video with this social media rant: "Look at the bias, hatred and rudeness on behalf of 60 Minutes and CBS." Trump, who seemed to like to preempt everything that might be controversial to his presidency, also attacked the moderator for that evening's presidential debate: "Tonight's anchor, Kristen Welker, is far worse!"

In publishing the video, the White House broke an agreement with CBS that it would not publish before it was officially aired on the network. But Trump also did something else by posting this video: he reinforced in many minds that he, a sitting president, was the one who interrupted and attacked, going so far as telling Stahl that she had discredited herself. "No, you're doing that," Stahl said in response.[6]

CBS, the same day, released a statement, saying on social media that the president's actions had not deterred the news station from broadcasting the interview with its "full, fair and contextual reporting."

The White House's unprecedented decision to disregard their agreement with CBS News and release their footage will not deter 60 MINUTES from providing its full, fair and contextual reporting which presidents have participated in for decades. 60 MINUTES, the most-watched news program on television, is widely respected for bringing its hallmark fairness, deep reporting and informative context to viewers each week. Few journalists have the presidential interview experience Lesley Stahl has delivered over her decades as one of the premier correspondents in America and we look forward to audiences seeing her third interview with President Trump and subsequent interview with Vice President Pence this weekend.[7]

The early post by President Trump likely did what he intended it to do: fuel further contempt for the news media and further divide the country. The video did not likely sway his base followers, nor did it likely bring him new supporters. The country had seen this type of vitriolic attack many times during his presidency. He tweeted the night before releasing the video that he was not running against Biden, but "against the Corrupt Media, the Big Tech Giants, and the Washington Swamp."

That's how Donald Trump viewed the news media: corrupt, liberal, and against everything he ever did as president.

Was it true?

Obviously, those who watch the *60 Minutes* broadcast have differing opinions about it. Some said Stahl was biased and unfair, while others said it was the president who interrupted and was contentious.

So how do we judge the fairness of this or any other news report? We can glean some insights from the Society of Professionalism Journalists' Code of Ethics. In part, it says journalists should "Diligently seek subjects of news coverage to allow them to respond to criticism or allegations of wrongdoing."[8] The president of the United States, no matter who he or she might be, is the best subject of news coverage, especially during an election year and especially when there are allegations of incompetency. "Be vigilant and courageous about holding those with power accountable. Give voice to the voiceless."

And one more: A news reporter's coverage should "support the open and civil exchange of views, even views they find repugnant." Of course, a president's job is different than that of a reporter's, but from these ethical inputs from SPJ, a professional journalism organization—the standard in the profession—Stahl and other journalists who asked hard questions of political leaders and candidates, including an incumbent president, did nothing wrong. She, in fact, stayed true to her profession's guidelines and ethics policy.

A Disheartening Conversation

During a post-election conversation with someone close to me, but whose political differences vary from mine, the topic was brought up by the person I was speaking with how he had concerns if Biden were to move into the White House. Apparently, this person still believed Trump had a chance of winning that seat for four more years even though all of Trump's lawsuits had failed, including the Supreme Court saying there was no evidence of large-scale voter fraud. This same person said Trump, as far as he was concerned, was the best president in has lifetime.

I did not initiate the topic of conversation, nor did I say anything negative about any political candidate, including Trump, until I was berated with a tantrum-like offense about this man's political beliefs and why he was right. Then I said how I believed differently, that I did not believe there was wide-scale voter fraud. I said I had my reasons to believe that, just as the person I was speaking with had his reasons to believe the opposite. That's when I was told something I never would have expected from this person: he basically called me a name. The words cut me to the quick and still sting when I think of the conversation. He had no right to call me what he did when he knew nothing of my political persuasion.

This is the mindset of a great many people: If you don't agree with their political beliefs, you are labeled a name. Whatever happened to respect, to hearing or bantering lightheartedly about opposing viewpoints? Why the name-calling?

I have always tried to respect other people's beliefs, whether they be religious or political. I do not call people names, especially friends and others close to me and just because their beliefs may be different than mine. I feel sorry for this man, and many others, who cannot reason with their opponents, who cannot have friendly conversations about differing viewpoints. Those respectful discussions and shared opinions and news are what helps us all come to a better understanding of each other and, as we do so, the truth.

Robert Stevens, 2001
The Sun

A week after the terrorist attacks of September 2001, mail arrived at several offices in the United States containing anthrax, a lethal substance whose spores wreak havoc once inside the body. Those who received the suspicious and deadly packages included some media personalities at ABC News and CBS, as well as Robert Stevens, a photographer and photo editor for *The Sun* newspaper in Boca Raton, Florida. Stevens opened the mail and later was hospitalized with flu-like symptoms. A few days later he died after what doctors had learned was from pulmonary anthrax.

Stevens was the first person killed by the anthrax scares of 2001. In all 21 people were exposed to the content of the deadly mailings; five died because of the anthrax and at least 17 became seriously ill from the suspicious letters.[9]

The Sun, a tabloid owned by American Media, is the same company that published *The National Enquirer*. Journalism at such publications is not in the same vein as what you generally find in a daily newspaper, where city and county issues are reported upon. They might throw real news in the mix, but tabloids are often known for the absurd stories that attract a certain breed of readers. Such stories may be about two-headed cows, Martians invading a virgin's boudoir, or the birth of a bat-like humanoid. The crazy tales one might read in such publications spark a whole different discussion about this genre of "journalism." Nonetheless, Stevens was a lifelong media worker who died while in the line of doing his work.

Because the letters containing anthrax started showing up in people's mailboxes soon after the terrorist attacks of 9/11, federal authorities believed that perhaps al-Qaeda was behind them. After further investigation, however, it was revealed that the anthrax in the envelopes came from a military base in Fort Detrick, Maryland.

These were acts of domestic terrorism.

Authorities honed in on a suspect, but they later found that he didn't have anything to do with the deadly mailings. Another man eventually caught their attention, and this one was more promising. Dr. Bruce Ivins worked at the base and became the prime suspect in the investigation, which, unfortunately, continued for several years. Before authorities could arrest him, however, Ivins completed suicide in 2008.

Investigators believed Ivins had targeted Stevens, but was there more than one person behind the deadly mailings, or did Ivins work alone?

Stevens's wife, Maureen Stevens, filed a lawsuit against the U.S. government claiming it was "negligent in failing to stop someone from working at an Army infectious disease lab from creating weapons-grade anthrax used in letters that killed five people and sickened 17 others."[10] She said Ivins was "not just a little bit weird" but "certifiable, and he had been for years."[11]

It wasn't until February 19, 2010, that the investigation finally concluded with the Department of Justice, citing "Evidence developed from [the] investigation established that Dr. [Bruce] Ivins, alone, mailed the anthrax letters."[12]

However, a panel of independent scientists who studied the science that the FBI used in its investigation concluded that while Ivins could have been the perpetrator, it doesn't prove that he was. "The new report is limited to an evaluation of the scientific evidence and does not assess the guilt or innocence of anyone connected to the case."[13]

Investigation and suppositions are a quest for truth, but the fact remains: anthrax was mailed to a number of people in the early 2000s. Five people died from the anthrax in the mailings, and many more became seriously ill because of it, including the seven-month-old baby of a news producer at ABC News, who had visited the network's Manhattan office in late September 2001.[14]

And let it be remembered that the first person to die from the mailings was journalist Robert Stevens.

8

Regaining the Public's Trust Amidst a Multitude of Voices

Objective journalism and an opinion column are about as similar as the Bible and Playboy magazine.—WALTER CRONKITE

A challenge for journalists and newsrooms in today's uneasy world is that a great many people who read and watch the news do not believe what they are being told. A number of reasons exist for the mistrust, a virus that started long ago and which in recent years reached pandemic proportions. We can scan the headlines over the years to see whence some of that mistrust sprang—including from careless and hurried journalists and news organizations and their ill-vetted stories, the very institutions that should hold truth involatile and facts paramount.

Perceptions of bias foment distrust, and, as has been discussed in a previous chapter, there also is a deliberate disinformation campaign to dissuade and delegitimize news professionals. Not all of the blame for today's mistrust should be laid upon the shoulders of journalists, and yet we also must not shrug off those misdeeds that lay heavy upon them. Some of these issues have already been discussed. This chapter offers suggestions about what journalists and news organizations can do to help regain trust from their reading, listening, and viewing audiences.

The Public's Waning Trust of the News Media

America's legitimate news institutions and journalists—our community newspaper, television and radio news groups as well as the country's legacy media—must be trustworthy if they are to meet the obligations of their profession: educate and inform their audiences, be a voice for the weary and unheard, and defend the public's right to know. If an audience is always unsure of the truth they are being told, it makes it difficult for journalists and newsrooms to accomplish these tasks.

Reports of weapons of mass destruction in Iraq, which later proved to be untrue but gave fuel to start the U.S. invasion of Iraq in 2003, and the months-long reporting, based on polls and assumptions that told the country Hillary Clinton would win the White House, are just two examples of how the media got the story wrong, according to NPR's public editor, Elizabeth Jensen. In an address given in 2017 in Honolulu, Hawaii, she highlighted some of news media's grievances before offering her own suggestions to improve newsrooms. And then there is this—cable networks and their talking heads and print media and their "conflated opinion, analysis, and straight reporting," Jensen said. "It's all of a piece: policy, technology, changing society, business decisions, and just plain errors. It all led to a place where news consumers began drifting to ideological corners, trusting some media that reflected their own views, distrusting others."[1]

The climate of media distrust has only worsened over the years. The industry needs a restoration like no other time in its history. According to national statistics, public trust of news media has declined noticeably in just over a one-year period. Only 9 percent of consumers in the U.S., for instance, said they trusted mass media—newspapers, television and radio—"a great deal" to report the news fairly and accurately (down from 13 percent in 2019), while 31 percent said they trusted them "a fair amount" of time (up 28 percent from 2019), according to a Gallup report released in September 2020. In 2019, 28 percent said they trusted the news media "not at all," but in 2020 it had increased to 33 percent.

Political affiliation saw even starker numbers, with Democrats more likely to trust what they read and hear about in the news media, over Republicans. But both parties' trust declined in 2020. That year among Democrats, 16 percent said they trusted the news media "a great deal," down from 24 percent the year before. Only 3 percent of Republicans said they had the same trust in the news media, down from 4 percent in 2019. On the other end of that, 58 percent of Republicans in 2020 said they didn't trust the media at all (48 percent in 2019), while only 6 percent of Democrats said they didn't trust the media (down from 10 percent in 2019).[2]

Gallup has asked the same question of Americans nearly every year since 1972. "Trust ranged between 68% and 72% in the 1970s, and though it had declined by the late 1990s, it remained at the majority level until 2004, when it dipped to 44%," according to the report. "After hitting 50% in 2005, it has not risen above 47%."[3]

For the ethical journalist, sometimes it feels like we're fighting a losing battle, with the weapons drawn against us fiercer than they have ever been in the past. There seems to be a no-holds-barred assault on journalists and the work they do. The country cannot even hold a free and fair election anymore without a great many people calling fraud and blaming the media for alleged conspiracies.[4]

Take heed colleagues; now is not the time to let down our guard. We must shoulder much of the blame for today's mistrust—*but not all of it*—and redouble our efforts to the very cause of journalism, which means in many instances letting go of the hubris and returning to its basic tenets.

It is not my intent to point the finger of blame at a profession I deeply admire but instead to point out suggestions on how to regain some of the trust that has been lost. Trust is something that takes time to build, just as it does with any relationship that has been offended or hurt. And, as is the case with those same relationships, depending on the offense, trust can dwindle almost immediately. This fast and hard rule of life and relationships is the very reason journalists must be both diligent and vigilant while standing on the watchtower of truth. They must admit when they fall short of their obligation or make mistakes. As mentioned in a previous chapter, they must regret the error.

Regret the Error

Leading up to 2020's presidential election, the Society of Professional Journalists reminded those who work in news about the fundamentals of good political and election reporting: "When covering the election today," it posted on social media on November 3, "journalists should seek sources whose voices we seldom hear, support the open and civil exchange of views, take special care not to misrepresent or oversimplify in promoting, previewing or summarizing a story and keep in mind that neither speed nor format excuses inaccuracy." This is an exceptional reminder not only during an election season but all year long, 24 hours a day, seven days a week, all 52 weeks and 365 days of the year: accuracy is paramount.

Accuracy in reporting far outweighs being the first to broadcast and publish. Mistakes happen nonetheless, and when they do journalists and news organizations need to make amends. That starts, of course, with recognizing and regretting the error.

"Regret the error" should be the mantra in journalism when mistakes occur. During my nearly seven-year stint at a newspaper in south-central Idaho, corrections printed in the paper always ended with the words, "The *Times-News* regrets the error." That's a good practice the outlet should implement and enforce immediately, if it is not already in place. Having a clear corrections policy in place helps reporters stand accountable for their mistakes. It also goes a long way in helping further the transparency of the news outlets and their journalists. Regretting the error is not a retraction but an acknowledgment that an error in reporting has occurred; it attests to readers that efforts are made to correct the mistake. It shows readers journalism's humanity.

Many other errors occur in reporting that don't necessarily fit into a correction, but they should nonetheless be addressed by news organizations and journalists alike. I believe many of the mistakes that happen in news reports are caused by the industry's rush to be first to broadcast and publish. Even though many long-standing news organizations have shuttered in recent years, which reduced the number of legitimate news outlets, the competition to be first has only increased with digital technology. Also, to recap what has been said previously, shrinking newsrooms cause reporters to take on more responsibility. Many of them cover more than one beat and juggle the tasks of reporter, photographer, online editor, videographer, and social media publicist. While these are tougher hurdles to overcome, with no easy solution in sight, there are some things outlets should consider adopting. They are things that journalists and news organizations can do to help regain the public's trust, to dig for those roots that need replanting. They include the following:

Have a code of ethics policy: The Society of Professional Journalists has an ethics code, which serves as the industry standard, but that doesn't mean that individual newsrooms cannot develop their own. Many newsrooms have created their own policy, which is good form for at least a couple of reasons. First, it allows the organization's journalists to know that the company is serious about its obligations to basic journalism standards; it gives them insight into the measures that will be taken if such policies are broken; and it highlights specific topics the newsroom may want to focus on, such as enforcing the standard that reporters obtain multiple sources and viewpoints for their stories. Second, it allows the news audience to become more familiar with and hold the organization accountable to the standards set forth in the policy. Adopting a code of ethics policy may also better educate the public about the role of journalism in their community, especially if the policy is published and easily accessible for consumers to view. An ethics standard should also make clear its corrections policy, as mentioned previously, which addresses how to treat errors when they occur. This, among the other items mentioned, will help bring more transparency to the newsroom.

Improve transparency: An ethics policy allows for more transparency, an important virtue of any newsroom. Transparency is something journalists urge from public officials and their agencies, and we fight for and defend the right to public information, but not a lot of journalists take the time to consider the same virtue in their own professions. And yet transparency in journalism is significant, because, like government offices, it allows the public a peek inside and validates journalists' work. What does transparency look like? According to the SPJ, it involves "explaining one's decisions to the public."[5] Another definition, this one by the Knight Foundation, is "disclosing potential conflicts of interest and making additional reporting material available to readers."[6] What does nontransparency resemble? The opposite of these beneficial traits. Student journalists know about the importance of transparency. Take a look at this counsel from a student newspaper at the University of Oregon: "There needs to be a shift in transparency in news publications," reads an article from the *Daily Emerald*. "If news publications are more transparent in where and how they are crafting these stories and acquiring information, there will be a positive shift in public trust of news."[7]

   Remember where opinions belong: "Objective journalism and an opinion column," said famed journalist Walter Cronkite, "are about as similar as the Bible and *Playboy* magazine."[8] A chapter has been devoted to the topic of fairness and allegations of bias, but for now let's remember that there is a difference between articles and opinions. Journalists know this, of course, but much of the public seems not to grasp the concept. I cannot count how many times someone has shared a post on social media, saying something like, "Look at this article!" Sometimes I would, only to immediately find it was not an article but an opinion column. That might seem like a minor thing, perhaps an unintentional mislabeling by the person who posted the item, but more often than not I believe it speaks volumes of why the public needs to be educated about journalism, what it is and what it is not. They know that fairness should be a journalist's trait, but they don't seem to know the difference between a news article and an opinion column. Leave editorializing to the opinion writers, radio commentators and television's talking heads.

   Diversify newsrooms and stories: Journalists speak highly of their profession, which they should, often believing their position is a higher call to service. They believe their work can influence public policy, which it can, but the fact is not all of the public is served by every news report. That's obvious, but sometimes whole newspapers and television broadcasts do not necessarily serve the minorities in their communities. It is true that each news publication or station has their primary target audience, but journalism is a broad sweep of the broom that should attract and include as much diversity as possible. Diversity should be developed in stories, but it should also cross into the newsroom. Those news agencies that will "thrive now and in the future will be those that can understand and serve the whole of their communities."[9] It is important for newsrooms to be diverse, especially those in diverse communities, not for political correctness but because it is the best way to serve the various groups in their communities. Many newsroom jobs, when posting for new talent, often mention that it is a plus if applicants are bilingual; others encourage reporters in minority groups to apply. While editors and organizations should not overlook the qualifications, skills and experience of any reporter, trying to diversify the newsroom will go a long way in letting readers and viewers know that the outlet is there to serve all people. Or that it is at least making strides to do so. As Steve Buttry said, newspapers are not often the voice of the voiceless. We need to do a better job at gaining and telling that voice and diversifying stories.

Share multiple viewpoints: Likewise, as has been mentioned previously, it is always good practice to have multiple sources of attribution in stories, but the reasons are many and important. The reason varied attribution might be missing from news stories may be because of time constraints to meet deadlines, sources not getting back with the reporter before deadline, and a host of other factors. But whenever possible it is a good thing to have multiple sources of attribution, even if it is in follow-up stories. Every journalist should build and retain a source network but also seek a diverse network of sources. It is good practice also for newsrooms themselves to have a consistently updated source (and resource) list for its reporters.

Help consumers become invested in the story: There has been a movement over the years by many news organizations to better engage their audiences. They call this interaction "audience engagement." In part, it means soliciting feedback, including asking consumers what they want from the newspaper. For a period of time in the late fall 2020, Forum Communications Company, headquartered in Fargo, North Dakota, but with newsrooms across several upper Midwest states, did just that. It invited readers who visited its websites to take a survey that asked them what they wanted from their news. Among other benefits, which are many, audience engagement can help the journalist and newsroom to get those multiple points of view for their story topics, as mentioned above. Forum also made further strides in its ongoing efforts to build public trust when it launched a company-wide Editorial Advisory Board in the summer of 2021. The goal was not only to promote its network of properties but to provide audiences with relevant conversations about regional interests. As such it tapped the expertise of diverse contributors and promoted community efforts to better educate the public about journalism and the business of news. It also invited audience members to participate in the discussions online. These are examples of how one news organization with multiple platforms has taken seriously its audiences experiences and input.

Promote the positives in communities: Journalists are familiar with the old saying, "If it bleeds it leads." Meaning, crime stories generally lead the front page and news broadcasts. This perhaps teeters on the verge of sensationalism, but it is because newsroom managers know they are the kind of stories that will grab people's attention. They are the stories that attract viewership, sell papers, and hike the access views on their websites. More importantly, it is information the public should know if it happened in their community so they can take precautions, if necessary.

During my time as a reporter, I have heard from a number of readers that the newspaper, whichever it was I was working for at the time, focused too much on the negativity, the bad events in their communities, and not enough on the positives. My ready reply, at least to my own thinking, was: "Why don't you read past the front page? If you did, you'd find feature sections with human interest stories—stories about arts and entertainment, faith topics, new businesses and other community-related news, stories about outdoor recreation, sporting events and celebrations, community announcements and milestones. All positive news!"

Of course, not every news outlet is a newspaper with its multiple sections, but even a broadcast station—radio or television—can in this day and age have a website that has these categories online; what's more, news organizations, no matter their platform, can dive deeper into the positive stories in their communities, making them not just hidden gems tucked away under a certain section but up front and center in the news category. They don't have to be only for the feature pages; they can have a news angle that fits nicely on the front page but with a positive focus. These are the types of stories journalists should be thinking about, as well as the more heavy-handed stories that most people expect.

Educate the community about journalism and why it matters: Taped to a wall near my desk in my current newsroom is a plain sheet of paper with the word "TEACH" scribbled on it in ballpoint pen. As mentioned in the acknowledgments section of this book, I put it there as a reminder of my obligation as a journalist to teach my readers, through my stories, something they may not have known previously. The paper was meant as a visual aid from my publisher after I joined the news organization. He would have tossed the scribble in the wastebasket, but I asked if I could keep it. To me it meant more than a piece of paper to be discarded into the trash bin; I wanted it to remind me of the moment between publisher and editor and as a reminder of what my obligation was as a journalist and writer. It remains on my wall at the time of this writing: TEACH.

Journalists know better than anyone else what their role and responsibility are to the public. They know theirs is a constitutionally defended profession and that, in essence, they are servants to the public. They know why journalism has mattered in the past and why it still matters today. Journalists know so much about journalism and its obligations, in fact, that they assume everyone else does as well. After all, journalism is one of the country's oldest institutions, a pillar of democracy, and so why wouldn't people know more about it? Why wouldn't they understand it?

People believe the press should be objective, but beyond that they seem to know or give little thought to other responsibilities and obligations of the free press. They may not understand why it matters. Newsrooms may be reluctant to dive into this topic because they don't want to insult their audience's intelligence or they believe such education should have happened in the schools, according to *Columbia Journalism Review*. "Whatever the reason, under Donald Trump,"—or in the aftermath of Trump—"there is no longer any excuse for *not* educating readers about what journalism is and why it matters."[10]

The education process may be part of audience engagement, teaching consumers about the roles and responsibilities of journalists and the news organization, how reporters go about finding stories, what the process is of putting out a news product, and why it matters.

What Other Ways Do You Believe Newsrooms Could Do Better?

If journalists and their editors and publishers truly regret the error, and if they wish to regain trust from the public, they must make changes. They cannot be like the man who says he is sorry for stealing the wallet off a blind man, only to continue to pickpocket from would-be passersby; they cannot say they regret the error and do nothing to correct it. They must do what they can to make amends. That might be soliciting audience engagement, diversifying the newsroom, or inviting reader comment—but most likely it means all of the above.

The suggestions mentioned here are only that—suggestions, but perhaps they are a good place to start if an organization is having trouble trying to decide how best to do its part to build or regain public trust. If one is having problems coming up with a plan, fall back to that one suggestion—audience engagement. Ask your local news consumers what you can do to build their trust. Spark a dialogue and see where it goes.

As you think outside the box and experiment with ideas, perhaps you will find other ways to improve your reporting staff and newsroom focus.

Doing so will help put you on the path to building more trust with the public.

Chauncey Bailey, 2007
Oakland Post

The typical sounds of a midsummer Thursday morning were shattered by gun blasts. On the ground, along a mundane street in the business district of downtown Oakland, California, lay the body of 57-year-old Chauncey Bailey, editor of the *Oakland Post*. Nearby was a McDonald's bag.

It was 7:30 a.m. on August 2, 2007.

This wasn't a mugging gone bad. Bailey had been shot at close range by a gunman dressed in dark clothing. Witness reports say he was shot at least three times, once in the face as Bailey lay prostate and bleeding.[11] It was a vicious attack on a decent man who cared deeply for his community and his profession.

The high-profile killing of the newspaper editor grabbed headlines nationwide, but so did Bailey's legacy as a journalist, which spanned not only his California community but several other communities in the Golden State and beyond.

Bailey, who loved being a journalist, had found his calling in life years before.

Born on October 20, 1949, in Oakland, Bailey's first foray into the world of news, as is the case with many newshounds at that time period, was delivering newspapers in his neighborhood. For Bailey it was the *Hayward Daily Review*. It was during this time that an incident occurred, perhaps on another early morning long before he became editor, that pointed him to his future career: a white woman complained that she didn't like having a Black boy deliver her newspaper. The racist comment made all the difference for young Bailey. "I decided that day that I was going to be a journalist," he later told the *San Francisco Chronicle*, because a byline, he realized, did not tell readers the race of the writer.[12]

Bailey's journey into journalism started when he wrote for the student newspaper at Hayward High School. He continued pursuing his dream in higher education, attending first Merritt Community College in Oakland, where he earned his associate degree, and earning his journalism degree in 1972 from San Jose State University. His career path took him to a number of newsrooms, including the *Hartford Courant* in Connecticut, United Press International in Chicago and the *Detroit News* in Michigan, but eventually he returned to his California roots and began working in the 1990s at the *Oakland Tribune*. It was at the *Tribune* that he became reacquainted with his community, and eventually he was named editor of the *Oakland Post*, a newspaper he originally freelanced for in 1970. It seemed to be the perfect fit. The paper served the Bay area's African American community, and Bailey had already established himself as someone who was deeply invested in the community and its topics and issues.

These are the twists of the screw that turned Bailey's fate.[13]

In 2007 Bailey started looking into a story about a local business called Your Black Muslim Bakery and its alleged financial troubles and crime connections. Though Bailey had written other stories about the bakery, some of them favorable, his big story about the company's financial challenges and legal problems was never published because his publisher said the story needed to be fleshed out with more attribution. His investigations, however, sparked the ire of the bakery's 24-year-old owner, Yusuf Bey IV. Bey had inherited the family shop from his father, Yusuf Bey, and he apparently also was angered at Bailey for writing articles about the child molestation charges that his father was facing at the time of his death at age 67 in 2003.[14] These efforts by the reporter seemed to have prompted Bey to order a hit on Bailey.

On the morning of August 2, as was his routine, Bailey stopped at a McDonald's for breakfast and then headed to work, walking just a few short blocks to his office. But Bey, it later was revealed, had his hitman follow Bailey to find out his daily routine. A white van followed the reporter that fateful morning; a figure, wearing a ski mask and dark clothing and wielding a shotgun, exited the van and approached Bailey.

And then shots rang out, and another American journalist fell to his death.

During the investigation police said the shooting appeared to have been an "assassin-style hit."[15] This wasn't a mugging gone wrong. Bailey was shot three times at close range, once to the face.

Two days later, on August 4, police arrested 19-year-old Devaughndre Broussard, already a convicted felon, and three days later he was arraigned on charges of murder and possession of a firearm by a convicted felon. Broussard, who confessed to pulling the trigger that ended Bailey's life, worked at the Your Black Muslim Bakery as a handyman, but investigations revealed he likely didn't act alone. It was Bey who had ordered the hit on Bailey.

Broussard, who was labeled as a sociopath,[16] agreed two years later while in prison to testify against Bey, who had been investigated for other crimes in the community, in exchange for a lower sentence.[17] In 2011,

Broussard testified for the prosecution of Bey and Antoine Mackey, another bakery employee, and both were found guilty of first-degree murder.

It determined that Bey had ordered the hit on two other men—Odell Roberson, Jr., 31, and Michael Wills, 36—during that same summer of 2007. Mackey was found guilty in Wills's death, but the jury deadlocked on the count against him for Roberson's death, according to reporting at the time.[18]

The prosecution's key witness in the murder trial was Broussard, who admitted that he had fatally shot Bailey and Roberson but said he did so because Bey ordered him to in exchange for a line of credit. Broussard also implicated Mackey in all three murders, saying Mackey killed Wills at Bey's direction and participated in the fatal shootings of Bailey and Roberson.

Broussard had been charged with two counts of murder, but prosecutors allowed him to plead guilty to two counts of the lesser charge of voluntary manslaughter in exchange for his testimony against Bey and Mackey.[19]

Bey likely will spend the rest of his life behind bars for masterminding the killings, while Bailey will roam freely in the hearts of journalists everywhere for his dedication to the journalistic ideology of uncovering crime and making its perpetrators stand accountable.

Bailey's career, which spanned the better part of four decades, was an honorable one. He had found his calling early and devoted his life to it, effecting change and touching many lives along the way.[20] Journalism was all he ever wanted to do. "He loved anything about journalism," his sister, Lorelei Waqia, told the *Mercury News* in a report just a few days after his death.[21]

In August 2019, a local councilwoman announced that a memorial plaque would be erected in honor of the slain journalist.[22] Originally scheduled to be installed in October 2019, the group later said it would delay the project to broaden its scope.[23] As of this writing, no date has been announced. But according to news reports in March 2022, an Oakland street was named after the slain journalist.

"I'm very teary," Bailey's cousin Wendy Ashley-Johnson said after the trial that convicted Bey. "Journalists have a job to do and they should not be squashed in what they do, and that's what they tried to do to Chauncey. That's why the family decided to talk to the press, because that's what Chauncey would have wanted us to do."[24]

9

Brave Journalism

The power to mould the future of the Republic will be in the hands of the journalists of future generations.—JOSEPH PULITZER

On a chilly Saturday evening on the first day of spring in the year 2021, while ghostly sounding winds whipped among the eaves outside the windows of my apartment in North Dakota, I opened a small book that had arrived by mail earlier that day: *Ten Days in a Mad-House.* The book, popular among those who are interested in journalism's past and its intrepid reporters, tells of the firsthand experiences of one of the industry's most intrepid, Nellie Bly, who had committed herself into an insane asylum to see how patients were being treated at the facility.

Bly, age 24 at the time she went undercover for *The World* newspaper in New York, was assigned the story by her editor. Bly had already proven herself a tenacious and reliable reporter whose only hindrance at the time was being a woman in a male-dominated society. She had previously worked at the *Pittsburg Gazette.* Her ambitions looked beyond the day's norm, which had women reporters do mostly lifestyle and society stories, not impactful news. She tired of the fluff pieces that women reporters were often responsible to write and wanted stories that were heavier hitting. But afterward, she found herself back at the fluff desks. Deciding she was going to make her mark, she packed her bags and headed to New York City's newspaper row, a section of the city where many newspaper offices were located. She visited with editors, trying to sell her skills and ambition as a writer. Eventually, one bought. The editor of Joseph Pulitzer's *The New York World* asked her how she felt about going undercover at Blackwell's Island Insane Asylum for Women. There had been rumors that patients at the facility were not treated kindly by its doctors, that occupants were malnourished and neglected.

Bly, whose real name was Elizabeth Cochrane and who would later compete in a race around the world in a real-life dramatis personae of Jules Verne's novel *Around the World in Eighty Days*, didn't hesitate, and later when she set words to paper she admitted she had experienced anxiety about tackling such as assignment, not knowing if she was a good enough actress to fool the hospital staff and doctors. She and her editor made plans on how she would commit herself into an institution and what the plans were for getting her out. Her editor added to her anxiety when he said he wasn't sure what the retrieval plans were at the time, but they would come up with something. Bly's courage and confidence sometimes waned when she wondered: what if something goes wrong and, somehow, I get stuck there, becoming a permanent resident? But intrepid reporters know the risks before they tackle their stories and go anyway. That's what makes them intrepid. Later, after her ordeal, she was able to confidently write: "On the 22D of September I was asked by the *World* if I could have myself committed to one of the asylums for the insane in New York, with view to writing a plain and unvarnished narrative of the treatment of the patients therein and the methods of management, etc. Did I think I had the courage to go through such an ordeal as the mission would demand? ... I said I believed I could. ... I said I could and I would. And I did."

And so the task was set. She had agreed to commit herself to the city's Blackwell Island Asylum for the mentally insane in the hopes to witness firsthand how the patients were being treated at the mental facility. According to rumors, there had been grave mistreatment at such facilities, but she wanted to find out for herself if the rumors were true or not, and, in so doing, she would let the reading public know as well. Of her ambition and goal, she writes:

> If I did get into the asylum, which I hardly hoped to do, I had no idea that my experiences would contain aught else than a simple tale of life in an asylum. That such an institution could be mismanaged, and that cruelties could exist 'neath its roof, I did not deem possible. I always had a desire to know asylum life more thoroughly—a desire to be convinced that the most helpless of God's creatures, the insane, were cared for kindly and properly. The many stories I had read of abuses in such institutions I had regarded as wildly exaggerated or else romances, yet there was a latent desire to know positively.
>
> I shuddered to think how completely the insane were in the power of their keepers, and how one could weep and plead for release, and all to no avail, if the keepers were minded. Eagerly I accepted the mission to learn the inside workings of the Blackwell's Island Insane Asylum.

This was brave journalism if there ever was any—not because Bly went incognito into a mental institution but also for the *purpose* of so doing and its end result: "writing a plain and unvarnished narrative" of the details as she witnessed and experienced them. Bly likely needed no reminding of journalism's ideals in seeking truth, but her editor reminded her just the same, telling her: "We do not ask you to go there for the purpose of making sensational revelations. Write up things as you find them, good or bad; give praise or blame as you think best, and the truth all the time."[1] Then he perhaps jested, "But I am afraid of that chronic smile of yours." Bly later intoned, perhaps with a nod to the same good nature: "I had little belief in my ability to deceive the insanity experts, and I think my editor had less."

Bly explains in the book, which in my copy comprises just 88 pages of text, that after she received her assignment she went to "practice the role in which I was to make my debut on the morrow." Her assignment took her first to a boarding house for women—but not before she spent the previous night practicing her crazy stare in the mirror—where she portrayed a woman who was unnerved and confused. Using the name of Nellie Brown—a pseudonym on top of pseudonym—to keep the initials N.B., she thought if she could fool the nurses at the boarding house that she had a good chance of being committed to the institution at Blackwell's Island. Once she secured lodging at the home, she played her part well, giving the glazed, incoherent stare, telling the nurses she was afraid of the women at the home, muttering nonsense about luggage that she couldn't find, and staying up all night to make sure she stayed in the zone.

Her plan had worked. She had duped the folks at the women's boarding house and, through her ensuing interactions and examinations with law enforcement and doctors, she was now on her way to Blackwell's Island, where she would spend the next ten days supposedly as a woman who doctors and nurses deemed crazy.

Once inside, Bly sadly discovered that the rumors she had heard were true. Some of the nurses and doctors at Blackwell's institution did treat patients cruelly. Among the transgressions witnessed were nurses making the female patients take cold baths, choking and punching them, teasing and making fun of the women, and ignoring those who sometimes needed medical attention. Perhaps in a twist of fate was that some of the women in the institution were not what was called insane, but only destitute. If they were not mentally challenged when they arrived, they surely would be if they stayed at the facility with such treatment for long, which surely many of them did. Bly herself said she had felt on the verge of mental collapse after spending several days in the facility. She was saved when the paper's lawyer showed up to release her, telling authorities at the hospital that her friends had assumed responsibility and would take care of her.

As she breathed the fresh air of freedom once more, she felt sorrow at having left behind the many other women at the asylum, knowing firsthand how they were being treated. She worried for their welfare and was hopeful her account would spark much-needed improvements at the facility in the way patients were treated. Perhaps through her reporting the women left at Blackwell's Island would be helped.

When Bly's story ran in a two-part series in *The World* on October 9 and 16, 1887, and later in book form the same year, it did what journalism is supposed to do: cause change. The story turned heads not only in New York but in other places too and plummeted Bly into the pantheon of America's great reporting sleuths. Readers were outraged at the treatment of the women and curious to see firsthand what Bly had reported; she was summoned to appear before a grand jury to answer questions about her experiences at the asylum. "If I could not bring them [the patients] that boon of all boons, liberty," she wrote near the end of her report, "I hoped at least to influence others to make life more bearable for them." She was requested to accompany the jurors back to Blackwell's Asylum, but news of their planned arrival leaked to officials at the facility, and when the group visited the institution, they did not see the same things that Bly had described in her articles. The kitchen was clean, whereas when she was there it had been unsanitary; salt, which was kept from patients at mealtime, was set out; and the bread, which had been moldy and hard, was freshly baked and on display. Halls were cleaned, bedding was improved, and wash basins that patients used, which before contained dirty water, were clean. And the women she had known were removed out of sight.

"The institution was on exhibition, and no fault could be found," she writes, explaining later: "I hardly expected the grand jury to sustain me, after they saw everything different from what it had been while I was there," she writes. "Yet they did, and their report to the court advises all the changes made that I proposed."

"I have one consolation for my work," she concluded, "on the strength of my story the committee of appropriation provides $1,000,000 more than was ever before given for the benefit of the insane."

It's a Jungle Out There

The same day that my book by Bly arrived, I took from a bookshelf my copy of the novel *The Jungle* by Upton Sinclair, which, while mostly fictional, dramatized the real-life experiences the author had witnessed in Chicago's meatpacking industry. To gain fodder for his novel Sinclair went undercover, working for several weeks at the stockyards in 1904, where he witnessed firsthand the atrocities he reported in *The Jungle*, a book that was published in 1906. His first accounts, however, found their home in a newspaper called *Appeal to Reason*, with a socialist bent.

While the scenes depicted in the novel, however disturbing they still may appear, on another level may seem tame compared to other exposés done since then. But at the time, Sinclair's reporting—his vivid descriptions of inhumane and unsanitary conditions inside the meatpacking facility— had effected change at the highest levels of the food and drug administration. While his aim may have been to bring more awareness to the plight of exploited immigrant workers, it was the health violations that caught readers' attention. Later, realizing this, Sinclair said, "I aimed at the public's heart, and by accident I hit it in the stomach."[2]

These books—one a true account and the other a work of fiction with muckraker skills thrown in for good measure—caused me to reflect upon journalism, literary or otherwise, that has helped spark societal changes. Some of the bigger stories some people are familiar with, rehashed here by their primary names, include the Pentagon Papers that unveiled previously hidden government goings-on during the Vietnam War era; Watergate in which reporters uncovered scandals at the Nixon White House; and the Spotlight investigations of sexual abuse in the Catholic Church. But I also thought of the lesser-known gems found in community journalism, whether it's a deep dive from the local daily newspaper or broadcast series by the local television or radio station. In these digital days, such investigations may also come from online-only news publications. Such was the case when Forbes Digital Tool, now Forbes.com, found through the dogged determination and curiosity of reporter Adam Penenberg and editor Kambiz Foroohar that *The New Republic* writer Stephen Glass had fabricated stories he wrote for the *Republic* and other national publications in the late 1990s.[3]

The Crusading Journalist

What Nellie Bly did has been called by some as "stunt journalism" and is frowned upon today. Ethically, a journalist should let potential sources and targets of investigation know he or she is a reporter investigating the given topic. And yet stunt reporting—the prelude perhaps to today's modern muckraking—has accomplished much over time. Kim Todd wrote an excellent book about early female stunt reporters, called *Sensational: The Hidden History of America's "Girl Stunt Reporters,"* of whom Nellie Bly was one ... but there were many others.

There also have been many above-the-board instances of muckraking or investigative reporting, the kind that is more proper, which also has accomplished much good. A few have already been mentioned, but here's another instance of brave journalism: Vern Marshall.

A canning factory in Cedar Rapids, Iowa, that was a front for illegal liquor sales and gambling in the days of prohibition, was raided by police on December 12, 1934. Vern Marshall, editor of the *Cedar Rapids Gazette,* caught wind of the story and, like a good reporter, kept digging until he uncovered that the scheme reached all the way to the state capitol.

Such efforts are not without their own threats of peril.

A journalist named Victor Riesel covered labor unions when on April 5, 1956, an irate reader—whom the *New York Times* called a "thug" in its April 6, 1956, edition—threw sulfuric acid at him. At the time of the incident, which happened after the reporter exited a restaurant in Manhattan, Riesel had been reporting on alleged corruption in the International Union of Operating Engineers. While the acid did not kill him, it caused him to be permanently blind.[4]

The Year of the Journalist

Brave journalism has been reported ever since man took up the pen and started scribbling the news of the day. When German-born goldsmith Johannes Gutenberg founded the printing press in 1440 AD, allowing for a much easier and wider distribution of news and opinions, that bravery accelerated. Today, despite the seemingly endless challenges that face newshounds, including backlash from an unappreciative society, there remains many instances of courageous journalism. We can pinpoint a number of examples just from 2020, a year that presented a number of challenges to the profession.

I am no eye doctor, but I know that ophthalmologists use the term 20/20 to describe normal visual acuity, or the clarity of vision measured at 20 feet. As the year 2020 began, I thought of this term frequently, seeking to apply it to my own New Year's resolutions. I wanted to experience 20/20 vision for the new year and new opportunities. Just a few months previous I had landed a new editor's position for a business magazine, and as the new year began, I had set the bar high with new goals and aspirations. Those ambitions were soon tweaked, my perspective shortened, as world conditions changed and then accelerated. By mid–March the coronavirus pandemic was declared, and I spent the rest of the year working remotely. As I heard of colleagues being laid off work, my vision clouded, and I wondered and feared about my own future. Anxiety about my career and colleagues mounted as journalists in many states were assaulted and arrested, sometimes on live television, during nationwide demonstrations over issues about racism. A sitting president assaulted the press over social media and at his rallies, with many of his supporters doing much the same thing. It was not the year for the journalist, I thought.

But then I thought again.

It *was* the year of the journalist. And the journalist came out on top.

I saw many instances of brave journalism—from the national media to hometown newspapers and television stations. While the naysayers complained and name-called, I knew differently. I was proud of my colleagues, whether I worked with them or watched them on the nightly news, and I was happy to be among this selected and slim body of scribblers.

Some of the brave journalism that came out of 2020 included stories about how the coronavirus was affecting families, businesses and hospitals; stories about racism and the need for change in our institutions and agencies to confront systemic racism; what businesses and families were doing to stay afloat during tough economic times; and continuing tallies of health care workers' efforts to combat the deadly virus, among many other stories.

Besides my stories with the business magazine, which sometimes depicted how industries were adapting to the uncertain times, I also helped report on governor's meetings about the pandemic and state-related initiatives to help businesses and people most affected. It was a surreal time to work as a journalist, especially since much of the reporting was done remotely, in virtual meetings or by telephone. It was always a boon when I could get in front of someone face-to-face, but my publisher stressed the importance of staying safe above all else.

It was the year of the journalist, not just because of the stories that were produced but because of the way it brought a community of journalists all over the country together to tell the stories of the unprecedented times in which we then lived.

I like to think that the year 2020 helped many of us become better reporters and, more importantly, better people. As such, it will help us carry the torch of brave journalism into the future.

Brave Journalism Going Forward

In early April 2021 the National Intelligence Council released a quadrennial report called Global Trends 2040. It didn't paint a happy picture for the world over the next 20 years. In part, the report describes the coronavirus pandemic as "a preview of crises to come."[5] It discussed a number of items, including climate change, which will likely "exacerbate food and water insecurity for poor countries,"[6] public health, relations between the U.S. and China, and potential chaos related to technology. The report mentioned that these "global challenges—including climate change, disease, financial crises, and technology disruptions—are likely to manifest more frequently and intensely in almost every region and country." Such challenges, some without human invention, "will produce widespread strains on states and societies as well as shocks that could be catastrophic."[7]

Of the COVID-19 pandemic, the authors of the report noted that it "marks the most significant, singular global disruption since World War II, with health, economic, political, and security implications that will ripple for years to come."[8] Furthermore, with regard to technology and communication, the report claims that over the next two decades "the pace and reach of technological developments are likely to increase ever faster, transforming a range of human experiences and capabilities while also creating new tensions and disruptions within and between societies, industries, and states. State and nonstate rivals will vie for leadership and dominance in science and technology with potentially cascading risks and implications for economic, military, and societal security."[9] Also, people will likely gravitate "to familiar and like-minded groups for community and security, including ethnic, religious, and cultural identities as well as groupings around interests and causes, such as environmentalism," while noting that a "combination of newly prominent and diverse identity allegiances and a more siloed information environment is exposing and aggravating fault lines within states, undermining civic nationalism, and increasing volatility."[10]

In this light, what will journalism look like in the future and what will be its role in society? While it no doubt will continue to adopt the latest technology to gather and disseminate news, it is tough to predict exactly how it will look or what its main thrust will be 20 years down the road. It is tough to predict what it will look like in even five or ten years. As the dividing lines in politics and government become more pronounced, it is likely partisan gaps will widen between some news organizations—conservative and liberal—which in their haste to be correct in their own view of things may find they have become the embodiment of the very groups they initially opposed, as such community news organizations—who knows if there will be news-"papers" at that time—will be competing with businesses and government agencies who will be disseminating their own brand of PR news. Many such organizations have already started doing this, as some companies, local government and civic agencies have their own newsletters and other publications to "inform" their citizens. As such, it will be imperative for news organizations to do what they do best: uncover and vet stories.

But there is another view of journalism's future that is more optimistic. According to an article titled "For US Journalism, the Future Is Brighter Than You Think" by the Boston Consulting Group, many of our legacy papers are still read and discussed. "Traditional forms of journalism remain vibrant," it said. "Newspapers such as the *New York Times*, the *Washington Post*, and the *Wall Street Journal* are showing that consumers will pay for high-quality online journalism. We believe that other online outlets with distinct coverage and a clear voice can also generate revenues from consumers."[11]

This reflects positivity in the industry, despite the naysayers: people still turn to the tried-and-true sources of news. They want real news, from real professionals, and our legitimate news organizations remain the best, most viable way to obtain it. That will continue as long as journalists continue to be brave. Adapting to the changing environment of journalism is both courageous and innovative.

What the journalism landscape will look like in the future, of course, is anyone's guess, but my own perspective, besides the likelihood of continued volatility mentioned above, is that people will, by and large, continue to turn to legitimate news sources for their daily facts. Even if newsprint were to go the way of the dodo bird, those same organizations will still be producing relevant and timely news through other mediums. Trained, professional, working journalists, reporters and editors will still be needed. Online news within these same organizations and among journalists will continue to grow.

Some challenges the industry and its reporters will face will be the continued and increasing use of social media. They will be faced with the continued task of correcting disinformation from ill-intended campaigns that deliberately seek to dissuade and discourage the public, stir a different kind of controversy, and belittle the legitimate press and make it seem irrelevant. Politicians and business leaders with their own agendas will likely lead this charge as they try to tell their own narrative *the way they want it told*. The term "fake news" seems to now be a part of the public's perception and vocabulary whenever they hear or read a report they don't agree with, and so we can expect to see and hear this negative labeling even when the news we read is true.

Newsrooms likely will continue to shrink, and more technologies will replace the legacy tools newsrooms are used to using; journalists will be tasked, much as they are now, with juggling different responsibilities; thus the needed skill sets that newsrooms seek from the rising generation of reporters will continue to tighten; and the industry will find more ways to be creative in telling and marketing their stories in an increasing world of pop culture and self-populated "news reports."

News media will continue to be gatekeepers, watchdogs of the government, but in the modern world with the 24-hour news cycle and a never-dormant online presence, it also will continue to set the news agenda, especially from the powerhouse institutions. However, the community news outlet must find their own narratives, create their own policies and ethical standards, and continue to educate the public in these opportune times.

The industry will most likely continue to evolve. What may have worked in the past may not work in the future. These are additional reasons journalists must be brave, their reporting courageous. Some will fall out of favor with their profession as demands and controversy increase, but others will remain on the front lines.

There will be financial challenges, and newsrooms will seek further ways to innovate and remain viable in the communities in which they serve. Partnerships may be formed, but they must not be at the expense of independent news reporting. Layoffs may happen, news organizations may shutter or shrink, papers may stop being printed, but there will always be a need for the ambitious and ethical scribbler to tell our stories and pass to the public the information that best helps them to make the decisions that impact their lives and livelihoods.

And the journalist will continue to tell relevant stories, seeking the big story while telling the daily grind of breaking and spot news. It will continue to find causes to champion, changes to promote, and that which is detrimental to our democracy it will uncover and expose. It will find new ways to tell old stories.

I have faith in journalism, because I know many ethical and passionate journalists who seek nothing but the best for the industry and the communities in which they work and serve. I have faith in the future of journalism because of the rising generation of talented newsies. And I have faith in my profession because it is defended under the Constitution of the United States, and I have faith in that document and the principles by which we all are made free. They are principles that journalists and journalism must defend. It must defend its own household and its very foundation.

There will always be a need for journalism because the mantra rings true: Journalism Matters. Especially brave journalism. Many have died for that kind of reporting, for those kinds of truths. It is likely that there will be more journalist martyrs, media workers who defend the rights and privileges of a free press and the public's right to know. In spite of the fallen, or perhaps because of them, the press will remain fundamentally the Fourth Estate. It is not fortuitous that it does so; it will be because of a concerted and deliberate effort to defend the constitutional liberties that make the press free.

Going forward, journalists must continue to be courageous in their reporting, namely because the environment in which they work and report will likely be volatile. There also will be old and new challenges to confront. One of them, if pundits are correct, is the continuing influence of Trumpism in American politics.

The political pendulum keeps swinging wider between right and left, forcing moderation off the stage. As the partisan divide grows, it poses a great risk of lengthening the divide between the public and the press. But brave journalism—journalism based on fact and not opinion—that emboldens positive change and lengthens the stride of truth will be needed more than ever.

These glorious words from Joseph Pulitzer are just as relevant now as they were when he spoke them in his day: "The power to mould the future of the Republic will be in the hands of the journalists of future generations."

The future begins now.

Alison Parker and Adam Ward, 2015
WDBJ7-TV

A member of the press is a member of a global community of free-thinkers and idealists. When one member falls, we all mourn. The journalism community mourned the killing of two reporters that occurred during a live broadcast in late August 2015 in Moneta, Virginia.

Alison Parker and Adam Ward worked for the television station WDBJ7 in Roanoke, Virginia, and were doing a feel-good story about the 50th anniversary of Smith Mountain Lake, a popular destination in the region for outdoor enthusiasts and recreationists. At a little before 7 a.m. on the morning of Wednesday, August 26, Parker stood with microphone in hand on the balcony of the Bridgewater Plaza, an office and retail center on the lakeshore, interviewing the local Chamber of Commerce president. Ward was filming the interview.

Not long after the broadcast started, a man dressed in black approached Ward from behind and fired several shots. As Ward fell, so did his camera, but continuing gunfire and screams could be heard in the background. Both journalists and the chamber president were shot.

Meanwhile, colleagues back at the studio were shocked at what they were witnessing. Their fellow journalists in the field, two of the station's bright spots, were under attack. Viewers in the region also were disturbed by the live scenes of tragedy in the making. Could this really be happening?

Parker and Ward both died at the scene—not in a combat zone or volatile civil demonstration, but in a peaceful setting during what was supposed to be a commemorative event in the area's lakeshore history. The shooting was a senseless act of violence that ended the budding lives and promising careers of two young people who already were making a difference in their careers and communities. In an emotional broadcast later, WDBJ7's general manager Jeff Marks said: "I cannot tell you how much they were loved, Alison and Adam, by the WDBJ7 team. Our hearts are broken."[12]

Both of the reporters had previously interned at the station before being hired full time. Both were dedicated journalists, personable and fun to be around, and loved their colleagues as much as their colleagues loved them. They were described as being able to "brighten up the room."[13] Both of them also had new chapters in their personal lives to look forward to.

Parker, 24, who had just been hired by the station the year previous, was dating the station's evening anchor and had recently moved in with him. Ward, 27, had recently gotten engaged to a producer at the station. According to one report, she was in the control room watching the live broadcast when the shooting occurred.[14]

Parker and Ward's passing left a void in the hearts of loved ones and in those of their journalist colleagues, not only in Virginia but across the country and around the globe. They died long before they should have and in a way that never should have happened, but the journalists did not die in vain. They will be remembered for their examples, friendship and kindness, how they impacted those closest to them and what they did for their communities. They also will be remembered for their love of impactful storytelling, of journalism and its ideals. As with anyone worthy to be called a journalist, they had put their all into the stories they covered, whether reporting on a hard news topic or on a celebratory feature about a regional lake.

"Alison Parker and Adam Ward loved their jobs as journalists," Pat Thomas of WDBJ wrote on the five-year anniversary of their deaths, August 26, 2020.[15] Perhaps it is the story they covered at the end that brings another level of sadness to the tale. It was not a hard news story. It was not one that uncovered conspiracy or crime or put the faces or names of criminals on the air. It was a light feature in honor of a regional icon, and yet a criminal had come to them anyway. "They are missed, and we continue to remember them with smiles and fond memories because that's exactly how they would want it," Thomas continued. "They will forever be in our hearts."

Playing the Violin

Chamber of Commerce President Vicki Gardner, whom Parker was interviewing at the time of the senseless tragedy, also was shot but thankfully survived after being taken to the hospital where she underwent emergency surgery.

As for the gunman, he was later identified as Vester Lee Flanagan II, a 41-year-old former employee of WDBJ7 who went by the on-air name of Bryce Williams. Flanagan was described as being "an unhappy man" and "difficult to work with."[16] After a history of conflicts at the station, including what has been described as instances of rage while in the workplace, he was relieved of his post, escorted from the building, and apparently ever after harbored ill feelings toward the station and his former colleagues. He was described as "a skilled broadcaster, but also volatile, combative, threatening and prone to seeing himself as persecuted."[17]

As the story unfolded on the morning of August 26, so did more details about the gunman. After the shooting, Flanagan, who had himself also recorded the violence with his own camera, posted the video on social media and faxed a 23-page missive to ABC News in New York. In it he referenced past mass shootings, claimed there was a race war going on, and alleged he had been harassed and discriminated against for being Black and gay. His emotional issues apparently ran deep, and when they came to the surface they boiled into rage. His past grievances in the workplace were only sporadic drops in the torrent that had been building and, when released, would cost the lives of two young journalists, his former colleagues.

Flanagan turned the gun on himself hours later after being cornered by police on a highway about 200 miles away, ending his own life.[18]

Workplace Violence

Workplace violence has become an issue over the years, grabbing media attention after a series of post office shootings that occurred in the 1980s and '90s. Incidences of workplace violence have happened in a number of industries, with particular attention to health care and protective services. Incidences of workplace violence that resulted in injured victims requiring days off work to heal and recuperate were, on average, four times higher in health care than in the private sector.[19]

There were about 700 workplace homicides every year between the years 1992 and 2012, some 14,770 victims in all.[20] According to a report by CNN in 2015, the same year that Parker and Ward were killed, the "most common but least reported types of workplace violence are bullying, intimidation and threats."[21]

Jumping ahead a few years and looking at a broader spectrum, according to the U.S. Bureau of Labor Statistics, 453 individuals were killed in incidences of general workplace violence in 2018. Eighty-two percent of them were male, 47 percent were white, and 66 percent were between the ages of 25 and 54. Twenty percent of the victims were working in sales or related occupations, and 19 percent were performing protective services. According to the same statistics, 20,790 workers in private industry were injured or experienced nonfatal trauma related to workplace violence. Seventy-one percent of that number were female; 73 percent worked in the health care or social assistance industry; and 20 percent required more than a month away from work to recover from their injuries.

Such violence costs not only bodily harm and in some cases death; it costs in lost wages and productivity. Journalists, as we have seen, are not immune from workplace violence or its threat. However, the incident that took the lives of Alison Parker and Adam Ward is rare, especially among news and media workers. More of their physical threat comes from outside the newsroom, the subjects they are reporting on.

We do not mourn Flanagan's passing as we do Parker's and Ward's, but we are saddened that a former news worker would turn to such senseless violence. The sane mind cannot comprehend the insane, just as the high-perched eagle cannot fathom the thoughts of a spider. Likewise, good cannot comprehend evil, only that it is dark and foreboding and painful, but to what depths only those who have welcomed the evil know. In short, it is difficult for the bread and butter of society to understand how a person could harbor such feelings of violence, let alone act upon them. Those who had worked with Flanagan, who knew of his short temper and self-aggrandizing personality, perhaps knew he was a person capable of violence, but they perhaps still had a tough time grasping that such a deliberate and evil act could be perpetrated on anyone, let alone one of their own. When it happened, they were shocked that a former employee, someone who had once worked in the news profession, could turn not only traitor but killer.

It didn't make sense—and still doesn't today—just as all such acts, no matter how deliberate or targeted, do not make sense to most people. The killing of Parker and Ward was a senseless act of cowardice and shame, no matter what lingo is thrown out there about race wars and prejudice and discrimination.

Leaving Their Mark

While the gunmen left his mark—a senseless act of violence committed by a warped mind—Parker and Ward have left a much different mark on the world. They have reinforced with their own blood that journalism, no matter the story, means something other than meeting a deadline.

Journalism, to a great many people who practice it, means more to them than just a means to pay the bills. It is a noble profession, defended by the Constitution, and carries a heavy mantle of public trust. For the committed journalist, the profession is not a job only; it is a calling to serve and defend. That might sound highbrow, self-absorbed and prideful, but after working in newsrooms for most of my working career, I have seen, heard, and felt that passion and perspective from my colleagues. And it is one I share with them.

Journalism is a calling, and for us print types we bleed ink.

For others, like Parker and Ward, who die while doing their work, their blood serves as a testament to the martyr's cause.

"Both extremely good people, will be missed," Jay Webb, the news director at WHSV, another local station and who had previously worked with Ward at WDBJ, told ABC News in an interview on the day the reporters were killed. "I think it's been said this morning, just two journalists that were just trying to do a good job."[22]

10

Blood and Ink

Covering a war means going into places torn by chaos, destruction, death and pain, and trying to bear witness to that.—MARIE COLVIN

During my time spent as an Outdoors writer, I had the privilege of reporting about hometown heroes, returning veterans who were wounded while serving their country in far-off lands. These wounded warriors were then and remain now an inspiration to me because they gave something so personal in the defense of their country—convictions that ultimately stir the heart of America.

The man I most closely worked with on some of these feature and spot news stories, the person who developed and organized the fishing and hunting excursions for these veterans, also has remained an inspiration to me. Monte Bruhn has passed away since we met and worked together—he being my source; I, the reporter—but I remember well the days we would chat, including the first time I met him and other American warriors at an early morning breakfast in a small community in southern Idaho.

Monte Bruhn, who at the time lived in Buhl, Idaho, never served his country in the military, but he had found a way to serve those who had. He and his wife, Diane, founded the nonprofit Idaho "N" Heroes Outdoors Inc., formerly the Doug Bridges Memorial Hunts. Part of the national The Link-up, every year Bruhn would take wounded veterans into Idaho's backcountry to hunt or fish. Some of the veterans came from out of state, others from just around the corner. It was exciting for the veterans, the donors, the volunteers and me. Even if I didn't go with them on the hunts, I was excited to know the work being done and the dreams being fulfilled by these brave men and women who served our country. Like Bruhn told me, it was time to give them a little something back. The veterans were ecstatic. "I've already got my bags packed," Bill Woods of Grand Rapids, Michigan, said in July 2010, a month before the actual hunt took place. "My wife says, 'You haven't even made it through the baseball season yet.' … It might not ever happen again, but hunting in Idaho is something I've always wanted to do. If it's going to happen, this will be the year. And maybe someday I can take my own son out west."

Here's a salute to all of the wounded veterans. And to Monte Bruhn. Here is a salute to my own father, Floyd, who served in the U.S. Army during the Korean War; to my father-in-law, Don Snyder, who served in the U.S. Air Force; to my nephew Mason, who is serving in the U.S. Marines; and for the uncle I never met, Homer Weeks, who died while serving his country in the U.S. Army, also during the Korean War, just a week before he was supposed to return home. He did return, but not in the way his loved ones had anticipated and prayed.

They have all taught me, in their own ways, what it means to serve. They also helped broaden my perspective that while many have made the ultimate sacrifice, many others, just as passionate about their country and defending its freedoms, find ways to serve without taking up arms. Sometimes they take up a pen and paper, sometimes it's a camera.

Viewing Conflict with a Third Eye

James Foley believed in humanity and went into the reaches of hell to fight for it by showing humankind its inhumanity. He believed that being a firsthand witness to the tragedies and civil unrest could help bring more humanity to the world because it would witness the cruelty and depravity of conflict.

Born on October 18, 1973, in Evanston, Illinois, James Foley was the eldest of five children of John and Diane Foley. He grew up in Wolfeboro, New Hampshire, and when he became of age and after graduating from Marquette University in Milwaukee, Wisconsin, and later from the Master of Fine Arts program in writing at the University of Massachusetts, he set out for a career in education and worked with Teach For America for a time, but his career and life's path took a different direction when the Medill School of Journalism at Northwestern University in Illinois gave him the opportunity to become a conflict reporter.

His journalism adventures took him to Afghanistan, Iraq and Libya, where he reported for *Stars and Stripes* and the *GlobalPost*. Sometimes he gave away his videos without remuneration just so they could be seen because he felt it was important to share the information with the world. Foley's third eye was the lens of his camera in which he detailed and saw the world in millimeters and sound bites. Without the images and the stories behind them, he had said, you can't really tell the world its troubles or find the solutions to overcome them.

In 2011, while reporting in Libya, Foley was taken by Gaddafi loyalists and held for 44 days before being released. It was but a foretaste of what was to come. He returned home to his family, but he felt uneasy, much like a fish out of water. Such feelings may be difficult for some people to understand. According to the documentary film *Jim: The James Foley Story*, they were longings his family and friends had a tough time understanding.

Ultimately, the distant lands of conflict drew him back to conflict. This time his destination was war-torn Syria. His life turned on a dime on November 22, 2012. While visiting an internet café in the town Binnish in Syria's northwest province of Idlib, Foley sent off a series of emails to colleagues and friends before catching a taxi to his next destination. While en route to the border, the taxi was ambushed by four mask-wearing jihadis. The next time his family and friends saw him was in an orange jumpsuit, which "heralded the announcement of Islamic State on the world stage."[1]

Foley was held in a dank prison with captured media workers from France. Sometimes the confined men quarreled and fought with each other, but over the ensuing months they became friends. But what can a friend do for the other when all are held prisoner and beaten by their captors? Eventually, the other journalists were released, but Foley, who celebrated his 40th birthday in a prison in a foreign land, was not released. His captors negotiated with his family for money and made demands through them to the U.S. government, but eventually all contact with the captors ceased until one last email arrived saying they planned to execute Jim. The next the family heard about Jim was from a video by his brutal captors, showing his execution.

So much could be written about James Foley, but thankfully we have a fine documentary about his life and career and the impact he had on his family and so many others. He was a good person, his imprisoned colleagues said of him, an honest man without a bad bone in his body. He was a deeply caring man who made others feel comforted in the dank cell of their capture. He brought smiles and laughter to the faces of his colleagues when he worked with them, friendship to his sources and contacts and the people he interviewed, and he brought important information to the world by the issues he covered.

What does the death of James Foley and other journalists who have lost their lives while covering conflict tell us about journalism's role in society, the country, and the world? Perhaps Foley himself said it best: "I believe frontline journalism is important," Foley said of his conflict reporting, as shown in the HBO documentary film *Jim: The James Foley Story*. "Without these photos and videos of firsthand experiences, you can't really tell the world how bad it might be."

His death by the hands of militants brings another layer to just how important reporting conflict is: it stirs the ire of those who oppose, who are doing the endangering, and brings further to light their evil deeds.

In honor of Foley and other slain and missing journalists, as well as those who continue the work of journalism today, the James Foley Foundation (jamesfoleyfoundation.org) was created, which, in part, offers proactive ways for journalists to implement a higher level of safety measures while reporting. It also advocates for the release of journalists held hostage in foreign lands.

There have been others like Foley who have put themselves in harm's way to bring information to the public. Here are only a few, Americans and otherwise:

Ralph Barnes worked for the *New York Herald Tribune* when he was sent overseas to cover Mussolini's invasion of Greece in 1940. Barnes was flying with the Royal Air Force when the plane he was on crashed on November 17 in Yugoslavia. He was the first war reporter killed during World War II. Colleagues, including well-known radio broadcaster William L. Shirer, praised Barnes's work, and in 1943 a ship was christened in his honor: the SS *Ralph Barnes*.[2]

Robert Perkins Post was among a group of journalists who achieved the honor of flying with the United States Eighth Air Force, also during World War II. Nicknamed the Flying Typewriters, or Legion of the Doomed, the group comprised eight journalists, including one correspondent by the name of Walter Cronkite. Another one was Andy Rooney. On February 26, 1943, they took off in B-24 and B-17 bombers for the Focke-Wulf aircraft factory in Bremen, Germany, which they were to bomb, but because skies over Bremen were cloudy, the group was dispatched to the submarine pens at Wilhelmshaven. It was during this run that the group was attacked by German fighters, knocking down Post's plane. He and several crew members died in the crash. The other plane carrying the remaining journalists returned safely to base.

Byron Darnton worked for the *New York Times* when he was killed in 1942 while covering stories in the Pacific theater. Adding another layer of sorrow, his death on October 18 was caused by friendly fire from American forces. He was traveling on a U.S. wooden trawler off the coast of Pongani in New Guinea, when an American B-25 crew mistook the ship and its fleet of vessels for Japanese craft and let loose a barrage of bomb and machine-gun fire. Darnton, who had won the accolades of his colleagues and servicemen, including General MacArthur, was the tenth American war correspondent killed in the war.[3]

Joseph Morton worked for the Associated Press in the European theater, also during World War II, when he was executed by Nazi soldiers on

January 24, 1945. Having joined the AP in 1937 in Lincoln, Nebraska, Morton reported in several cities until he was assigned to be a foreign correspondent in May 1942. His first assignments took him to Africa, North Africa and Sicily. But when Rome fell on June 1, 1944, his editors at the AP encouraged him to expand his coverage in the Balkans. On December 26, 1944, a Nazi counter-partisan unit stormed a log cabin on Homolka Mountain in present-day Slovakia. A number of allied intelligence and others, including Morton, were in the cabin and taken by the Nazis. His press card did little for him, and instead of being treated as a prisoner of war, according to the Geneva Convention of 1929, Morton and the others were executed in a concentration camp. He was the only Allied correspondent to be executed during the war.[4]

William R. Moore, a journalist who worked for *The Oklahoman*, served a stint in the U.S. Army but returned to the war zone two years later, in 1948, to cover the Korean War. He went to war to help his countrymen understand the dynamics and penalties of conflict. He was one of the first reporters during the war to reach the front lines and the first reporter to uncover atrocities committed by the North Korean government. He died far from home on July 30, 1950, while trying to help soldiers who had been hit by enemy fire near Masan.

Georgette Louise Meyer, perhaps better known as Dickie Chapelle, was an American photojournalist who seemed to never stop covering conflict. She reported during World War II to her last foray in the Vietnam War. While embedded with a U.S. Marine platoon doing a search-and-destroy operation on November 4, 1965, Meyer died after a tripwire set off an explosive. A photojournalist colleague, Henri Huet, who was with her at the time of her passing, captured her last moments on film. Huet would later also be killed while photographing the war, but he would not be the last journalist to die in a war zone. As for being the first American female reporter to be killed in action, that goes to Meyer.[5]

A little more than five years after Meyer's death, her French photojournalist friend and colleague **Henri Huet** died on February 10, 1971, while covering South Vietnam's invasion of Laos, when the aircraft he was flying in was shot down by enemy fire. He died with two other journalist colleagues on board—Larry Burrows of *Life* magazine and Keizaburo Shimamoto of *Newsweek*.[6]

It is believed that **Dana Stone**, a freelance photojournalist for CBS News, died sometime in 1971 after being captured a year earlier by members of the People's Army of Vietnam. The capture happened like this: They were in Phnom Penh on rented Honda motorbikes looking to find the front lines of fighting in Cambodia. Investigations by fellow photojournalist Tim Page, reported in the UK *Sunday Times* on March 24, 1991, indicate that Stone and colleague Sean Flynn were taken first to the village of Sangke Kaong and then to other villages before being handed over to the Khmer Rouge.[7]

Byron G. Highland, a U.S. Marine Corps combat photographer, was killed by a land mine on February 21, 1967, just days after his 33rd birthday. Like some other journalists who have died in war zones, he did not die alone. War correspondent and historian **Bernard B. Fall** also died from the land mine.[8]

These intrepid correspondents—and many, many others in all wars—have been the stuff of films, pulling heartstrings in the theaters or on the home viewing screen because of their sheer determination to reveal truth while risking their everything. And in real life, many of them have not only risked their lives but lost them in these conflict zones. It was Edmund Burke who said, "All that is necessary for the triumph of evil is that good men do nothing." For journalists in general, but perhaps conflict reporters in particular, this maxim is close to the vest. The practice of journalism is their way of "doing something." A musician may write a song, a poet a poem, a writer a novel. A journalist goes into action as an eyewitness to world events and brings it home for his countrymen and women to witness. They know once they leave their homeland to report on turmoil far from home they may not be coming back. And yet like soldiers, they go anyway. It may be idealistic, but like soldiers, these conflict reporters know the risks. And it doesn't lessen the lesson: journalism, especially war reporting, is idealistic. But so is truth.

"Without these photos and videos of firsthand experiences, you can't really tell the world how bad it might be," Foley said. He even went so far as saying that journalists needed to get as close to action as possible. During a speech at Northwestern in 2011, he said: "That's part of the problem with these conflicts. We're not close enough to it. If we don't try to get really close to what these guys … are experiencing, you don't understand the world, essentially."[9]

Journalism is a means to better understanding the world, both for the journalist and for the reading and viewing public.

Marie Colvin was another one who lost her life while reporting in turmoil. Colvin, an American journalist who at the time of her death worked for the British newspaper *The Sunday Times*, was killed on February 22, 2012, while covering the siege of Homs in war-torn Syria. In a November 2010 speech delivered during a service at St. Brides Church in London, she addressed the topic of conflict reporting, saying: "War reporting is still essentially the same—someone has to go there and see what is happening," she said. "You can't get that information without going to places where people are being shot at, and others are shooting at you."[10] During the same address: "Our mission is to speak truth to power," she said. "We send home that first rough draft of history. We can and do make a difference in exposing the horrors of war especially the atrocities that befall civilians."[11]

Not for conflict's sake, but in the hopes that by their reporting, future conflicts may be avoided and the current one they are witnessing may have an end. The naysayers, which may at times even include family and friends, question such idealistic thinking, especially since the world has shown over and over again that reporting on war has done little to lesson or eliminate it. The terrible cost of war continues to be felt, even after more than two centuries of American scribblers reporting on it. Still, the journalist must go to tell the stories of conflict.

As of this writing, another journalist is believed to still be kept by his captors in Syria. Austin Tice was covering the war in Syria when he went missing in 2012. As of April 2021, nine years after he went missing, it was believed he was still alive and in Syrian captivity. That same month a bipartisan group of 80 members of U.S. Representatives and Senators, urged by more than 2,000 citizens, signed a letter addressed to President Joe Biden stating they would support every diplomatic means necessary to secure Tice's release. It noted that Tice's parents, Marc and Debra, have worked tirelessly over two past administrations to promote their son's return and that according to the intelligence community, Tice is believed to still be alive.

It is disheartening that in nine years' time he has remained, in the best-case scenario, in captivity. He should have been home with his family long ago, but ceaseless prayers and efforts continue to be made to bring him home.

Ideals and values aside, there is another reason brave journalists—solders with pen and camera—go to war. Something innate drives them to conflict, to experience the adrenaline that comes from serving in these hostile environments where their daily actions might be dodging bullets and potential kidnappers. When they're back home, away from the chaos, they feel a stirring, a longing to return, just as Foley did.

Why?

It's another question not easily answered. Some may say it is a flaw in their character, their personality, but I believe otherwise. These journalists may have been adrenaline junkies, who, while not craving conflict, perhaps they felt as fish out of water when they were not covering it; they may have found an unwary solace in covering turmoil, just as conflict reporters do today. It takes a special kind of journalist to want to become a conflict reporter and then go through the steps to actually make that life and work a reality. It bespeaks of an inner drive or motivation that few seem to find.

Whatever the reasoning, whatever draws journalists to report on war up close and personal, they are patriots of the highest caliber, and like our veterans who go into battle, we owe them a great deal of gratitude and thanks. We at home sitting in our armchairs with our smartphones in hand, or the books we take down from our shelves to learn about history and social consequences, wouldn't be as well educated about the world if not for the journalists who report the goings-on of war and governments. Many of them have paid the ultimate price for such knowledge—for us.

Ernie Pyle, one of the most respected war reporters to come out of World War II, was one of them. Today's journalists, both abroad and at home, can learn something from his work experiences.

Pyle was fatally shot on April 18, 1945, while embedded with troops on the small island of Ie Shima in the war's Pacific theater.[12] His body lay in a ditch for hours before a soldier was able to retrieve it. If one did not know he was dead, a person could assume he was sleeping. A photograph of Pyle's body shows him lying on his back in peaceful repose. He is dressed in helmet, boots and his army fatigues, his head tipped slightly to his right and with hands folded at the waist.[13] An article that announced his passing reads:

> COMMAND POST, IE SHIMA, April 18 (AP)—Ernie Pyle, war correspondent beloved by his co-workers, GIs and generals alike, was killed by a Japanese machine-gun bullet through his left temple this morning.[14]

When word spread about Pyle's death, it wasn't only those closest to him who mourned. Servicemen, civilians and generals alike all mourned his passing, knowing that one of the great Americans—and great American journalists—left this world all too soon. Even the president of the United States sorrowed at his passing. When he died, it was President Harry Truman who said of him: "The nation is quickly saddened again by the death of Ernie Pyle."[15] The nation had only recently laid to rest President Franklin Roosevelt, and now the nation's greatest reporter. As James Tobin writes in his excellent book *Ernie Pyle's War*, "no one thought it strange for President Truman to equate the death of Franklin Roosevelt with a newspaper reporter. For Pyle had become far more than an ordinary reporter, more even than the most popular journalist of his generation. He was America's eyewitness to the twentieth century's supreme ordeal."[16]

Pyle, thin at five feet, eight inches tall, was a giant of a man, according to those who knew him best. He had a flair for storytelling that went above and beyond battle coverage. He focused his stories on the people, the soldiers, most readily impacted by the battles—what we'd today call human-interest stories. Such tales of heroism and valor impacted his readers, giving them a glimpse of the life and struggle of those who fought in the battle zones but also how they dealt with war when away from battle and in the camps at night.

Before he went to war, Pyle wrote about aviation and once served as the editor of the *Washington Daily News*. In a memo to his staff, he wrote: "We have to make people read this paper," he said in the memo, and then explained how he envisioned that was to happen, "by making it so alert and saucy and important that they will be afraid of missing something if they don't read it."

> Keep your eyes open. There are swell stories floating around your beats every day that you either don't see or don't bother to do anything about when you do see them.
>
> You can hardly walk down the street, or chat with a bunch of friends, without running into the germ of something that may turn up an interesting story if you're on the lookout for it. News doesn't have to be important, but it has to be interesting. You can't find interesting things, if you're not interested. ... Always look for the story—for the unexpected human emotion in the story.
>
> Write a story as tho it were a privilege for you to write it. ... You don't have to be smart-alecky or pseudo-funny. Be human. Try to write like people talk [as quoted in *Ernie Pyle's War*, page 24].

Good advice, indeed, especially since the act of news gathering and reporting is the same whether in conflict or on the beat.

Five in Annapolis, 2018
The Capital Gazette

The year 2018 was not a good one for journalists, American or otherwise. By the time the year was over a number of journalists in the USA had been assaulted, threatened, or killed. Some examples: two reporters were punched by strangers during their reporting duties in New York and North Carolina, and three journalists covering a vehicle crash had their own vehicle damaged when a man wielding a metal object attacked. "Those were among the lower-profile attacks on journalists in 2018," according to an ABC News report. "Others received more widespread attention, like when a series of mail bombs was sent to a major news network's headquarters, among other targets."[17]

That October suspicious packages arrived at a number of Democrat officials' offices, including former President Barrack Obama, Secretary of State and former First Lady Hillary Clinton, and two at the office of then-former Vice President Joe Biden. One package also was sent to CNN. Each package contained a suspicious device.

President Donald Trump called the sending of the bombs "abhorrent" and "despicable acts." Vice President Mike Pence tweeted: "We condemn the attempted attacks against fmr Pres Obama, the Clintons, @CNN & others. These cowardly actions are despicable & have no place in this Country." Trump shared Pence's tweet, writing "I agree wholeheartedly!"

The man who sent the deadly packages was a right-wing fanatic whose van when discovered was decked out with fliers and stickers, all political propaganda, including a decal showing a sniper's crosshairs on Hillary Clinton and CNN. As the drama played out, it seemed as if the country was on the verge of something terrible. Already school shootings had made headlines all too frequently—and now this? The atmosphere it seemed to create, as does any national emergency, was something similar to what happened after the terrorist attacks in 2001, when mail containing anthrax was sent to a number of people and businesses in an attempt to frighten and threaten and, ultimately, cause harm.

A few months prior to the suspicious mail deliveries, on a sun-filled day in late June, gun blasts rang out inside the *Capital Gazette* newsroom, piercing eardrums and shattering glass. A man who had been offended by reporting by the newspaper entered the building and, with smoke canisters and shotgun in hand, blasted his way into the newsroom in Annapolis, Maryland. By the end of the premeditated violence, five people were dead and several wounded.

According to news reports at the time by the *Capital Gazette*'s own staff, the gunman had entered the back of the building with a shotgun and smoke grenades and used a barricade to block the back door. He released a smoke grenade in the hallway and went directly to the newsroom. Finding it locked, he blasted through the door. As the shots rang out, journalists and sales staff began to run for cover, some finding refuge under their desks. Others had fallen injured or were killed by the blasts. As one reporter who lived through the ordeal described it, the scene was like a war zone. "There is nothing more terrifying than hearing multiple people get shot while you're under your desk and then hear the gunman reload," Phil Davis, a *Capital Gazette* police reporter, tweeted shortly after the shooting.

Staff members who were outside wondered about the fate of their colleagues left inside the building. Calls had already been made to the police, including one by the gunman. "This is your shooter. The shooting is over. I surrender," he said.[18] But not before irreparable damage had been done.

Lives had been lost, and because of that, there was no turning back, no making amends, no reversals that could change the outcome. Ever after would the memory of that tragic day live in the memory of those who were most affected by the assault—the families of the victims, those who sustained injuries, and those who saw their colleagues and friends fall to their deaths.

By most accounts state and federal law officers responded to the scene quickly. When they entered the building in search of the gunman, the scene before them was chaotic. It looked like something from a battlefield, only in this episode one person fired a weapon instead of many. Police found the man who caused the tragedy hiding under one of the desks. They couldn't immediately identify him because, according to one report at the time, his fingerprints had apparently been altered. Another report said police officers asked his name, but the man replied: "You don't know my name?"[19]

Ironic that he did not offer them his name since he had called police to say he was the gunman. Others knew of the man, whom they described as an irate reader named Ramos. With help from facial recognition software, police confirmed the man's identity as 38-year-old Jarrod Warren Ramos of Laurel, Maryland, who harbored a deep grudge against the paper and some of its reporters and editors. According to reports, he had a long history of conflict with the newspaper. In 2011, for instance, the paper published a column about a harassment case filed by a woman against Ramos; after it ran, Ramos "wrote angry letters to the newspaper and filed rounds of lawsuits, claiming defamation."[20] In 2012, according to the paper, Ramos had filed another defamation claim against the *Gazette*, but the case was dismissed. He had apparently sued a number of journalists for defamation and waged "a social media campaign against them."[21] He wouldn't let his grudge go. Later, when police searched his apartment after the shooting, "detectives found a CD with computer files that included photos of newspaper staffers, articles that listed their names and a video surveillance Ramos captured of the office's back hallway."[22] His was not a spur-of-the-moment decision. Like most mass shooters, he had been planning his attack for some time.

His anger exploded on June 28, when he went to the newsroom bent on revenge. "This was a targeted attack on the *Capital Gazette*," according to Anne Arundel County Deputy Police Chief Bill Krampf, noting that at the time they did not know if Ramos was targeting anyone specific. "This person was prepared to shoot people. His intent was to cause harm."[23]

And that is exactly what he did.

"Unspeakable Grief"

When it was over, four journalists and one sales assistant were dead. Their names: Gerald Fischman, Rob Hiaasen, John McNamara, and Wendi Winters; and Rebecca Smith.

Touching tributes about each of the slain media workers were published in the *Capital Gazette*, as well as other newspapers such as the *Baltimore Sun*. Colleagues, sharing memories that touched the heartstrings, expressed how each of them were gifted workers and loved what they did. They enjoyed working with people and telling the stories of their community. They were savvy wordsmiths, gifted writers, sharp editors and liked to coach young reporters. As individuals and as a collective team, they had deep intuitional knowledge and keen understanding of their community.

Never had such tragedy struck an American newsroom. When they were killed, it caused other newsrooms across the country to reevaluate their buildings' access and security, but it also gives other food for thought: How should editors and reporters deal with irate readers or viewers?

As grief-stricken and shocked as *Gazette* team members were at the tragedy that had befallen their newsroom that day, knowing that many of their colleagues had been injured or killed, they still went to work getting the next edition to press. They also continued to post updates and details as they became available online and on social media, never wearying of letting readers know what was happening. In doing so they fulfilled their obligation as defenders of the public trust and "worked the story" for the people's right to know what was happening in their community.

Reporters interviewed, while photographers captured images and video recordings. In the frenzied, anxious melee of law enforcement and media workers from other outlets, the journalists and editors of the *Gazette* never missed their deadline and got the next day's newspaper out on time.

Some people may question the work and motivation behind such work, wondering if reporting on their own newsroom's tragedy is self-aggrandizement, self-deprecation, or if journalists are just immune to such tragedies and use them as a means to sell their product.

None of it is true.

Violence and sex in news, like on the silver screen, sells, but getting the story out is more than just banking a profit, especially when lives have been lost. Journalists cover tragedy because it is the public's right to know of the terrible things that happen in their communities and country, but perhaps the more personal reason for doing so is a means to cope with the senselessness of it all. For journalists, reporting on the topsy-turvy world in which we all live can serve as a sort of catharsis, to try to make sense of the senselessness. It is a way that many journalists cope. It is never easy to cover tragedy, and journalists have been known to experience anxiety and depression, a sense of post-traumatic stress disorder, because of it. Many have sought counseling or other means to get out of their funk. The memories and anguish never go away, of course, but perhaps the work they do helps lessen the hammering over time.

What does the newsroom of the future look like? The coronavirus pandemic has taught many news organizations that reporters and editors do not necessarily have to be in the newsroom to put out a good product. It helps collaboratively to be all together in one place, and there are instances when such in-person team building is most conducive to the product and morale of the journalists, but with today's technology, reporting can be done anywhere, by any means. Perhaps by having reporters work remotely in their own designated spaces, the chances of newsroom tragedies such as the one that happened in Annapolis may be averted or lessened.

As for those five who senselessly and tragically lost their lives that day in June, *Time* magazine collectively named them "Person of the Year" for 2018. The *Capital Gazette* received a Pulitzer Prize Special Citation on April 15, 2019, for its work covering the unfolding drama in their own newsroom. The citation was given in "honor of the journalists, staff and editorial board of the Capital Gazette, Annapolis, Maryland, for their courageous response to the largest killing of journalists in U.S. history in their newsroom on June 28, 2018, and for demonstrating unflagging commitment to covering the news and serving their community at a time of unspeakable grief."[24]

11

What About Khashoggi?

When Jamal Khashoggi went to the Saudi Arabian consulate on October 2, 2018, in Istanbul, it was supposed to be a routine visit. He was there to pick up a marriage license for an upcoming wedding. While his fiancé waited outside the consulate, hours passed and still no sign of his return. She wondered what could be keeping him. Little did they know that when Khashoggi walked into the building that he never would come out of it alive.

Khashoggi, a 59-year-old journalist who wrote columns for the *Washington Post*, had been born in Saudi Arabia in 1958 but fled the country in September 2017 because of the hardships imposed upon him by the government he reported about. Besides writing for the *Washington Post*, Khashoggi also was the editor of Al-Arab News Channel and a published book author. In his writings he had been critical of the Saudi government, especially after he went into self-imposed exile.

When he didn't return from the consulate on October 2, rumors began to spread that he had been killed while inside. What's more, the killing of the journalist was very horrific in its nature. Investigations by the Turkish police, and later by the CIA, uncovered the awful truth: Khashoggi had been tortured and dismembered and his body cremated.

What should have been a firm verdict pronounced by the U.S. on the Saudi government, primarily Crown Prince Mohammed bin Salman, whom investigators said likely ordered the killing, instead turned to what amounted as a slap on the wrist. President Donald Trump, when asked about reports from members of his own intelligence team that Khashoggi was killed on orders from the Crown Prince, instead of supporting such intelligence it appeared as if Trump believed the Saudis even more.

It was another cruel slap in the face to journalism by a sitting president. It was an example of weakness from a man who touted strength, and it was an irreverent response for the family and friends who lost one of their loved ones at the hands of evil men.

The actions of the president—whether verbal or otherwise—have ramifications far beyond the moment. President Trump's response belittled his own intelligence briefings, shored up the defense of those who perpetrated the crime, and sent a message to his own country and the world that, at least under his administration, journalists were not worth the time and effort to protect. In so doing, it also hinted that perhaps to the government that is supposed to provide freedom and protection to all people that not all life is of equal value.

While this may have been a political stance for Trump, it should have been a human rights and human decency case for the sitting president. America's power and influence in the world, while never able to bring the slain journalist back to life, could have done something more to bring justice to Khashoggi and his memory.

"A declassified intelligence report, released in February, said that an 'operation of this nature' would not have taken place without the authorization of Prince Mohammed, and that the prince supports the use of violent measures to silence dissidents abroad, including against Khashoggi," according to reporting done by *The Hill*.[1]

Two months later, in April 2020 the U.S. House of Representatives passed legislation to restrict arms sales to Saudi Arabia because of the killing of Khashoggi. The legislation, called the "Protection of Saudi Dissidents Act of 2021," passed the House with bipartisan support, but it was unclear if the Senate would take up the measure.[2]

Khashoggi may have been quickly swept under the rug by those in power, but he was not soon forgotten by journalists and human rights defenders across the globe.

Like the five individuals who were killed in their own newsroom in Annapolis, Maryland, just a few months before his own death in Istanbul, Khashoggi was featured as Person of the Year on the front cover of *Time* magazine in early December 2018. The magazine labeled the journalist as a "Guardian of the Truth." "Khashoggi put his faith in bearing witness," Karl Vick writes of the slain journalist. "He put it in the field reporting he had done since youth, in the newspaper editorship he was forced out of and in the columns he wrote from lonely exile." Vick explains that what led to the journalist's death was tempering his own conclusions with troubling facts, which the kingdom did not like. He had trusted "the public to think for itself."[3]

Author's Note

Community Journalism

When my editor told me to take a hike, he meant it—literally.

My boss told me one day soon after taking over my new beat as the paper's Outdoors editor that he wanted me to, at least once a week, explore a different place in south-central Idaho's Magic Valley, an eight-county segment that is named because of the plentiful supply of water found in underground aquifers that during the area's initial farming efforts had turned the otherwise desert landscape into a bountiful agriculture region. For me, it held a different kind of magic.

Growing up in California and Utah, and having parents who instilled within me a love of nature, I had always appreciated the Great Outdoors—its calm serenities as well as its thunderous extremes. Now, being able to explore and write about it was a boon and a blessing that not only allowed me to get to know my new state better but also taught me important lessons about myself and journalism.

Something that stands out: like a person's faith that she or he carries with them no matter the setting or where they may journey, I came to realize that while there might be different approaches to reporting, journalism is basically the same no matter the beat or location. I also learned by the examples of my colleagues, many who were engaged in community activities outside their work, that journalists make up an important and vibrant part of any community, both while at work and in other aspects of life. And, depending on the size of your community, you may run into a journalist, perhaps unbeknownst to you, in circumstances and places you may not expect. Perhaps even in the Great Outdoors.

Take a hike, my editor had told me. And so I did, almost every week.

I toted along a camera with a long lens to snap photos of the people and places I visited, but eventually my editor assigned a photographer to go with me on my adventures. I was excited. The photographer, Justin Jackson, and I had become friends, and now we would be working together at least once a week on a devoted section of the newspaper. We'd select a spot, an activity, and every Thursday we'd pack our gear and head to a destination. Over the next couple of years, we tallied quite the list of places we had visited. We explored trails by foot, on bicycle, while riding our motorcycles or driving four-wheelers; we covered stories about horseback riders and joggers who used these same trails. We explored fish hatcheries, lakes, ponds, reservoirs and rivers. We went birding and, on an excursion, went in search of wild turkeys. We explored mountain terrain and desert landscapes. We went skiing, snowshoeing, and tubing in the winter months, even tried ice fishing, and we got up before dawn one cold morning to spend the day with a resort owner in a large tractor while he groomed a mountain for that day's ski run. We traversed places in my two-wheel drive Nissan Sentra, driving it places we wondered if we'd be able to get back out of, sometimes down steep canyon grades and rocky, potholed terrain. We hiked, we fished, sought out beaver dams and hummingbird nests, explored old mines and caves, and hiked some more.

One of my most memorable experiences was exploring parts of the Oregon Trail, as it ran through the Magic Valley. My idea was to showcase the trail in several areas of the valley, tell the history of the trail through the historical record, and discuss the contemporary settings and talk to real people who lived near the trail more than 100 years later. I envisioned a larger series, but it wound up being two lengthy ones with charts and photos. Places I had visited along the historic trail, about seven different places in all, stretched from Massacre Rocks near American Falls in the southeast end of the valley to Three Island Crossing outside the valley some 140 miles away in Glenns Ferry. My favorite location was the trail site at a place called Stricker Ranch in Kimberly, just a 30-minute jaunt from where I lived in Twin Falls. Here, outside a white and green clapboard ranch house, rumored to be haunted by spirits of the past, the trail, imprinted into the hard crust of the earth, is fading, as it is in much of the land across Idaho and other parts of the country. When the trail fades completely, all that will be left will be the historical record.

White posts stick out of the ground, alerting visitors to the historic trail, in which they can walk for several yards among old relics of a bygone era—an old storehouse and cellar, stone markers and grave sites, and rusted pieces of farm equipment. A newer barn also sits on the property known as Stricker Ranch, as does a modern interpretive center with informative kiosks that tells about the history of the trail and the site that first came into prominence in 1864 when Ben Holladay came to town.

He was followed by German-born Herman Stricker. As the community grew, a young woman by the name of Lucy Walgamott caught Stricker's fancy, and the two courted for a period of time before tying the knot. They started out their lives together in a small, wooden farmhouse, but bad luck befell them when a few years later it burned to the ground. Instead of moving on, the couple built a new house—this one a much larger mansion style (for the time) completed in 1901, in which Lucy took great pride. Here she would host parties.

In its heyday the Stricker Ranch site had as many as 90 buildings and encompassed some 900 acres, but when the trail use dwindled and transportation became more modern, fewer people came to the site and the parties lessened. The hustle and bustle of the place was eventually silenced and, by all appearances, became a ghost town. Today the official site encompasses only six acres.

Park benches sit under thick pine and oak trees outside of the ranch house, where sometimes hoot owls are heard hooting and, if you listen closely and believe the stories, the quiet moaning of spirits past. Off in the distance, to the north, lay the Sawtooth mountain range, their tips rising like jagged teeth on the horizon.

A person could get lost in thoughts out here, not wanting to go back to civilization that sits just a few miles to the north and west. Sitting here, taking in the surroundings, is almost like being in a time warp, where the past and all of its ghosts, literal or figurative (it's up to you to decide), seem very real in the modern world. It's a great place to ponder and pray and reminisce and plan.

Perhaps a better definition is that a person could find one's self here at Stricker, or at least in part. That was the case with me. I also found a friend here named Gary Guy, caretaker of the property, while working on the Oregon Trail series. Gary passed way in March 2020, but I will always remember fondly the way he treated me from the day we first met to the last time we talked. A bit rotund, and with silver hair and nicely trimmed beard, Gary was always willing to share stories about the old property. He had amassed a collection of books during the time he spent at the ranch house, researching the history of the land that saw thousands upon thousands of travelers wend their way through Rock Creek Station on their way to other points west. While working on my trail series, Gary and I stood on the front lawn of the house, where he reminisced about the old days as if he had been an occupant of the house when the Oregon Trail was alive with wagon trains.

You stand here, waiting, and soon you hear the clop of horses' hooves and the turn of wagon wheels. And then, out of the dust, you catch the first sight of the emigrants and stagecoaches approaching, tired and worn and dusty. A party goes to greet them, offers them water. While here, the travelers refresh themselves and buy needed supplies at the store and visit with other travelers.

"You can sit out here and visualize a Friday night with the cowboys coming in, wanting to get a little drink and play some cards," Gary said. "You can almost see them riding their horses, laughing and carrying on or leaving on their horses."

Gary had painted a picture for me, and within my mind's eye I could see what he described: the cowboys coming down the trail, dust kicking up at their heels and wheels.

An owl hooted and erased the vision from my mind, but it has returned many times since—just as I have returned many times to Stricker Ranch.

Gary, once a source, had become a friend.

A few miles to the south of Stricker Ranch lie the South Hills.

During the hike on a multiuse trail, Justin and I encountered a couple of horseback riders. As we hiked the trail, enjoying the autumn colors and fresh air, we encountered two riders. I approached them, introduced ourselves, and queried to see if I could ask them a few questions about their experience in the outdoors that day. They agreed, but I could tell by the looks on the faces that they were unsure if we were really who we claimed to be. "You are journalists?" the female rider asked.

They had a bit of the same skepticism that Gary displayed to me when I first visited the ranch property. Why was a journalist spending so much time taking photos of the old ranch house and surrounding area? Didn't he have his story yet?

"We are," I replied to the woman. And then, perhaps feeling a bit witty or just downright honest, I told the couple: "Watch out, you never know where you might run into a journalist."

Think about this: A journalist might be your neighbor, someone you unknowingly meet in the supermarket or movie theater or at the dentist's office or post office. She might be one you wave to while strolling along the sidewalk on an evening hike, or he might be someone you nod to while pumping gas at the local convenience store. You'll find them at city and county meetings, at community picnics and parades, at new construction sites and grand openings, at your high school sporting events, and at your state legislature. You find them outdoors, indoors, wherever a story might be told—from fluff pieces to hard topics.

You will even find them at church.

While I was serving as the Outdoors editor, my boss eventually laid another section on my plate: Religion. I at first was a bit nervous about this beat, because of all the things I had covered in my journalism career so far, religion was not one of them. How do you do religion reporting, I wondered? What would I write about? Was there anything newsy going on in the faith community that was worthy of weekly news and feature stories?

Little did I know that the beat was one that I would very much enjoy, as I spoke with various faith leaders in the community—Anglican, Baptist, Catholic, Jehovah's Witness, Latter-day Saint, Mennonite, Muslim, Pentecostal, Seventh Day Adventist, among many others from local congregations. Through my reporting I gained the trust of religious leaders, many who had expressed doubt when I first took over the religious page, wondering how I'd slant the news. Some were afraid—I know this because they verbally expressed it to me—that the section would lean heavily toward my own faith. I assured them that would not be the case.

I became friends with several of the local pastors and other religious leaders and enjoyed learning about not only their beliefs and what made them believe the way they do, but about their involvement in the community. It gave me a broader understanding of the role that churches and people of faith play in communities.

Churches sit as citadels on the corner block—or along rural bypass roads—inviting all to come inside and take a peek, say a prayer, and walk away with new friends.

But not everyone has positive experiences within congregations. No matter what side of the church door a person is on, inside or outside, no one is perfect.

Journalism also is a community service, and like churches and people's experiences with them, it can either build trust or knock it down. Journalists are people too and, as such, are not perfect.

But of course, you know that.

The news media and their representatives are far from perfect. They are told that all of the time, but it's not something we need to be reminded of constantly.

Or is it?

In some respects, my whole career has been spent being told I was never good enough. There was always someone better.

Journalism, I learned early on, isn't always easy. Some days are most excellent when you feel like you're riding on cloud nine. Other days it feels like you've fallen through the cloud and landed on your face. Journalism, for me, has been at times a love-hate relationship. Obviously more love than hate, but there have been times when I have considered my life would be less stressful if I found another line of work. Constant deadlines, always being scrutinized by the public, dealing with irate readers, always trying to come up with new story ideas and angles, kicking myself when a mistake has been made—it all is like working under the pressure of a steel trap that is ready to spring. But then I have the good days, when everything seems to fall into place: sources talk with me, I uncover facts and get information, the story comes together and when I sit down to write the words flow. And then it is published, and readers respond. It catches attention, and I begin to see the impact of my work. I'm on cloud nine.

But there are those other days.

And, unfortunately, as we have seen, for some journalists the trials and backlash are much more severe. It's not only conflict reporters and investigative journalists who receive the hate. Attacks against journalists and the free press have happened on all beats, against men and women, Black and white, American and those from other countries.

While in North Dakota during the coronavirus pandemic—and a politically volatile year in 2020—I was worried for my colleagues in the news profession. I kept hearing of reporters being arrested by police or assaulted by law officers or protesters or threatened by those angry at the media. One reporter friend of mine went to Bemidji, Minnesota, to cover a Trump rally. While he was not assaulted, he said he felt on edge being in a crowd that seemed to dislike reporters and threw verbal barbs their way. Another reporter friend in California had an object thrown at him and caught some of the police officers' pepper spray while covering protests in the Golden State. He saw other reporters who received harsher treatment. I feared for my colleagues in many places—California, Idaho, Minnesota, North Dakota, South Dakota, Utah. This wasn't what we signed up to do.

Or was it?

Journalism is full of ups and down, of glorious days and hard-knock, drag-out days. And the journalist must be—and usually is—adaptable and tough-skinned enough to handle the swaying diversity of the profession.

But we are never prepared for our own communities, our own audiences, to turn on us. And yet that seems to be what happens more and more these days.

Some weaknesses and transgressions of the free press have been discussed within these pages, but there are others. However, I cannot help but consider the possibility that the root problem goes much deeper than the media's transgressions. Those might have been the jumping off points, but what is it that keeps the spiral in motion?

Personally, I think it's a combination of multiple modern-day issues, no less the heavy-handedness of social media that allows everyone to be everybody else's worst critic at the push of a few buttons. Where once people took the time to sit down and craft a letter to the editor, buy postage, and send it to the local newspaper, now anyone with a smartphone or computer can knock out senseless drivel and push blame without vetting any facts whatsoever. It's a real-life scenario that has, in some ways, dumbed down society but also has made us a more contentious, unforgiving, and weary people.

It also has made the journalist's job a lot harder.

But thankfully—let's hope—the assaults against journalists we saw on the streets of America in 2020 and early 2021 were only a moment in time and will not be part of the "new normal" for journalists.

We are community citizens, who do community journalism, for our fellow community residents. We need to work together, the public and the press, and come together in forms of audience-journalist engagement. "We need not only the giants but the small voices you can find nowhere else than in community journalism," said Rick Hutzell, editor of the *Capital Gazette* in Annapolis, Maryland. "Democracy begins in the small town, in the city hall, in the county council."

My views of journalism are idealistic—a view I do not apologize for—and it is through that lens that I contemplate and work, believing that the ethical and determined journalist can and does make a positive difference in the world, a world in which we all live and work. I believe in small-town reporting, national watchdog reporting, and the importance of conflict journalism. If this book has come across as idealistic, that is my view of my profession. However smug or unrealistic it may sound, I truly believe that America's best hope at retaining its democratic values lies, to a great extent, in the responsibilities and work of the free and independent press. I also believe that despite their faults—we're all human, after all—the majority of journalists are decent, country-loving people who are trying to do the right thing and report the news fairly. To some who work in the newsroom it might seem like just a job; but I believe that more often than not there are the journalists who treat their positions with respect and consider it an honor, like I do, to be a member of the free press. Idealistic? You bet, and perhaps a little heady, too. But that's territory explored for the journalist, who believes the work she or he does truly does impact lives.

Starting with their own.

My explorations in community journalism have not always been wonderful experiences for me. It hasn't always been easy, but it has been worth meeting the challenges along the way.

Will I always be a journalist?

There have been times when I have thought about moving on to something new and different, not because I have fallen out of love with what I do but because it is a taxing profession and sometimes, as the years wear on me, it takes a little more effort to find the stamina to meet the daily grind.

But I will always consider myself a journalist, even if one day I am not working in a newsroom. But for now I remain a member of the American free press—not a secret society but a special society of professional men and women who love their country and seek to make their world a better place through their reporting. Journalism is a quest for truth, a journey that is fraught with anxious and ambitious reporters trying to meet their deadlines while also trying to tell their community's story, whether that community is their local neighborhood or the country as a whole—we are all part of a community. And together we can make a better community not only for ourselves but future generations.

Give the Fourth Estate a chance. Or a second or third chance.

It is indeed an anxious time to be a journalist, but it also is a thrilling time to be a journalist. Because I believe the Constitution, I believe in press freedom. Because I believe in press freedom, I believe it is one of America's great pillars of democracy. You don't have to believe a certain religion to believe in the right to worship by the dictates of one's own conscience. Likewise, you don't have to agree with everything the press reports to believe in its importance. There have been many chips taken out of that pillar, but it still stands strong and will remain immovable as journalists and the public band together to defend this remarkable institution and its service in protecting the public's right to know. Your right to know!

Otherwise, we could be closer to this vision: "If you want a vision of the future, imagine a boot stamping on a human face—forever." That was from George Orwell, who gave us the dystopian novel *1984* some 40 years before the title's date arrived.

Journalism is not the answer to all of society's problems. Unethical and unvetted journalism has in many cases made the climate worse. But if there is hope for our politically divided world—a time when truth is under attack perhaps like never before—then determined, ethical and persistent journalism must be put in its rightful place. It is one of the pillars of democracy, and if it falls as the gatekeeper, then who else will be left at the gate?

An extreme vision of the future, perhaps, but maybe not so much if realized in our democratic values. If we lose democracy, it'd be like having our faces stomped on day after day.

Journalism is not the sole means to protecting that democracy, but it is one of the pillars that lets us know it still stands. And it is one of the ways in which we can fight and defend. Such has always been the case, from the Founders' politically contentious times to our own. Journalists like the ones mentioned in these pages—and many others, too many to mention—have been on the front lines.

"Journalism can never be silent: that is its greatest virtue and its greatest fault," Henry Grunwald said. "It must speak, and speak immediately, while the echoes of wonder, the claims of triumph and the signs of horror are still in the air."

Chapter Notes

Introduction

1. "Don Bolles' tragic death," *The Michigan Daily*, June 16, 1976. https://news.google.com/newspapers?id=VP9JAAAAIBAJ&pg=3922,2003692&dq=don+bolles&hl=en.

2. Tal Axelrod, "Report: U.S. joins ranks of world's most dangerous places for journalists for first time," *The Hill*, December 18, 2018. https://thehill.com/homenews/media/421848-report-us-joins-ranks-of-worlds-most-dangerous-places-for-journalists-for-the.

3. Bruce D. Brown, "Attacks on the press are a threat to your freedom. Here's how you can help," Special to McClatchy, *Miami Herald*, November 7, 2019. https://www.miamiherald.com/article237076929.html.

4. "Federal reporter's shield law proposed," Reporter's Committee for Freedom of the Press, November 22, 2004. https://www.rcfp.org/federal-reporters-shield-law-proposed/.

Chapter 1

1. Pete Danko and Sheryl Oring, "Kissing the Newsroom Goodbye," as quoted in *AJR*, June 1995. https://ajrarchive.org/article.asp?id=1480&id=1480.

2. Thomas Peele, "Death stalks some reporters working their beats in U.S.," *The Plain Dealer*, August 1, 2012; updated January 12, 2019. https://www.cleveland.com/opinion/2012/08/death_stalks_some_reporters_wo.html.

3. "As long as our government is administered for the good of the people, and is regulated by their will," President Andrew Jackson said, "as long as it secures to us the rights of persons and of property, liberty of conscience and of the press, it will be worth defending." We need government, but in its rightful place—as a servant to the people—and we need the free press to serve as watchdog of the government for the people.

4. Tweet by Jim Acosta, July 31, 2018. https://twitter.com/Acosta/status/1024467940257738752?ref_src=twsrc%5Etfw%7Ctwcamp%5Etweetembed%7Ctwterm%5E1024467940257738752%7Ctwgr%5Eshare_3%2Ccontainerclick_0&ref_url=https%3A%2F%2Fwww.bbc.com%2Fnews%2Fworld-us-canada-47208909.

5. Brian Stelter, "Trump calls journalists 'bad people' at rally a week after newsroom shooting," CNN, July 6, 2018. https://money.cnn.com/2018/07/06/media/trump-montana-rally-media-attacks/index.html.

6. "Trump supporter attacks BBC cameraman at El Paso rally," February 12, 2019. https://www.bbc.com/news/world-us-canada-47208909.

7. Jonathan Chait, "Trump Says Reporters Covering Protests Deserve to Be Attacked," *New York* magazine, September 22, 2020. https://nymag.com/intelligencer/2020/09/trump-reporters-covering-protests-deserve-to-be-attacked.html.

8. "Minnesota journalist attacked by Trump supporter at rally," Associated Press, October 1, 2020. https://apnews.com/article/election-2020-joe-biden-donald-trump-journalists-minnesota-546e102d48ef79cb460857115ddee695.

9. Tweet by Jim Acosta, October 28, 2020. https://twitter.com/acosta/status/1321605737534009344?lang=en.

10. Kevin Breuninger, "GOP quiet on Trump praising Rep Greg Gianforte for assaulting reporter, amid Khashoggi crisis

and criticism of alleged Democratic 'mob' tactics," October 19, 2018. https://www. cnbc.com/2018/10/19/gop-quiet-on-trump-praising-greg-gianforte-for-assaulting-reporter.html.

11. Khashoggi was a Saudi journalist but wrote for the *Washington Post*. He had been critical of the kingdom's royal family. It was discovered that the journalist had been tortured, murdered and dismembered by the Saudi government after he entered its consulate in Istanbul on Oct. 2. For more, see Chapter 11.

12. Daniel Arkin, "Donald Trump Criticized After He Appears to Mock Reporter Serge Kovaleski," NBC News, November 26, 2015. https://www.nbcnews.com/politics/2016-election/donald-trump-criticized-after-he-appears-mock-reporter-serge-kovaleski-n470016.

13. The complete phrase by Pulitzer is: "Our republic and its press will rise or fall together. An able, disinterested, public-spirited press, with trained intelligence to know the right and courage to do it, can preserve that public virtue without which popular government is a sham and a mockery. A cynical, mercenary, demagogic press will produce in time a people as base as itself. The power to mould the future of the republic will be in the hands of the journalists of future generations." This means that, even as Taylor Batten editorialized in the *Charlotte Observer* on May 31, 2014, "each institution needs to recommit itself to Pulitzer's vision. ... Today the American media landscape includes more cynical, mercenary and demagogic elements than it has in a very long time. As Pulitzer predicted, that is creating a people as base as itself, and threatening to make popular government a sham." See Taylor Batten, "The importance of a courageous press," *The Charlotte Observer*, May 31, 2014. https://www.charlotteobserver.com/opinion/opn-columns-blogs/taylor-batten/article9126314.html.

14. The comment has often been attributed to have been coined by Graham, but a column in *Slate* says it might not have been Graham who first spoke the words after all, referencing a book review in the *New Republic*. See Jack Shafer, "Who Said It First? Journalism is the 'first rough draft of history,'" *Slate*, August 30, 2010. https://slate.com/news-and-politics/ 2010/08/on-the-trail-of-the-question-who-first-said-or-wrote-that-journalism-is-the-first-rough-draft-of-history.html.

15. That's not to say that pointing out error is wrong. Contrary, it is a positive thing for the public to bring attention to journalists' errors and mistakes. Of all the journalists I have worked with, however, any errors that I have observed in newsrooms have been done unintentionally. Facts are a journalist's bread and butter, and it's a reporter's obligation to get them right; as Craig Silverman says, reporters and news organizations should always "regret the error."

16. April Thorn, "Fifteen journalists die while covering war in Iraq," *The News Media & The Law*, Spring 2003, page 7. https://www.rcfp.org/journals/the-news-media-and-the-law-spring-2003/fifteen-journalists-die-whi/.

17. Adam Miller, "Kidnappers: 24 Hours More, Then He's Dead," *New York Post*, February 1, 2002. See also, Transcript, "E-mail Extending Kidnapper's Deadline Not Yet Authenticated," CNN, January 31, 2002. http://edition.cnn.com/TRANSCRIPTS/0201/31/lt.05.html; Peter Grier, "Journalist's kidnapping a puzzling power play," *The Christian Science Monitor*, February 1, 2002. https://www.csmonitor.com/2002/0201/p01s04-wosc.html.

18. "Killings of journalists rise as reprisal murders more than double in 2020," Committee to Protect Journalists, December 22, 2020. https://cpj.org/2020/12/killings-of-journalists-rise-as-reprisal-murders-more-than-double-in-2020/.

19. *Ibid.*

20. *Ibid.*

21. Cameron Scott, "Mexico's Most Wanted Journalist," *Mother Jones*, May 1, 2007. https://www.motherjones.com/politics/2007/05/mexicos-most-wanted-journalist/.

22. Michael Safi, Jonathan Watts, Oliver Holmes, Kareem Shaheen and Shaun Walker, "'You can get killed': journalists living in fear as states crack down," *The Guardian*, November 29, 2017. https://www.theguardian.com/media/2017/nov/30/journalists-living-in-fear-states-crackdown-press-freedom.

23. "Killings of journalists rise as reprisal murders more than double in 2020," Committee to Protect Journalists, De-

cember 22, 2020. https://cpj.org/2020/12/killings-of-journalists-rise-as-reprisal-murders-more-than-double-in-2020/.

24. Committee to Protect Journalists, https://cpj.org/data/killed/2018/?status=Killed&motiveConfirmed%5B%5D=Confirmed&type%5B%5D=Journalist&start_year=2019&end_year=2019&group_by=location.

25. Robert Leger, "A Dangerous Job: Journalists, too, have a role in the fight for freedom, and sometimes the risks of reporting are great." Society of Professional Journalists. https://www.spj.org/dangerousjob.asp.

26. Department of Veterans Affairs, https://www.va.gov/opa/publications/factsheets/fs_americas_wars.pdf.

27. At 42 years old, Theodore Roosevelt was a year younger than Kennedy when he became president for the first time, but he was not elected. Instead, Roosevelt had gained the presidency after the assassination of President William McKinley in 1901.

28. See This Day in History: May 11, "President Kennedy orders more troops to South Vietnam," History. https://www.history.com/this-day-in-history/president-kennedy-orders-more-troops-to-south-vietnam.

29. Edwin L. Dale Jr., "What Vietnam Did to the American Economy," *The New York Times*, January 28, 1973. https://www.nytimes.com/1973/01/28/archives/what-vietnam-did-to-the-american-economy-worsening-payments-deficit.html.

30. *On Two Fronts: Latinos & Vietnam*, PBS, 2015. https://www.pbs.org/video/stories-service-two-fronts-latinos-vietnam-full-episode/. See also, "Vietnam War Casualties by Race, Ethnicity and Natl Origin," The Names of Vietnam War Personnel, 1945 to 1970, The American War Library. https://www.americanwarlibrary.com/vietnam/vwc10.htm; Juan Castillo, "'On Two Fronts': The Vietnam Experience Through Latino Family Lens," NBC News, September 22, 2015. https://www.nbcnews.com/news/latino/two-fronts-vietnam-war-through-latino-familys-lens-n419001; Steve Cuevas, "the Invisible Force: Latinos at War in Vietnam," KQED, May 25, 2015. https://www.kqed.org/news/10534280/the-invisible-force-latinos-at-war-in-vietnam.

31. Raul A. Reyes, "Prominent Latino journalist Ruben Salazar killed 50 years ago, tackled racism, identity," *USA Today* network, published on NBC News, August 28, 2020. https://www.nbcnews.com/news/latino/prominent-latino-journalist-ruben-salazar-killed-50-years-ago-tackled-n1238011.

32. "Salazar's Beginnings As A College Student Journalist," Ruben Salazar Project. https://rubensalazarproject.com/2013/08/27/salazars-beginnings-as-a-college-student-journalist/.

33. Ruben Salazar, "25 Hours in a City Jail: I lived in a Chamber of Horrors," *El Paso Herald*, May 9, 1954, as quoted in Ruben Salazar: 25 Hours in City Jail, *El Paso Times*, August 26, 2020. https://www.elpasotimes.com/story/news/2020/08/26/ruben-salazar-25-hours-city-jail-lived-chamber-horrors-el-paso-article-herald-post/5638166002/.

34. Carribean Fragoza, "Truths Unsilenced: The Life, Death and Legacy of Ruben Salazar," August 27, 2020. https://www.kcet.org/shows/lost-la/truths-unsilenced-the-life-death-and-legacy-of-ruben-salazar.

35. *Ibid.*

36. See the *Ruben Salazar Project*, particularly Kira Brekke, "Salazar's Beginnings as a College Student Journalist," August 27, 2013. https://rubensalazarproject.com/2013/08/27/salazars-beginnings-as-a-college-student-journalist/.

37. Gustavo Arellano, "READING RUBEN SALAZAR: He was no radical. He was a prophetic reporter," *Los Angeles Times*, August 23, 2020. https://www.latimes.com/projects/chicano-moratorium/ruben-salazar-reporting-legacy-la-impact/.

38. Robert J. Lopez, "Ruben Salazar had clashed repeatedly with LAPD in months before slaying," *Los Angeles Times*, August 29, 2010. https://www.latimes.com/archives/la-xpm-2010-aug-29-la-me-salazar-20100829-story.html.

39. "The Ruben Salazar Files," *Los Angeles Times*, https://documents.latimes.com/ruben-salazar/.

40. Carribean Fragoza, "Truths Unsilenced: The Life, Death and Legacy of Ruben Salazar," KCET, August 27, 2020. https://www.kcet.org/shows/lost-la/truths-unsilenced-the-life-death-and-legacy-of-ruben-salazar.

41. "Some people feel that there has

yet to be a definitive accounting of Salazar's death," according to a column by Raul A Reyes. See "Prominent Latino journalist Ruben Salazar, killed 50 years ago, tackled racism, identity," *USA Today* network, published on NBC News, August 28, 2020. https://www.nbcnews.com/news/latino/prominent-latino-journalist-ruben-salazar-killed-50-years-ago-tackled-n1238011.

42. Dave Smith and Paul Houston, "Deputy Says He Did Not Know Kind of Missile," *Los Angeles Times*, October 6, 1970.

43. Robert J. Lopez, "No evidence Ruben Salazar was targeted in killing, report says," *Los Angeles Times*, February 19, 2011. https://www.latimes.com/archives/la-xpm-2011-feb-19-la-me-ruben-salazar-20110220-story.html.

44. Robert J. Lopez, "Journalist's Death Still Clouded by Questions: Friends say Ruben Salazar, whose stories often criticized police treatment of Mexican Americans, believed he was in danger. His 1970 slaying left a lasting wound," *Los Angeles Times*, August 26, 1995. https://www.latimes.com/archives/la-xpm-1995-08-26-mn-39122-story.html.

45. Ruben Salazar Park, Los Angeles Conservancy. https://www.laconservancy.org/locations/ruben-salazarpark#:~:text=On%20September%2017%2C%201970%2C%20East,march%20on%20August%2029%2C%201970.

46. Adolfo Flores, "Plaque to honor memory of journalist Ruben Salazar," *Los Angeles Times*, August 29, 2014. https://www.latimes.com/local/la-me-ruben-salazar-plaque-20140830-story.html.

47. Zita Arocha, "Ruben Salazar questioned his own ethnic identity and the role of journalism in American society," April 24, 2014. https://borderzine.com/2014/04/ruben-salazar-questioned-his-own-ethnic-identity-and-the-role-of-journalism-in-american-society/ Retrieved October 3, 2020.

CHAPTER 2

1. Many different strains of the coronavirus exist, often found in bat and bird species, which are believed to act as natural hosts, according to the WHO. Science tells us that the most recent common ancestor of these viruses existed around 10,000 years ago. COVID-19 is a novel, or new, coronavirus that before its detection in late 2019 had not previously been seen in humans. COVID, also known as SARS-CoV-2, is rendered from the words "corona" (CO), virus (VI) and disease (D) and the year in which it was detected.

2. Once again Trump fanned the flames of mistrust.

3. According to a running tally by the *Washington Post*, 967 black people were shot by police in a one-year period, according to data retrieved on June 5, 2021. https://www.washingtonpost.com/graphics/investigations/police-shootings-database/.

4. Jason Hanna and Amir Vera, "CNN crew released from police custody after they were arrested live on air in Minneapolis," CNN, May 29, 2020. https://www.cnn.com/2020/05/29/us/minneapolis-cnn-crew-arrested/index.html.

5. Grynbaum, Michael M. and Marc Santora, "CNN Crew Is Arrested on Live Television While Covering Minneapolis Protests." *The New York Times*, May 29, 2020. https://www.nytimes.com/2020/05/29/business/media/cnn-reporter-arrested-omar-jimenez.html.

6. Brian Stelter, "Arresting reporters at a protest is an affront to the First Amendment," CNN Business, May 29, 2020. https://www.cnn.com/2020/05/29/media/reporters-arrest-minneapolis-first-amendment/index.html.

7. "Press Rights at a Protest," p. 10. https://www.rcfp.org/wp content/uploads/2018/12/Police_Protesters_and_the_Press_2018.pdf See also, https://www.rcfp.org/wp-content/uploads/imported/20180614_100229_rcfp_protest_tip_sheet_0618.pdf.

8. "Police, Protesters, and the Press," Reporters Committee for Freedom of the Press, updated June 2020, https://www.rcfp.org/wp-content/uploads/2020/06/Police-Protesters-Press-2020.pdf.

9. Brian Stelter, "Arresting reporters at a protest is an affront to the First Amendment," CNN, May 29, 2020. https://www.cnn.com/2020/05/29/media/reporters-arrest-minneapolis-first-amendment/index.html.

10. In a June 1, 2020, article Tirado wrote for THINK, she explained that more than once she had woken only to remember that she had been shot in the eye and left partially blind. It is something that no

journalist expects to have happen to them, but given the political climate and hate-mongering toward the news media "it's always been only a matter of time. ... The targeting of journalists—and it's hard to feel as though those of us identified as press aren't being targeted—feels like something we might hear about in another country, in another era. But it is 2020." See Linda Tirado, "I came to the Minneapolis protests to cover police aggression. Then I became the victim of it," THINK, NBC News, June 1, 2020. https://www.nbcnews.com/think/opinion/i-came-cover-aggression-minneapolis-then-i-became-victim-it-ncna1221241.

11. "Editorial: There is no excuse for government-sanctioned violence against the free press," *Los Angeles Times*, June 2, 2020. https://www.latimes.com/opinion/story/2020-06-02/police-attacks-media-protests-george-floyd.

12. "Journalist arrested amid protests in Lincoln, Nebraska," U.S. Press Freedom Tracker, May 31, 2020. https://pressfreedom tracker.us/all-incidents/journalist-arrested-amid-protests-lincoln-nebraska/.

13. "Police shove, make AP journalists stop covering protest," June 3, 2020. https://apnews.com/article/us-news-new-york-city-manhattan-ny-state-wire-journalists-1d2d9e4afdd822b27bfcce570e0cbdb5, https://www.nbc12.com/2020/06/03/police-shove-make-ap-journalists-stop-covering-protest/.

14. Trump supporters still call him a businessman—I have heard it firsthand—seemingly not willing to acknowledge that he is now a politician. But the fact is, once a person enters the political realm he or she becomes a politician, just as one may be called a journalist once the person starts reporting for a news organization. Trump is both businessman and politician.

15. It was reported by *The New Republic* in an article titled, "Why were so many journalists killed in 2018," that many other politicians and leaders, following Trump's example, started using the same media-bashing lingo. See Joel Simon, "Why Were So Many Journalists Murdered in 2018?" *The New Republic*, December 19, 2018. https://newrepublic.com/article/152676/many-journalists-murdered-2018.

16. As disturbing as these developments are, however, and with no excuse for a president of the United States to say such things that in effect attack the First Amendment that he took an oath to protect, these instances should serve as a teaching moment for journalists and news organizations. A little self-evaluation, perhaps long overdue, is a good thing, especially since, according to statistics, the public's distrust of news media had been declining long before Trump took office. According to a poll conducted by *USA Today*, CNN and Gallup, only 36 percent of Americans believed news organizations get the facts right, compared with 54 percent of Americans in mid-1989. Another poll, this one by American Society of Newspaper Editors, found that 80 percent of Americans believe journalists chase sensational stories to sell newspapers, "not because they think it is important news." A large percentage of Americans also believed news organizations do not report adequately on issues that affect the majority of the population and that news outlets have short attention spans, leaving one headline or broadcast in favor of the next big scoop. Polls also found that nonprofit media organizations had far higher confidence ratings from the public than for-profit organizations, such as CNN, NBC and Fox News.

17. President Donald Trump, according to former National Security Advisor John Bolton, made remarks that journalists should be jailed so they'd divulge their sources. Going to the extreme, Bolton said in his book *The Room Where It Happened: A White House Memoir* that the president even said some journalists should be put to death. "These people should be executed," Trump purportedly said in June 2019. "They are scumbags."

The Poynter Institute's Tom Jones, in an article dated June 18, 2020, about Bolton's book and the alleged Trump comments, wrote that it was stunning but perhaps not surprising seeing who it came from, to hear such talk from a U.S. president. "This kind of talk not only goes against everything a democracy should stand for, but continues to potentially put journalists at risk from those who view Trump's words as more than a catchphrase at a rally or remark in administration meetings. His words are dangerous. But, sadly, not that surprising." Tom Jones, "President Trump thinks some journalists should be executed, according to John Bolton's upcoming book," Poynter,

June 18, 2020. https://www.poynter.org/newsletters/2020/president-trump-thinks-some-journalists-should-be-executed-according-to-john-boltons-upcoming-book/.

18. Meghan Roos, "Louisville Protesters Throw Brick Into Car Windshield of Local Camera Crew," *Newsweek*, June 16, 2020. https://www.newsweek.com/louisville-protesters-throw-brick-car-windshield-local-camera-crew-1511207.

19. Tina Moore, Amanda Woods and Lia Eustachewich, "Cops arrest man for alleged wooden board attack on Post reporter," *New York Post*, July 14, 2020. https://nypost.com/2020/07/14/cops-arrest-man-who-attacked-post-reporter-with-wooden-board/.

20. See Section 230 of the Communications Decency Act, 47 U.S.C. § 230, a Provision of the Communication Decency Act, as found at Electronic Frontier Foundation. https://www.eff.org/issues/cda230. The EFF is a nonprofit organization that defends civil liberties in the digital world.

21. Ken Dilanian and Tom Winter, "Here's what happened when NBC News tried to report on the alleged Hunter Biden emails," NBC News, October 30, 2020. https://www.nbcnews.com/politics/2020-election/here-s-what-happened-when-nbc-news-tried-report-alleged-n1245533.

22. Terrance Smith, "Trump has long-standing history of calling elections 'rigged' if he doesn't like the result," ABC News, November 11, 2020. https://abcnews.go.com/Politics/trump-longstanding-history-calling-elections-rigged-doesnt-results/story?id=74126926.

23. Emily Stephenson and Alana Wise, "Trump charges U.S. election results being rigged 'at many polling places,'" Reuters, October 16, 2016. https://www.reuters.com/article/us-usa-election-trump-rigged/trump-charges-u-s-election-results-being-rigged-at-many-polling-places-idUSKBN12G0SU.

24. "These Are the 5 People Who Died in the Capitol Riot," *The New York Times*, https://www.nytimes.com/2021/01/11/us/who-died-in-capitol-building-attack.html.

25. Tweet by Shomari Stone, January 6, 2021. https://twitter.com/shomaristone/status/1346941715895250949?ref_src=twsrc%5Etfw%7Ctwcamp%5Etweetembed%7Ctwterm%5E1346941715895250949%7Ctwgr%5E%7Ctwcon%5Es1_&ref_url=https%3A%2F%2Fthehill.com%2Fhomenews%2Fnews%2F533022-videos-show-protesters-outside-capitol-destroying-journalists-equipment.

26. Tiffany Hsu and Katie Robertson, "Covering Pro-Trump Mobs, the News Media Became a Target," *The New York Times*, January 6, 2021. https://www.nytimes.com/2021/01/06/business/media/media-murder-capitol-building.html?fbclid=IwAR2Bb25N0UJ0ZtjMBf5bdPLU0zXaLz2uTk6N1jYyq0KaoQ2b8VH9VG1an10.

27. Tweet by Samantha-Jo Roth, January 6, 2021. https://twitter.com/SamanthaJoRoth/status/1346984853149868033.

28. Sophia Eppolito, "Trump supporters gather at Utah capitol in mostly calm event," January 6, 2021. https://apnews.com/article/election-2020-joe-biden-utah-elections-salt-lake-city-52666c5949ea26f15fd952929361e6f5.

29. See https://twitter.com/slcmayor/status/1346951864995041282.

30. As quoted in Ted Anthony, "A moment in America, unimaginable but perhaps inevitable," Associated Press, January 6, 2021. https://apnews.com/article/joe-biden-donald-trump-senate-elections-united-states-michael-pence-e3c49772b8516c84676e1c2afd4362a2.

31. Denise Lavoie, "Daunte Wright: Doting dad, ballplayer, slain by police," Associated Press, April 14, 2021. https://apnews.com/article/daunte-wright-shooting-minnesota-f70fb7fc4c205740507b7ec53d7315f0.

32. Hollie Silverman, "Minnesota governor expresses regret for mistreatment of journalists during Daunte Wright demonstrations," CNN, April 18, 2021. https://www.cnn.com/2021/04/18/us/daunte-wright-minnesota-shooting-sunday/index.html.

33. Todd Richmond, "Journalists allege police harassment at Minnesota protests," Associated Press, April 17, 2021. https://apnews.com/article/death-of-daunte-wright-shootings-journalists-minnesota-minneapolis-2f567f3c306d99ed146a6acb43c587a2.

34. *Ibid.*

35. Hollie Silverman and Andy Rose, "Minnesota governor expresses regret for mistreatment of journalists during Daunte Wright demonstrations," CNN, April 18, 2021. https://www.cnn.com/2021/04/18/

us/daunte-wright-minnesota-shooting-sunday/index.html.

36. See https://twitter.com/GovTim Walz/status/1383539678704390149.

37. "Reporter, colleague arrested while documenting Elizabeth City protests," U.S. Press Freedom Tracker, May 19, 2021. https://pressfreedomtracker.us/all-incidents/reporter-colleague-arrested-while-documenting-elizabeth-city-protests/.

38. Devlin Barrett, "Trump Justice Department seized Post reporter's phone records," *Washington Post*, May 7, 2021. https://www.washingtonpost.com/national-security/trump-justice-dept-seized-post-reporters-phone-records/2021/05/07/933cdfc6-af5b-11eb-b476-c3b287e52a01_story.html.

39. Letter by Jan Neuharth, chair and chief executive officer, Freedom Forum. https://www.freedomforum.org/2020/06/05/this-first-amendment-moment/.

40. Tom Fitzpatrick, "Explosive Testimony," *Phoenix New Times*, March 3, 1993. https://www.phoenixnewtimes.com/news/explosive-testimony-6425909.

41. *Ibid.*

42. "Don Bolles murder reverberates 42 years later in a changed world," *The Arizona Republic*, June 1, 2018. https://www.az central.com/story/news/local/don-bolles/2018/06/01/arizona-republic-reporter-don-bolles-murder-reverberates-42-years-later/658390002/.

43. See Pamela Warrick, "What a long, strange trip it's been," *Los Angeles Times*, March 20, 1997. https://www.latimes.com/archives/la-xpm-1996-03-20-ls-49715-story.html.

44. Richard Ruelas, "40 years later, final words of murdered reporter Don Bolles still a mystery," *The Arizona Republic*, December 20, 2016. https://www.azcentral.com/story/news/local/phoenix-best-reads/2016/06/02/republic-reporter-don-bolles-final-words-emprise-mafia/84793594/.

45. Tatiana Hensley, "Bolles: Cautious man, dedicated journalist," *The Arizona Republic*, May 28, 2006. http://archive.az central.com/specials/special01/0528bolles-profile.html.

46. Steve Shadley, "New Podcast Revisits Murder Case of Arizona Republic Reporter Don Bolles," NPR's Knau, Arizona Public Radio, November 25, 2019. https://www.knau.org/post/new-podcast-revisits-murder-case-arizona-republic-reporter-don-bolles.

47. I believe reporting and investigating are redundant terms. All journalism should, to an extent, be investigative. Nonetheless, some topics and stories require more investigating than others. I will use the term "investigative reporter" and "investigative reporting" here to lessen confusion and to keep with the typical reference about the type of reporting that Bolles did.

48. Jeremy Duda, "Bombed car of assassinated Az reporter Don Bolles needs new home," *Tucson Sentinel*, October 30, 2019. http://www.tucsonsentinel.com/local/report/103019_bolles_car/bombed-car-assassinated-az-reporter-don-bolles-needs-new-home/.

49. Jeremy Duda, "Bombed car of assassinated Az reporter Don Bolles needs new home," *Arizona Mirror*, as posted at *Tucson Sentinel*, October 30, 2019. http://www.tucsonsentinel.com/local/report/103019_bolles_car/bombed-car-assassinated-az-reporter-don-bolles-needs-new-home/.

50. *Ibid.*

51. According to a *Los Angeles Times* story, Jon Sellers, the lead investigator on the case, said he had never seen a man suffer as much as Bolles. See Pamela Warrick, "What a long, strange trip it's been," *Los Angeles Times*, March 20, 1996. https://www.latimes.com/archives/la-xpm-1996-03-20-ls-49715-story.html.

52. "Don Bolles' tragic death," *The Michigan Daily*, June 16, 1976. https://news.google.com/newspapers?id=VP9JAAAAIBAJ&pg=3922,2003692&dq=don+bolles&hl=en.

53. "Reporters' probe of Arizona crime draws mixed reaction from press," *The Washington Post*, March 15, 1977. https://www.washingtonpost.com/archive/local/1977/03/15/reporters-probe-of-arizona-crime-draws-mixed-reaction-from-press/c683a57d-bc8c-4ea0-b8f5-c5e9c708dbfe/.

54. Jon Talton, "40 years later: Who murdered reporter Don Bolles," *Tucson Sentinel*, June 2, 2016. http://www.tucsonsentinel.com/local/report/060216_bolles_murdered/40-years-later-who-murdered-reporter-don-bolles/.

55. Jon Talton, Rogue Columnist. https://www.roguecolumnist.com/rogue_columnist/2015/09/who-murdered-don-bolles-i.html.

56. Mike O'Neil, "The Think Tank revisits the Don Bolles story," KTAR, December 6, 2019. https://ktar.com/story/2868171/the-think-tank-revisits-the-don-bolles-story/. Retrieved October 25, 2020.

57. "Don Bolles' tragic death," *The Michigan Daily*," June 16, 1976. https://news.google.com/newspapers?id=VP9JAAAAIBAJ&pg=3922,2003692&dq=don+bolles&hl=en.

58. EJ Montini, "Don Bolles: Decades later, speaking truth to power earns journalists scorn," *The Arizona Republic*, June 1, 2018. https://www.azcentral.com/story/news/local/don-bolles/2018/06/01/decades-after-arizona-republic-reporter-don-bolles-killed-reporters-scorned/656948002/. Retrieved October 23, 2020.

59. Steven Symes, "The Don Bolles Car Controversy," *Motorious*, February 14, 2020. https://buy.motorious.com/articles/news/398800/don-bolles-car-controversy. Retrieved October 25, 2020.

60. Jeremy Duda, "Bolles investigator hopes to find new home for famous car," *The Mirror*, October 30, 2019. https://www.azmirror.com/2019/10/30/bolles-investigator-hopes-to-find-new-home-for-famous-car/ See also http://www.tucsonsentinel.com/local/report/103019_bolles_car/bombed-car-assassinated-az-reporter-don-bolles-needs-new-home/. Retrieved October 25, 2020.

61. "Don Bolles murder reverberates 42 years later in a changed world," *The Arizona Republic*, June 1, 2018. https://www.azcentral.com/story/news/local/don-bolles/2018/06/01/arizona-republic-reporter-don-bolles-murder-reverberates-42-years-later/658390002/.

Chapter 3

1. See "Branches of the U.S. Government," USA.gov. https://www.usa.gov/branches-of-government.

2. See Delbert Tran, "The Fourth Estate As The Final Check," November 22, 2016. Media Freedom & Information Access Clinic, Yale Law School, November 22, 2016. https://law.yale.edu/mfia/case-disclosed/fourth-estate-final-check.

3. Holzer, Harold, *The Presidents vs. the Press*, p. xix.

4. These men were truly historians of the times and not necessarily deemed jour-

nalists as we know them today, but I mention the context of keeping with the idea that journalists are record keepers of their age.

5. "A Brief History of Journalism: How We Arrived to Where We Are." See https://www.universalclass.com/articles/writing/journalism-a-brief-history.htm.

6. See "'Publick Occurrences, Both Foreign and Domestic,' the First Newspaper Published in North America, Suppressed after a Single Issue," Jeremy Norman's HistoryofInformation.com, https://www.historyofinformation.com/detail.php?id=400#:~:text=Massachusetts%2C%20United%20States-,%22Publick%20Occurrences%2C%20Both%20Foreign%20and%20Domestic%2C%22%20the%20First,Suppressed%20after%20a%20Single%20Issue&text=This%20was%20the%20first%20newspaper,hand%20around%20with%20the%20newspaper.

7. The name that Benjamin Franklin chose as his pseudonym, Silence Dogood, is interesting. Silence has been used as a female's name, the gentler sex. Perhaps the name was meant to convey in a type of symbology that keeping his real name "silent" was meant to "do good" with his controversial columns in the society in which he then lived. Instead of the more frontal and aggressive attack of using a male's name, Silence was rather perhaps meant to gently persuade.

8. John Welsh and Gordon S. Wood, as found in "Benjamin Franklin: American author, scientist, and statesman," Britannica. https://www.britannica.com/biography/Benjamin-Franklin.

9. An interview with Todd Andrlik, author and editor of "Reporting the Revolutionary War," as seen on George Washington's Mount Vernon, https://www.mountvernon.org/george-washington/the-revolutionary-war/reporting-the-revolutionary-war-an-interview-with-todd-andrlik/#:~:text=Benjamin%20Rush%20wrote%20to%20General,that%20%E2%80%9Cin%20establishing%20%20American%20independence%2C.

10. Delbert Tran, "The Fourth Estate As The Final Check," November 22, 2016. https://law.yale.edu/mfia/case-disclosed/fourth-estate-final-check.

11. Holzer, Harold. *The Presidents vs. the Press*, p. 4.

12. Shannon Duffy, History Department Texas State University, as found in "Press Attacks," Washington Library, George Washington's Mount Vernon. https://www.mountvernon.org/library/digitalhistory/digital-encyclopedia/article/press-attacks/.

13. See, for example, Holzer's *The President vs. the Press*, p. 21.

14. Thomas Jefferson to John Norvell, June 11, 1807. Library of Congress. https://www.loc.gov/resource/mtj1.038_0592_0594/?sp=3&st=text. Retrieved October 21, 2020.

15. See "Image 3 of Thomas Jefferson to John Norvell, June 11, 1807," The Library of Congress. https://www.loc.gov/resource/mtj1.038_0592_0594/?sp=3&st=text.

16. Linda Barrett Osborne, Guardians of Liberty, p. 7.

17. Linda Barrett Osborne, Guardians of Liberty, Abrams Books for Young Readers, 2020, p. 4.

18. Jessica Chasmar, "Joe Biden snaps at CBS reporter for Hunter question: 'Another smear campaign, right up your alley,'" *The Washington Post*, October 19, 2020. https://www.washingtontimes.com/news/2020/oct/19/joe-biden-snaps-at-cbs-reporter-for-hunter-questio/.

19. Harold Holzer, *The Presidents vs. the Press*, Dutton, 2020, p. xviii.

20. "The 10 Most Censored Countries," CPJ, May 2, 2006. https://cpj.org/reports/2006/05/10-most-censored-countries/.

21. After a brief tour to wave to crowds outside Walter Reed Medical Center when Donald Trump was at the hospital receiving treatment for Covid-19 in early October 2020, he tweeted that he was grateful for his "fans," foregoing the usual reference from an American president of calling them "citizens."

22. Ironically, some people already think the mainstream media is "state controlled," promoting the leftist agenda.

23. Ann Telnaes, "Opinion: World Press Freedom Day," *Washington Post*, May 3, 2021. See https://www.washingtonpost.com/opinions/2021/05/03/world-press-freedom-day/.

24. "Statement by President Joe Biden on World Press Freedom Day," The White House, May 2, 2021. https://www.whitehouse.gov/briefing-room/statements-releases/2021/05/03/statement-by-president-joe-biden-on-the-occasion-of-world-press-freedom-day/.

25. "A Bloody End for an Anti-Drug Crusader," *Newsweek*, March 22, 1992. https://www.newsweek.com/bloody-end-anti-drug-crusader-196172.

26. "2 indicted in N.Y. journalist's killing Drug cartel said to order slaying," *Newsday* in *The Baltimore Sun*, May 11, 1993. https://www.baltimoresun.com/news/bs-xpm-1993-05-11-1993131217-story.html.

27. Richard Pyle, "Jury Convicts Colombian Teen in Slaying of Anti-Drug Journalist, Associated Press, March 9, 1994. https://apnews.com/article/e2066765b1851b57c92faa7171973a19.

28. Pope Brock, "A Crusader Falls," *People*, March 30, 1992. https://people.com/archive/a-crusader-falls-vol-37-no-12/.

29. *Ibid.*

30. *Ibid.*

31. *Ibid.*

32. Albor Ruiz, "Killed for Reporting the Truth," Al Dia, March 14, 2018. https://aldianews.com/articles/politics/op-ed-killed-reporting-truth/51996.

33. *Ibid.*

34. *Ibid.*

35. Albor Ruiz, "The death of a journalist," Al Dia, March 18, 2020. https://aldianews.com/articles/politics/opinion/death-journalist/57927.

CHAPTER 4

1. See Christopher Paul and James J. Kim, *Reporters on the Battlefield: The Embedded Press System in Historical Context*, RAND Corp., 2004, p. 118. https://www.jstor.org/stable/10.7249/mg200rc.14?seq=2#metadata_info_tab_contents.

2. *Ibid.*

3. Kristin Markway, "All agree on public's right to know," University of Missouri, as seen at National Freedom of Information Coalition. https://www.nfoic.org/all-agree-publics-right-know.

4. *Ibid.*

5. Clarence Page, "Trump's war against leakers shows why we need a 'shield law,'" *Chicago Tribune*, June 12, 2018. https://www.chicagotribune.com/columns/clarence-page/ct-perspec-page-trump-sessions-espionage-act-cpj-0613-20180612-story.html.

6. Martin A. Lee and Tiffany DeVitt, "Gulf War Coverage: Censorship Begins at Home," *Sage Journals*, January 1, 1991. https://journals.sagepub.com/doi/10.1177/073953299101200104.

7. Cecilia Friend, Don Challenger and Katherine C. McAdams, *Contemporary Editing*, p. 4.

8. "Pentagon Papers," History, August 2, 2011; updated August 21, 2018. https://www.history.com/topics/vietnam-war/pentagon-papers.

9. James L. Greenfield, "How the New York Times published the Pentagon Papers," December 17, 2017. https://www.salon.com/2017/12/17/how-the-new-york-times-published-the-pentagon-papers/. Retrieved October 24, 2020.

10. "Pentagon Papers," History, August 2, 2011; updated August 21, 2018. https://www.history.com/topics/vietnam-war/pentagon-papers.

11. See "NEW YORK TIMES COMPANY, Petitioner, v. UNITED STATES. UNITED STATES, Petitioner, v. The WASHINGTON POST COMPANY et al.," located at the Legal Information Institute, Cornell Law School, https://www.law.cornell.edu/supremecourt/text/403/713. See also the original court case here: https://supreme.justia.com/cases/federal/us/403/713/.

12. Carl Bernstein and Bob Woodward, *All the President's Men*, Simon & Schuster: New York, 1974. Watergate, the reporting duo wrote, "was an odd place to find the Democrats. The opulent Watergate on the banks of the Potomac in downtown Washington, was as Republican as the Union League Club. ... The futuristic complex with its serpent's-teeth concrete balustrades and equally menacing price ($10,000 for many of its two-bedroom cooperative apartments), had become the symbol of the ruling class in Richard Nixon's Watergate." Page 14.

13. David Von Drehle, "FBI's No. 2 Was Deep Throat: Mark Felt Ends 30 Year Mystery of the Post's Watergate Source," *Washington Post*, June 1, 2005. https://www.washingtonpost.com/politics/fbis-no-2-was-deep-throat-mark-felt-ends-30-year-mystery-of-the-posts-watergate-source/2012/06/04/gJQAwseRIV_story.html.

14. *Ibid.*, pages 345–346. The story of Watergate is a haunting memory that in some ways has been revisited in our own day but with a different twist. Instead of the Republicans rising up to convict Donald Trump during a second impeachment trial for inciting the invasion of the capitol, Republicans acquitted him over partisan politics.

15. Michael Rezendes, Matt Carroll, Sacha Pfeiffer, and Walter V. Robinson. "Church allowed abuse by priest for years," part 1 of 2, *The Boston Globe*, January 6, 2002. https://www.bostonglobe.com/news/special-reports/2002/01/06/church-allowed-abuse-priest-for-years/cSHfGkTIrAT25qKGvBuDNM/story.html.

16. "Three-part Herald video documentary, 'On the border,' captures snapshot of life on the border in northwest Minnesota," *Grand Forks Herald*, December 23, 2020. https://www.grandforksherald.com/news/6807940-Three-part-Herald-video-documentary-On-the-border-captures-snapshot-of-life-on-the-border-in-northwest-Minnesota; Also see Korrie Wenzel, "On the border: Struggles, successes in northern Minnesota come to the forefront," Grand Forks Herald, December 18, 2020. https://www.grandforksherald.com/opinion/columns/6806731-On-the-border-Struggles-successes-in-northern-Minnesota-come-to-the-forefront.

17. Joe Nelson, "Murder charges in fentanyl deaths? Riverside County carves new path in Southern California," *The Orange County Register*, March 8, 2021. https://www.ocregister.com/2021/03/08/murder-charges-in-fentanyl-deaths-riverside-county-carves-new-path-in-southern-california/.

18. Karcin Harris, "'It just hurts my heart'—How COVID dissent pushed some Latter-day Saints away from their church," *The Salt Lake Trubune*, May 2, 2021. https://www.sltrib.com/religion/2021/05/02/it-just-hurts-my-heart/.

19. *Ibid.*

20. See The Sunshine Project, *The Laconia Daily Sun*. https://www.laconiadailysun.com/news/local/the-sunshine-project--series/collection_c5fce562-f050-11e9-bdf7-07debb13e4ba.html.

21. Richard Cole, "Haitian Radio Show Host Killed in Miami With PM-Haiti," Associated Press, October 25, 1993. https://apnews.com/article/608057e1f92d4bb0d5c9c20cda7b5c55.

22. Aristide, who had an on-again, off-again presidency, was also ousted in 2004 in which he claimed the U.S. played a part. The George W. Bush administration denied

such allegations. "That's nonsense," according to White House press secretary Scott McClellan in a CNN report. "I've seen some of the reports [and they] do nothing to help the Haitians move forward to a better, more prosperous future." See "Aristide says U.S. deposed him in 'coup d'état,'" CNN, March 2, 2004. http://edition.cnn.com/2004/WORLD/americas/03/01/aristide.claim/.

23. See https://www.sun-sentinel.com/news/fl-xpm-1993-12-07-9312070104-story.html.

24. Larry Rhoter, "In Miami's Little Haiti, Fears of Assassination," *The New York Times*, March 20, 1994, https://www.nytimes.com/1994/03/20/us/in-miami-s-little-haiti-fears-of-assassination.html.

25. "Exile: Slain Haitian Named on Hit List," Associated Press, as found in *Boca Raton News*, October 26, 1993. https://news.google.com/newspapers?nid=1290&dat=19931026&id=7xZUAAAAIBAJ&pg=5620,5845368.

26. "Dime a Dance Place is Shot Up After Slaying," *Sarasota Herald-Tribune*, July 31, 1949. https://news.google.com/newspapers?id=GB8hAAAAIBAJ&pg=2698,2953697&dq=southwick+alice+mason&hl=en.

27. Laura Smith, "This brash Jewish radio host was murdered by white supremacists for denouncing anti–Semitism," *Timeline*, November 6, 2017. https://timeline.com/alan-berg-jewish-murder-denver-57f54b2989dd.

28. Thomas J. Knudson, "Trial Opens in Slaying of Radio Talk Show host," Special to *The New York Times*, October 31, 1987. https://www.nytimes.com/1987/10/31/us/trial-opens-in-slaying-of-radio-talk-show-host.html.

Chapter 5

1. Jeff Jarvis in Craig Silverman's book, *Regret the Error*, p. ix.

2. Kyle Pope, "Here's to the return of the journalist as malcontent," CJR, November 9, 2016. https://www.cjr.org/criticism/journalist_election_trump_failure.php.

3. *The Grand Forks Herald*, June 18, 2020, https://www.grandforksherald.com/opinion/editorials/6537375-Our-view-Going-slow-is-best-with-social-media.

4. *Ibid.*

5. Jean Kim, "Is Social Media Destroying Our Attention Spans?" *Psychology Today*, December 14, 2018. https://www.psychologytoday.com/us/blog/culture-shrink/201812/is-social-media-destroying-our-attention-spans.

6. Kelly Lawler, "Morning TV anchors try to parse election results on Day 2: 'Big Dumps' and deep breaths," *USA Today*, November 4, 2020. https://usatoday.com/story/entertainment/tv/2020/11/04/how-tv-networks-covered-2020-election-day-2-no-winner/6158722002/.

7. Steve Buttry, "The voiceless have a voice. A journalist's job is to amplify it," CJR, May 18, 2016. https://www.cjr.org/first_person/buttry_story.php.

8. Some readers may find it interesting that I write this, since parts of this book may be perceived as being biased. But here's a difference: I am writing this book as a personal endeavor and not as a reporter sanctioned by a news organization to produce it. I mentioned in the preface that if this book comes across as biased, I am OK with that because I am biased toward journalists and my profession. As for what I have written about Donald Trump, which some may take as biased against him, I disagree with that assumption. If Joe Biden, Barack Obama, or George W. Bush, et cetera, called journalists names and belittled the profession at press conferences and rallies, et cetera, I would have written similar things of them. My stance on Trump as may appear in these pages is not a political motive but an ethical one—in defense of my colleagues and the constitution as I view them.

9. William Davies, "Why can't we agree on what's true anymore?" *The Guardian*, September 19, 2019. https://www.theguardian.com/media/2019/sep/19/why-cant-we-agree-on-whats-true-anymore.

10. Gina Piccalo and Kurt Streeter, "Venice Anti-Gang Activist Killed in His Driveway," *Los Angeles Times*, October 19, 2000. https://www.latimes.com/archives/la-xpm-2000-oct-19-me-38801-story.html.

11. See https://www.latimes.com/archives/la-xpm-2000-oct-19-me-38801-story.html.

12. Pat Morrison, "Slaying of Venice Acitvist Proves Danger of Truth-Telling," *Los Angeles Times*, October 20, 2000. https://www.latimes.com/archives/la-xpm-2000-oct-20-me-39300-story.html.

13. James Edwin Richards, "Neighborhood News Killed in California," CPJ, Octo-

ber 18, 2000. https://cpj.org/data/people/james-edwin-richards/.

14. "Was an LA Activist Shot for His Anti-Crime Efforts?" ABC News, January 7, 2006. https://abcnews.go.com/U.S./story?id=95310&page=1#.UFJybrJlRQQ.

15. "LAPD Announces Arrest of Suspect Who Murdered Community Activist," Los Angeles Police Department news release, March 11, 2002. https://www.lapdonline.org/march_2002/news_view/22295.

16. *Ibid.*

17. *Ibid.*

18. *Ibid.*

19. Margaret Sullivan, "What's a journalist supposed to be now—An Activist? A stenographer? You're asking the wrong question," *Washington Post*, June 6, 2020, https://www.washingtonpost.com/lifestyle/media/whats-a-journalist-supposed-to-be-now—an-activist-a-stenographer-youre-asking-the-wrong-question/2020/06/06/60fdfb86-a73b-11ea-b619-3f9133bbb482_story.html.

20. Gina Piccalo and Kurt Streeter, "Venice Anti-Gang Activist Killed in His Driveway," *Los Angeles Times*, October 19, 2000. https://www.latimes.com/archives/la-xpm-2000-oct-19-me-38801-story.html.

21. https://www.venicenc.org/files/081103-Rosendahl-Designate10-18Jim RichardsDay.pdf.

22. *Ibid.*

CHAPTER 6

1. See John 18:33–38, King James Version of the Bible.

2. After President Donald Trump's inauguration in January 2017, Press Secretary Sean Spicer told the news media, and in turn the world, that his new boss had the largest inauguration crowd in U.S. history. That caused a stir, some questioning the assertion. Later, on a Meet the Press interview, Trump advisor and former campaign manager Kellyanne Conway defended Spicer, saying the new press secretary was providing "alternative facts."

3. In what might seem like a comical post from the master of horror fiction, Stephen King tweeted on June 17, 2021, a response to a *New York Times* column. "Frank Brunl worries (in today's *NY Times*) that he and other opinion columnists have helped fuel the toxic atmosphere

of American politics," King tweeted. "This presupposes that anyone cares about opinion columnists, other than their moms." See Stephen King, @StephenKing, Twitter, June 17, 2021. https://twitter.com/StephenKing/status/1405480358011969536.

4. It is likely true that most journalists are more liberal-minded than not, because one of the crucial traits that reporters are taught in J-School is to think outside the box, peer into other boxes, and see the story with more than two eyes. The reason we have journalism is to vet stories, investigate facts, and relay to our audiences what those facts are, uncovered to the best of our ability at that moment in history.

5. Russ Buettner, Susanne Craig and Mike McIntire, "The President's Taxes," *The New York Times*, September 27, 2020. https://www.nytimes.com/interactive/2020/09/27/us/donald-trump-taxes.html.

6. Josh Boaks, "NY Times: Trump paid $750 in U.S. income taxes in 2016, 2017," Associated Press, September 27, 2020. https://apnews.com/article/donald-trump-business-ny-state-wire-ap-top-news-nyc-wire-f0e2af5f9f99de9d30dc6b9097121188.

7. Carl Bernstein, "The Idiot Culture: Reflections on Post-Watergate Journalism." http://carlbernstein.com/magazines_the_idiot_culture.pdf.

8. Disinformation campaigns are murky bends of truth, lies and sincere beliefs—lessons from the pandemic," The Conversation. Retrieved November 13, 2020. https://theconversation.com/disinformation-campaigns-are-murky-blends-of-truth-lies-and-sincere-beliefs-lessons-from-the-pandemic-140677.

9. *Ibid.*

10. James Warren, "The real problem with fake news? Citizen stupidity," Poynter, December 2, 2016. Retrieved November 27, 2020. http://www.poynter.org/2016/the-real-problem-with-fake-news-citizen-stupidity/441029/.

11. Mike Wendling, "The (almost) complete history of 'fake news,'" BBC, January 22, 2018. Retrieved November 14, 2020. https://www.bbc.com/news/blogs-trending-42724320.

12. Elisa Shearer, "Two-thirds of U.S. adults say they've seen their own news sources report facts meant to favor one side," Pew Research Center, November 2, 2020.

Retrieved November 14, 2020. https://www.pewresearch.org/fact-tank/2020/11/02/two-thirds-of-u-s-adults-say-theyve-seen-their-own-news-sources-report-facts-meant-to-favor-one-side/.

13. Ali Swenson, "Photo of newspaper was edited to add 'President Gore' headline," Associated Press, November 8, 2020. Retrieved Nov. 14, 2020. https://apnews.com/article/fact-checking-9702032985.

14. Cydney Henderson, "John Krasinski sells 'Some Good News' web series to CBS; some fans aren't happy," *USA Today,* May 22, 2020. https://www.usatoday.com/story/entertainment/celebrities/2020/05/22/john-krasinski-sells-some-good-news-cbs-fans-call-him-sellout/5247315002/.

15. Taylor Lorenz, "The News Is Making People Anxious. You'll Never Believe What They're Reading Instead," *The New York Times*, April 14, 2020. https://www.nytimes.com/2020/04/14/style/good-news-coronavirus.html.

16. Natasha Daly, "Fake animal news abounds on social media as coronavirus upends life," *National Geographic*, March 20, 2020. https://www.nationalgeographic.com/animals/article/coronavirus-pandemic-fake-animal-viral-social-media-posts.

17. *Ibid.*

18. Amy Harmon, "The number of people with the virus who died in the U.S. passes 300,000," *The New York Times*, December 14, 2020. https://www.nytimes.com/live/2020/12/14/world/covid-19-coronavirus/the-number-of-people-with-the-virus-who-died-in-the-us-passes-300000?campaign_id=60&emc=edit_na_20201214&instance_id=0&nl=breaking-news&ref=headline&regi_id=141056041&segment_id=46904&user_id=4e6bd6ade8282ab70299356d05856e39.

19. Dave Zweifel, "Journalism matters because democracy matters," *Times-Republic*, October 11, 2019. Retrieved Nov. 13, 2020. https://www.timesrepublican.com/opinion/columnists/2019/10/journalism-matters-because-democracy-matters/.

20. "The parting shot," *The Irish Times*, December 22, 2001. https://www.irishtimes.com/news/the-parting-shot-1.343336.

21. Jerry Adler, "Shooting To The End," *Newsweek* (The Daily Beast), October 14, 2001. https://web.archive.org/web/20130
513081638/http://www.thedailybeast.com/newsweek/2001/10/14/shooting-to-the-end.html.

22. *Ibid.*

23. See his images at the William Biggart website, BillBiggart.com: http://www.billbiggart.com/911.html.

24. *Ibid.*

25. See http://www.billbiggart.com/.

26. See http://www.billbiggart.com/.

27. "Remembering the Only Photojournalist Lost on 9/11," 9/11 Memorial Museum. https://www.911memorial.org/connect/blog/remembering-only-photojournalist-lost-911.

28. As quoted in, "Bill Biggart killed at World Trade Centre," EPUK, September 18, 2001. http://www.epuk.org/news/bill-biggart-killed-at-world-trade-centre.

CHAPTER 7

1. Dave Zweifel, "Journalism matters because democracy matters," *Times-Republic*, October 11, 2019. https://www.timesrepublican.com/opinion/columnists/2019/10/journalism-matters-because-democracy-matters/.

2. "What's a journalist supposed to be now—an activist or stenographer?" *The Washington Post*, June 6, 2020. https://www.washingtonpost.com/lifestyle/media/whats-a-journalist-supposed-to-be-now—an-activist-a-stenographer-youre-asking-the-wrong-question/2020/06/06/60fdfb86-a73b-11ea-b619-3f9133bbb482_story.html.

3. "Writing on the Wall: An Interview with Hunter S. Thompson," *The Atlantic Monthly*, August 26, 1997. https://www.theatlantic.com/past/docs/unbound/graffiti/hunter.htm.

4. See Henry Grunwald Quotes, Brainy Quote. https://www.brainyquote.com/quotes/henry_grunwald_113731.

5. "Journalism Sayings and Quotes," Wise Sayings. https://www.wiseoldsayings.com/journalism-quotes/#ixzz6dXFdtK6U.

6. CBS Source. See also, Stephen Battaglio, "President posts unedited 60 Minutes interview," *Los Angeles Times*, October 22, 2020. https://www.latimes.com/entertainment-arts/business/story/2020-10-22/president-trump-posts-unedited-60-minutes-interview-facebook. He writes: "While the interview is combative, it is no more contentious than other sit-downs

Trump has done with journalists outside of the friendly confines of the opinion programs on Fox News."

7. *60 Minutes* (@60Minutes). Twitter, October 22, 2020. https://twitter.com/60Minutes/status/1319316652412919808.

8. SPJ Code of Ethics. https://www.spj.org/ethicscode.asp.

9. Tania Valdemoro, "Anthrax victim's widow breaks four-year silence," *Palm Beach Post*, as quoted in UCLA Department of Epidemiology, School of Public Health, November 5, 2005, http://www.ph.ucla.edu/epi/bioter/fouryearsilence.html; see also "FBI concludes investigation into 2001 anthrax mailings," CNN, February 19, 2010. http://www.cnn.com/2010/CRIME/02/19/fbi.anthrax.report/.

10. "Widow, U.S. Reach Settlement Deal In Florida Anthrax Death," CBS Miami/Associated Press, October 30, 2011. https://miami.cbslocal.com/2011/10/30/widow-us-reach-settlement-deal-in-florida-anthrax-death/.

11. "Anthrax victim's widow speaks out," BBC, August 7, 2008. http://news.bbc.co.uk/2/hi/7547823.stm.

12. "Special Series: The Anthrax Investigation. Timeline: How The Anthrax Terror Unfolded," NPR, February 15, 2011. https://www.npr.org/2011/02/15/93170200/timeline-how-the-anthrax-terror-unfolded.

13. *Ibid.*

14. "Baby of ABCNEWS Employee Has Anthrax," ABC News, January 7, 2006. https://abcnews.go.com/U.S./story?id=92279&page=1.

CHAPTER 8

1. Elizabeth Jensen, "Looking To The Future: Restoring Public Trust In The Media," National Public Radio, May 15, 2017. https://www.npr.org/sections/publiceditor/2017/05/15/528158488/looking-to-the-future-restoring-public-trust-in-the-media.

2. Megan Brenan, "Americans Remain Distrustful of News Media," Gallup, September 30, 2020. Retrieved November 20, 2020. https://news.gallup.com/poll/321116/americans-remain-distrustful-mass-media.aspx.

3. Megan Brenan, "Americans Remain Distrustful of Mass Media," Gallup, September 30, 2020. https://news.gallup.com/poll/321116/americans-remain-distrustful-mass-media.aspx.

4. There were many instances in which people blamed the media for what they deemed an unfair and faulty election. Donald Trump's former campaign manager Corey Lewandowski, in a conversation with Fox News' Chris Wallace, said as much as recently as early June 2021. He pushed his belief that Trump would be reinstated as president as early as that August and said the news media was in part to blame for the alleged election fraud. He said while he was in Philadelphia after the election his team contacted the news media, telling them they had found "at least one dead person who voted," Lewandowski told Wallace, "but the response from the media was 'but that person was a Trump supporter.'" Wallace pushed back, saying, "you keep blaming this on the media." Wallace pointed out that more than 60 court cases were submitted to the courts, but every one of them was thrown out. Also, Wallace highlighted that the Supreme Court refused to hear any of the Trump challenges, "so please don't blame this on the media—you had your day in court, and you lost." See Mark Joyella, "Chris Wallace: 'Please Don't Blame the Media, You Had Your Day In Court And You Lost,'" Forbes, June 6, 2021. https://www.forbes.com/sites/markjoyella/2021/06/06/chris-wallace-please-dont-blame-the-media-you-had-your-day-in-court-and-you-lost/?sh=66ba2c595f3f. For anyone who has followed the contested election results, it is known that "the media" has been blamed for pushing alleged voter fraud, if for no other reason, these naysayers claim, than wanting Trump out of office.

5. SPJ Code of Ethics. https://www.spj.org/ethicscode.asp.

6. "Indicators of news media distrust," Knight Foundation, September 11, 2018. https://knightfoundation.org/reports/indicators-of-news-media-trust/.

7. Emma Spaeth, "Spaeth: The importance of transparency in modern journalism," *Daily Emerald*, April 7, 2019. https://www.dailyemerald.com/opinion/spaeth-the-importance-of-transparency-in-modern-journalism/article_f5cc9d70-5972-11e9-a208-e7046b777390.html.

8. Walter Cronkite, as quoted in Lynn Walsh, "POINT OF VIEW: Journalists

seek the truth," *The Palm Beach Post*, December 29, 2016. https://www.palmbeach post.com/news/opinion/point-view-journalists-seek-the-truth/aRZirirGzrwv NqRg1aX6YI/.

9. American Press Institute, "Diversity and inclusivity in Journalism." https://www. americanpressinstitute.org/diversity-programs/.

10. Philip Eil, "5 ways journalists can regain trust from readers," April 11, 2018. Retrieved November 16, 2020. https://www. cjr.org/analysis/trust-journalism.php.

11. Christopher Heredia, Leslie Fulbright, Marisa Lagos, "Hit man kills newspaper editor on Oakland street," *The San Francisco Chronicle*, August 2, 2007. https://www.sfgate.com/bayarea/article/Hit-man-kills-newspaper-editor-on-Oakland-street-2549667.php.

12. See "Chauncey Baily, 1949–2007." Encyclopedia.com. https://www.encyclo pedia.com/education/news-wires-white-papers-and-books/bailey-chauncey. The site also lists several news sources covering Bailey's death and the court trials that followed.

13. A number of articles about Bailey and the trial of his killers can be found here: "Chauncey Bailey," KPIX 5, CBS SF Nay Area, https://sanfrancisco.cbslocal.com/tag/chauncey-bailey/.

14. Peele, Thomas, "Infamous Black Muslim leader Yusuf Bey IV tries to order hits from prison, authorities say," *Mercury News*, November 21, 2016. https://www. mercurynews.com/2016/11/21/infamous-black-muslim-leader-yusuf-bey-iv-tries-to-order-hits-from-prison-authorities-say/.

15. *Ibid.*

16. Thomas Peele, "Devaughndre Broussard: I want the families to know I am sorry," *East Bay Times*, Bay Area News Group, June 16, 2011; updated August 15, 2016. https:// www.eastbaytimes.com/2011/06/16/devaughndre-broussard-i-want-the-families-to-know-i-am-sorry/.

17. "Your Muslim Bakery Leader Guilty of Journalist Slaying," CBS SF, June 9, 2011, https://sanfrancisco.cbslocal.com/2011/06/09/your-black-muslim-bakery-leader-guilt y-of-journalist-slaying/ Retrieved June 20, 2020.

18. Terry Collins, "2 men found guilty in murder of Calif journalist," Associated Press, as printed in *The San Diego Union-Tribune*, June 11, 2011; "2 men found guilty

in murder of Bay Area journalist," ABC7NY, June 9, 2011.

19. *Ibid.*

20. One business owner said Bailey's reporting had helped her business to flourish. See Douglas Fischer and Josh Richman, "Bailey's career in news spanned globe for decades," Daily Climate, *Bay Area News Group, East Bay Times*, August 3, 2007. Retrieved June 20, 2020. https://www.east baytimes.com/2007/08/03/baileys-career-in-news-spanned-globe-for-decades/.

21. Kristin Bender, "Chauncey Bailey, veteran newsman, Oakland Post editor," *Bay City Times, The Mercury News*, August 2, 2007. Retrieved June 20, 2020. https:// mercurynews.com/2007/08/07/chauncey-bailey-veteran-newsman-oakland-post-editor/.

22. "Oakland councilwoman plans memorial for slain journalist Chauncey Bailey," *Bay City Times, The Mercury News*, August 2, 2019. Retrieved June 20, 2020. https://www.mercurynews.com/2019/08/02/oakland-councilwoman-plans-mem orial-for-slain-journalist-chauncey-bailey/.

23. Ali Tadayon, "Memorial for slain journalist delayed," *Bay Area News* Group, *East Bay Times*, October 18, 2019. Retrieved June 20, 2020. https://www.eastbaytimes. com/2019/10/18/memorial-for-slain-oakland-journalist-delayed/.

24. "Your Black Muslim Bakery head guilty," UPI, June 10, 2011.

CHAPTER 9

1. It is perhaps interesting that in seeking truth through reporting, Bly had to herself lie to get the story.

2. "I aimed for the public's heart, and … hit it in the stomach," *Chicago Tribune*, May 21, 2006. https://www.chicagotribune.com/news/ct-xpm-2006-05-21-0605210414-story.html.

3. Michael Noer, "Read The Original Forbes Takedown Of Stephen Glass," *Forbes* magazine, November 12, 2014. https://www. forbes.com/sites/michaelnoer/2014/11/12/read-the-original-forbes-takedown-of-stephen-glass/?sh=42b8cb1a683a.

4. A.H. Raskin, "Thug Hurls Acid on Labor Writer," *The New York Times*, April 6, 1956. https://www.nytimes.com/1956/04/06/archives/thug-hurls-acid-on-labor-writer-sight-imperiled-victor-riesel.html.

5. Shane Harris, "Intelligence forecast sees a post-coronavirus world upended by climate change and splintering societies," *Washington Post*, April 8, 2021. https://www.washingtonpost.com/national-security/intelligence-globe-future-crises-/2021/04/08/303c350e-97df-11eb-962b-78c1d8228819_story.html.

6. "Global Trends 2040," The National Intelligence Council, March 2021. https://www.dni.gov/files/ODNI/documents/assessments/GlobalTrends_2040.pdf page 2.

7. *Ibid.*, page 2.
8. *Ibid.*, page 2.
9. *Ibid.*, page 7.
10. *Ibid.*, page 8.

11. Neal Zuckerman, Alannah Sheerin and Anna Green, "For U.S. Journalism, the Future Is Brighter Than You Think," BCG, September 26, 2019. https://www.bcg.com/publications/2019/united-states-journalism-future-is-brighter-than-you-think.

12. Cassandra Vinograd, "WDBJ7 Reporter Alison Parker, Photographer Adam Ward Killed on Live TV," NBC News, August 26, 2015. https://www.nbcnews.com/storyline/virginia-tv-shooting/wdbj7-reporter-alison-parker-photographer-adam-ward-killed-live-tv-n416221.

13. Elizabeth Chuck, "Alison Parker and Adam Ward, WDBJ Journalists Killed on Live TV, 'Were Special People'," NBC News, August 26, 2015. https://www.nbcnews.com/storyline/virginia-tv-shooting/wdbj-journalists-alison-parker-adam-ward-were-special-people-n416256.

14. "Remembering Virginia TV reporter Alison Parker and cameraman Adam Ward," ABC7, August 26, 2015. https://abc7.com/allison-parker-adam-ward-journalists-killed-reporter/957809/.

15. Pat Thomas, "Virginia journalists Alison Parker and Adam Ward remembered," WDBJ, as posted on NBC12, August 26, 2020. https://www.nbc12.com/2020/08/26/virginia-journalists-alison-parker-adam-ward-remembered/.

16. *Ibid.*

17. Michael D. Shear, Richard Perez-Pena and Alan Blinder, "Ex-Broadcaster Kills 2 on Air in Virginia Shooting; Takes Own Life," *The New York Times*, August 26, 2015. https://www.nytimes.com/2015/08/27/us/wdbj7-virginia-journalists-shot-during-live-broadcast.html.

18. *Ibid.*

19. See "Workplace violence in Healthcare: Understanding the Challenge," Occupational Safety Health Administration. https://www.osha.gov/sites/default/files/OSHA3826.pdf.

20. Jeanne Sahadi, "How common is workplace violence?" CNNMoney, August 26, 2015. https://money.cnn.com/2015/08/26/news/workplace-violence-virginia-shooting/.

21. *Ibid.*

22. Veronica Stracqualursi, "Alison Parker and Adam Ward, Slain Virginia Reporter and Cameraman, 'Did Great Work Every Day'," ABC News, August 26, 2015. https://abcnews.go.com/U.S./alison-parker-adam-ward-slain-virginia-reporter-cameraman/story?id=33330993.

Chapter 10

1. Tom Seymour, "'The camera is not a shield: life and death as a war photographer," *The Guardian*, July 26, 2016. https://www.theguardian.com/tv-and-radio/2016/jul/26/life-and-death-as-a-war-photographer-netflix-series.

2. Marc Lancaster, "Ralph Barnes: First U.S. War Correspondent to Fall," World War II on Deadline, November 18, 2020. https://ww2ondeadline.com/2020/11/18/ralph-barnes-first-us-war-correspondent-killed-wwii/; and Barbara Mahoney, "Ralph Barnes (1899–1940)," *Oregon Encyclopedia*, Oregon Historical Society. https://www.oregonencyclopedia.org/articles/barnes_ralph/#.YMfBQZNKiIs.

3. "World War Correspondent Killed at New Guinea," *The Michigan Alumnus*, p. 139. https://books.google.com/books?id=u_rhAAAAMAAJ&pg=PA139&dq=Byron+Darnton+adrian+mi&hl=en&sa=X&ei=EOQMU7yNGca2yAHlyYGACw&ve d=0CCsQ6AEwAA#v=onepage&q=Byron%20Darnton%20adrian%20mi&f=false; and "U.S. Explorer Killed in New Guinea," The Sydney Morning Herald, October 23, 1942. https://trove.nla.gov.au/newspaper/article/17824904.

4. See "Joseph Morton, War Reporter, Slain by Germans," Associated Press, July 9, 1945. https://news.google.com/newspapers?nid=950&dat=19450709&id=d8wLAAAAIBAJ&pg=3622,1546710. See also, Joe Morton: War Correspondent Executed by

the Nazis," World War Two on Deadline. https://ww2ondeadline.com/2021/01/24/joe-morton-war-correspondent-ap-oss-ww2-dawes-mission/ https://ww2ondeadline.com/2021/01/24/joe-morton-war-correspondent-ap-oss-ww2-dawes-mission/; and Don North, "Inappropriate Conduct: Mystery of a Disgraced War Correspondent, iUniverse, 2013. https://books.google.com/books?id=2XnP3ypSH6MC&q=Joe+Morton+joined+the+AP+in+Lincoln,+Nebraska&pg=PT75#v=snippet&q=Joe%20Morton%20joined%20the%20AP%20in%20Lincoln%2C%20Nebraska&f=false.

5. See Haines, Don C. "With Her Eyes Wide Open," HistoryNet.com, https://www.historynet.com/eyes-wide-open.htm; "A Woman with Balls and Pearl Earrings," Charter for Compassion, https://charterforcompassion.org/dickey-chapelle-controversial-war-photojournalist/a-woman-with-balls-and-pearl-earrings; and "CHAPELLE, Georgette Meyer," Encyclopedia.com. https://www.encyclopedia.com/arts/news-wires-white-papers-and-books/chapelle-georgette-meyer, https://www.encyclopedia.com/arts/news-wires-white-papers-and-books/chapelle-georgette-meyer.

6. Richard Pyle, "4 photojournalists find resting place at last," NBC News, April 1, 2008. https://www.nbcnews.com/id/wbna23908336.

7. Perry Deane Young, "Two of the Missing: Remembering Sean Flynn and Dana Stone," Press 53, 2009.

8. See Fredrik Logevall, "Bernard Fall: The Man Who Knew the War," *The New York Times*, February 21, 2017. https://www.nytimes.com/2017/02/21/opinion/bernard-fall-the-man-who-knew-the-war.html; https://www.bernard-fall.com/; see also, "Bernard B. Fall: Vietnam War Author," HistoryNet, https://www.historynet.com/bernard-b-fall-vietnam-war-author.htm.

9. See Jennifer Levitz and Jon Kamp, "In Fear and Violence, Slain U.S. Journalist Found Humanity," *The Wall Street Journal*, August 20, 2014. https://www.wsj.com/articles/james-foley-u-s-journalist-killed-by-islamic-state-knew-risks-of-conflict-1408569500.

10. "8 Inspiring Quotes by War Correspondent Marie Colvin," The Circle,

February 9, 2018. https://thecircle.ngo/8-inspiring-quotes-war-correspondent-marie-colvin/.

11. An address titled "Truth at All Costs," presented at St. Bride's Church, London, 2010. Marie Colvin Foundation. https://mariecolvin.org/truth-at-all-costs-marie-colvin.

12. "This Day in History, April 18: War correspondent Ernie Pyle killed," History. https://www.history.com/this-day-in-history/journalist-ernie-pyle-killed.

13. "Death photo of war reporter Ernie Pyle found," Associated Press, February 3, 2008, as found at NBC News. https://www.nbcnews.com/id/wbna22980127.

14. *Ibid.*

15. James Tobin, *Ernie Pyle's War: America's Eyewitness to World War II*, page 2.

16. *Ibid.* Tobin, page 3.

17. Meghan Keneally, "From verbal taunts to shots fired: How journalists were attacked in 2018," ABC News, May 3, 2019. https://abcnews.go.com/U.S./verbal-taunts-shots-fired-journalists-attacked-us-2018/story?id=62778248.

18. Alex Mann and Jessica Anderson, "Capital Gazette shooting: Maryland man pleads guilty to attack that killed five as chilling details emerge," *The Capital Gazette*, October 28, 2019. https://www.capitalgazette.com/news/crime/ac-cn-capital-shooting-hearing-1028-20191028-nkxc5ukn4nbzjdwoltewbmqx6u-story.html.

19. *Ibid.*

20. *Ibid.*

21. Sabrina Tavernise, Amy Harmon and Maya Salam, "5 People Dead in Shooting at Maryland's Capital Gazette Newsroom," *The New York Times*, June 28, 2018. https://www.nytimes.com/2018/06/28/us/capital-gazette-annapolis-shooting.html.

22. *Ibid.*

23. Hollie Silverman, Janet DiGiacomo and Darran Simon, "Five dead in shooting at Capital Gazette in Annapolis, Maryland," CNN, June 29, 2018. https://www.cnn.com/2018/06/28/us/annapolis-maryland-newsroom-shooting/index.html.

24. "Announcement of the 2019 Pulitzer Prize Winners," The Pulitzer Prizes, April 14, 2019. https://www.pulitzer.org/news/announcement-2019-pulitzer-prize-winners.

CHAPTER 11

1. Laura Kelly, "House passes bill limiting arms sales to Saudi Arabia over Khashoggi killing, *The Hill*, April 21, 2021. https://thehill.com/policy/international/549617-house-passes-bill-limiting-arms-sales-to-saudi-arabia-over-khashoggi.

2. *Ibid.*

3. Karl Vick, "The Guardians and the War on Truth," *Time*, 2018. https://time.com/person-of-the-year-2018-the-guardians/.

Bibliography

Acosta, Jim. (@Acosta). Twitter, July 31, 2018. https://twitter.com/Acosta/status/10244 67940257738752?ref_src=twsrc%5Etfw %7Ctwcamp%5Etweetembed%7Ctw term%5E1024467940257738752%7C twgr%5Eshare_3%2Ccontainerclick _0&ref_url=https%3A%2F%2Fwww. bbc.com%2Fnews%2Fworld-us-canada-47208909.

Acosta, Jim (@Acosta). Twitter, October 28, 2020. https://twitter.com/acosta/status/1 321605737534009344?lang=en.

Adler, Jerry. "Shooting To The End." *Newsweek* (*The Daily Beast*), October 14, 2001. https://web.archive.org/web/2013051 3081638/http://www.thedailybeast.com/ newsweek/2001/10/14/shooting-to-the-end.html.

"America's Wars," Department of Veterans Affairs. https://www.va.gov/opa/ publications/factsheets/fs_americas_ wars.pdf.

"Announcement of the 2019 Pulitzer Prize Winners." The Pulitzer Prizes, April 14, 2019. https://www.pulitzer.org/news/ announcement-2019-pulitzer-prize-winners.

Anthony, Ted. "A moment in America, unimaginable but perhaps inevitable." Associated Press, January 6, 2021. https:// apnews.com/article/joe-biden-donald-trump-senate-elections-united-states-michael-pence-e3c49772b8516c84676e1 c2afd4362a2.

"Anthrax victim's widow speaks out." BBC, August 7, 2008. http://news.bbc.co.uk/2/ hi/7547823.stm.

Arellano, Gustavo. "READING RUBEN SALAZAR: He was no radical. He was a prophetic reporter." *Los Angeles Times*, August 23, 2020. https://www.latimes.

com/projects/chicano-moratorium/ ruben-salazar-reporting-legacy-la-impact/.

"Aristide says U.S. deposed him in 'coup d'état." CNN, March 2, 2004. http:// edition.cnn.com/2004/WORLD/ americas/03/01/aristide.claim/.

Arkin, Daniel Arkin. "Donald Trump Criticized After He Appears to Mock Reporter Serge Kovaleski." NBC News, November 26, 2015. https://www.nbcnews.com/ politics/2016-election/donald-trump-criticized-after-he-appears-mock-reporter-serge-kovaleski-n470016.

Arocha, Zita. "Ruben Salazar questioned his own ethnic identity and the role of journalism in American society." Borderzine, April 24, 2014. https://borderzine. com/2014/04/ruben-salazar-questioned-his-own-ethnic-identity-and-the-role-of-journalism-in-american-society/.

"Arrest in Slaying of Haitian Broadcasters." *New York Times*, November 19, 1994. https://www.nytimes.com/1994/11/19/ us/arrest-in-slaying-of-haitian-broad casters.html.

Axelrod, Tal. "Report: U.S. joins ranks of world's most dangerous places for journalists for first time." *The Hill*, December 18, 2018. https://thehill.com/homenews/ media/421848-report-us-joins-ranks-of-worlds-most-dangerous-places-for-journalists-for-the.

"Baby of ABCNEWS Employee Has Anthrax." ABC News, January 7, 2006. https: //abcnews.go.com/U.S./story?id=92279 &page=1.

Barrett, Devlin. "Trump Justice Department seized Post reporter's phone records," *Washington Post*, May 7, 2021. https:// www.washingtonpost.com/national-security/trump-justice-dept-seized-post-reporters-phone-records/2021/05/07/933cdfc6-af5b-11eb-b476-c3b287e52a01_story.html.

Battaglio, Stephen. "President posts unedited 60 Minutes interview." *Los Angeles Times*, October 22, 2020. https://www.latimes.com/entertainment-arts/business/story/2020-10-22/president-trump-posts-unedited-60-minutes-interview-facebook.

Batten, Taylor. "The importance of a courageous press." *The Charlotte Observer*, May 31, 2014. https://www.charlotteobserver.com/opinion/opn-columns-blogs/taylor-batten/article9126314.html.

Bender, Kristin. "Chauncey Bailey, veteran newsman, Oakland Post editor." *Bay City Times*, *The Mercury News*, August 2, 2007. https://www.mercurynews.com/2007/08/07/chauncey-bailey-veteran-newsman-oakland-post-editor/. Retrieved June 20, 2020.

Bernard Fall. https://www.bernard-fall.com/.

"Bernard B. Fall: Vietnam War Author." HistoryNet, https://www.historynet.com/bernard-b-fall-vietnam-war-author.htm.

Bernstein, Carl. "The Idiot Culture: Reflections on Post-Watergate Journalism." http://carlbernstein.com/magazines_the_idiot_culture.pdf.

Bernstein, Carl, and Bob Woodward. "All the President's Men." Simon & Schuster: New York, 1974.

Biden, Joe. "Statement by President Joe Biden on World Press Freedom Day." The White House, May 2, 2021. https://www.whitehouse.gov/briefing-room/statements-releases/2021/05/03/statement-by-president-joe-biden-on-the-occasion-of-world-press-freedom-day/.

BillBiggart.com. http://www.billbiggart.com/911.html.

"Bill Biggart killed at World Trade Centre," EPUK, September 18, 2001. http://www.epuk.org/news/bill-biggart-killed-at-world-trade-centre.

"A Bloody End for An Anti-Drug Crusader." *Newsweek*, March 22, 1992. https://www.newsweek.com/bloody-end-anti-drug-crusader-196172.

Bly, Nellie. Ten Days in a Mad-House. Reprint. New York: Ian L. Munro, 1887.

Boaks, Josh. "NY Times: Trump paid $750 in U.S. income taxes in 2016, 2017." Associated Press, September 27, 2020. https://apnews.com/article/donald-trump-business-ny-state-wire-ap-top-news-nyc-wire-f0e2af5f9f99de9d30dc6b9097121188.

"Branches of the U.S. Government" USA.gov. https://www.usa.gov/branches-of-government.

Brekke, Kira. "Salazar's Beginnings as a College Student Journalist," Ruben Salazar Project, August 27, 2013. https://rubensalazarproject.com/2013/08/27/salazars-beginnings-as-a-college-student-journalist/.

Brenan, Megan. "Americans Remain Distrustful of Mass Media." Gallup, September 30, 2020. https://news.gallup.com/poll/321116/americans-remain-distrustful-mass-media.aspx.

Breuninger, Kevin. "GOP quiet on Trump praising Rep Greg Gianforte for assaulting reporter, amid Khashoggi crisis and criticism of alleged Democratic 'mob' tactics." CNBC, October 19, 2018. https://www.cnbc.com/2018/10/19/gop-quiet-on-trump-praising-greg-gianforte-for-assaulting-reporter.html.

"A Brief History of Journalism: How We Arrived to Where We Are." https://www.universalclass.com/articles/writing/journalism-a-brief-history.html.

Brock, Pope. "A Crusader Falls." *People*, March 30, 1992. https://people.com/archive/a-crusader-falls-vol-37-no-12/.

Brown, Bruce D. "Attacks on the press are a threat to your freedom. Here's how you can help." Special to McClatchy, *Miami Herald*, November 7, 2019. https://www.miamiherald.com/article237076929.html.

Buettner, Russ, Susanne Craig and Mike McIntire, "The President's Taxes." *New York Times*, September 27, 2020. https://www.nytimes.com/interactive/2020/09/27/us/donald-trump-taxes.html.

Buttry, Steve. "The voiceless have a voice. A journalist's job is to amplify it." CJR, May 18, 2016. https://www.cjr.org/first_person/buttry_story.php.

Castillo, Juan. "'On Two Fronts': The Vietnam Experience Through Latino Family Lens." NBC News, September 22, 2015. https://www.nbcnews.com/news/

latino/two-fronts-vietnam-war-through-latino-familys-lens-n419001.

Chait, Jonathan. "Trump Says Reporters Covering Protests Deserve to Be Attacked." *New York* Magazine, September 22, 2020. https://nymag.com/intelligencer/2020/09/trump-reporters-covering-protests-deserve-to-be-attacked.html.

"CHAPELLE, Georgette Meyer." Encyclopedia.com. https://www.encyclopedia.com/arts/news-wires-white-papers-and-books/chapelle-georgette-meyer.

Chasmar, Jessica. "Joe Biden snaps at CBS reporter for Hunter question: 'Another smear campaign, right up your alley.'" *Washington Post*, October 19, 2020. https://www.washingtontimes.com/news/2020/oct/19/joe-biden-snaps-at-cbs-reporter-for-hunter-questio/.

"Chauncey Bailey," KPIX 5, CBS SF Nay Area. https://sanfrancisco.cbslocal.com/tag/chauncey-bailey/.

"Chauncey Baily, 1949–2007." Encyclopedia.com. https://www.encyclopedia.com/education/news-wires-white-papers-and-books/bailey-chauncey.

Cole, Richard. "Haitian Radio Show Host Killed in Miami With PM-Haiti." Associated Press, October 25, 1993. https://apnews.com/article/608057e1f92d4bb0d5c9c20cda7b5c55.

Collins, Terry. "2 men found guilty in murder of Calif journalist." Associated Press, as printed in *The San Diego Union-Tribune*, June 11, 2011.

Colvin, Marie. Address, "Truth at All Costs," St. Bride's Church, London, 2010. Marie Colvin Foundation. https://mariecolvin.org/truth-at-all-costs-marie-colvin.

Committee to Protect Journalists, https://cpj.org/data/killed/2018/?status=Killed&motiveConfirmed%5B%5D=Confirmed&type%5B%5D=Journalist&start_year=2019&end_year=2019&group_by=location.

Cuevas, Steve. "The Invisible Force: Latinos at War in Vietnam." KQED, May 25, 2015. https://www.kqed.org/news/10534280/the-invisible-force-latinos-at-war-in-vietnam.

Dale, Edwin L., Jr. "What Vietnam Did to the American Economy." *New York Times*, January 28, 1973. https://www.nytimes.com/1973/01/28/archives/what-vietnam-did-to-the-american-economy-worsening-payments-deficit.html.

Daly, Natasha. "Fake animal news abounds on social media as coronavirus upends life." *National Geographic*, March 20, 2020. https://www.nationalgeographic.com/animals/article/coronavirus-pandemic-fake-animal-viral-social-media-posts.

Danko, Pete, and Sheryl Oring. "Kissing the Newsroom Goodbye." Quoted in AJR, June 1995. https://ajrarchive.org/article.asp?id=1480&id=1480.

Davies, William. "Why can't we agree on what's true anymore?" *The Guardian*, September 19, 2019. https://www.theguardian.com/media/2019/sep/19/why-cant-we-agree-on-whats-true-anymore.

"Death photo of war reporter Ernie Pyle found." Associated Press, February 3, 2008, as found at NBC News, https://www.nbcnews.com/id/wbna22980127.

Dilanian, Ken, and Tom Winter. "Here's what happened when NBC News tried to report on the alleged Hunter Biden emails." NBC News, October 30, 2020. https://www.nbcnews.com/politics/2020-election/here-s-what-happened-when-nbc-news-tried-report-alleged-n1245533.

"Dime a Dance Place is Shot Up After Slaying," *Sarasota Herald-Tribune*, July 31, 1949. https://news.google.com/newspapers?id=GB8hAAAAIBAJ&pg=2698,2953697&dq=southwick+alice+mason&hl=en.

"Disinformation campaigns are murky bends of truth, lies and sincere beliefs—lessons from the pandemic." The Conversation. https://theconversation.com/disinformation-campaigns-are-murky-blends-of-truth-lies-and-sincere-beliefs-lessons-from-the-pandemic-140677.

"Diversity and inclusivity in Journalism." American Press Institute. https://www.americanpressinstitute.org/diversity-programs/.

"Don Bolles murder reverberates 42 years later in a changed world." The *Arizona Republic*, June 1, 2018. https://www.azcentral.com/story/news/local/don-bolles/2018/06/01/arizona-republic-reporter-don-bolles-murder-reverberates-42-years-later/658390002/.

"Don Bolles' tragic death." *The Michigan Daily*," June 16, 1976. https://news.google.com/newspapers?id=VP9JAAAAIBAJ&pg=3922,2003692&dq=don+bolles&hl=en.

Drehle, David Von. "FBI's No. 2 Was Deep Throat: Mark Felt Ends 30 Year Mystery of the Post's Watergate Source." *Washington Post*, June 1, 2005. https://www.washingtonpost.com/politics/fbis-no-2-was-deep-throat-mark-felt-ends-30-year-mystery-of-the-posts-watergate-source/2012/06/04/gJQAwseRIV_story.html.

Duda, Jeremy. "Bolles investigator hopes to find new home for famous car." *The Mirror*, October 30, 2019. https://www.azmirror.com/2019/10/30/bolles-investigator-hopes-to-find-new-home-for-famous-car/. See also http://www.tucsonsentinel.com/local/report/103019_bolles_car/bombed-car-assassinated-az-reporter-don-bolles-needs-new-home/. Retrieved October 25, 2020.

Duda, Jeremy. "Bombed car of assassinated Az reporter Don Bolles needs new home." *Arizona Mirror*, as posted at *Tucson Sentinel*, October 30, 2019. http://www.tucsonsentinel.com/local/report/103019_bolles_car/bombed-car-assassinated-az-reporter-don-bolles-needs-new-home/.

Duffy, Shannon. History Department Texas State University, as found in "Press Attacks." Washington Library, George Washington's Mount Vernon. https://www.mountvernon.org/library/digitalhistory/digital-encyclopedia/article/press-attacks/.

"Editorial: There is no excuse for government-sanctioned violence against the free press." *Los Angeles Times*, June 2, 2020. https://www.latimes.com/opinion/story/2020-06-02/police-attacks-media-protests-george-floyd.

"8 Inspiring Quotes by War Correspondent Marie Colvin," *The Circle*, February 9, 2018. https://thecircle.ngo/8-inspiring-quotes-war-correspondent-marie-colvin/.

Eil, Philip. "5 ways journalists can regain trust from readers." April 11, 2018. https://www.cjr.org/analysis/trust-journalism.php.

"E-mail Extending Kidnapper's Deadline Not Yet Authenticated." Transcript posted on CNN, January 31, 2002. http://edition.cnn.com/TRANSCRIPTS/0201/31/lt.05.html.

Eppolito, Sophia. "Trump supporters gather at Utah capitol in mostly calm event." Associated Press, January 6, 2021. https://apnews.com/article/election-2020-joe-biden-utah-elections-salt-lake-city-52666c5949ea26f15fd952929361e6f5.

"Exile: Slain Haitian Named on Hit List." Associated Press, as found in *Boca Raton News*, October 26, 1993. https://news.google.com/newspapers?nid=1290&dat=19931026&id=7xZUAAAAIBAJ&pg=5620,5845368.

Fatal Force. *Washington Post*. https://www.washingtonpost.com/graphics/investigations/police-shootings-database/.

"FBI concludes investigation into 2001 anthrax mailings." CNN, February 19, 2010. http://www.cnn.com/2010/CRIME/02/19/fbi.anthrax.report/.

"Federal reporter's shield law proposed." Reporter's Committee for Freedom of the Press, November 22, 2004. https://www.rcfp.org/federal-reporters-shield-law-proposed/.

Fischer, Douglas, and Josh Richman, "Bailey's career in news spanned globe for decades." *Daily Climate*, Bay Area News Group, *East Bay Times*, August 3, 2007. https://www.eastbaytimes.com/2007/08/03/baileys-career-in-news-spanned-globe-for-decades/ Retrieved June 20, 2020.

Fitzpatrick, Tom. "Explosive Testimony." Phoenix New Times, March 3, 1993. https://www.phoenixnewtimes.com/news/explosive-testimony-6425909.

Flores, Adolfo. "Plaque to honor memory of journalist Ruben Salazar." *Los Angeles Times*, August 29, 2014. https://www.latimes.com/local/la-me-ruben-salazar-plaque-20140830-story.html.

Fragoza, Carribean. "Truths Unsilenced: The Life, Death and Legacy of Ruben Salazar." KCET, August 27, 2020. https://www.kcet.org/shows/lost-la/truths-unsilenced-the-life-death-and-legacy-of-ruben-salazar.

Friend, Cecilia, Don Challenger and Katherine C. McAdams, *Contemporary Editing*. Chicago: NTC, 2000.

"Global Trends 2040." The National Intelligence Council, March 2021. https://www.dni.gov/files/ODNI/documents/assessments/GlobalTrends_2040.pdf page 2.

Grand Forks Herald, June 18, 2020. https://www.grandforksherald.com/opinion/editorials/6537375-Our-view-Going-slow-is-best-with-social-media.

Greenfield, James L. "How the New York Times published the Pentagon Papers." December 17, 2017. https://www.salon.com/2017/12/17/how-the-new-york-times-published-the-pentagon-papers/.

Grier, Peter. "Journalist's kidnapping a puzzling power play." *Christian Science Monitor*, February 1, 2002. https://www.csmonitor.com/2002/0201/p01s04-wosc.html.

Grunwald, Henry. Henry Grunwald Quotes, Brainy Quote. https://www.brainyquote.com/quotes/henry_grunwald_113731.

Grynbaum, Michael M., and Marc Santora. "CNN Crew Is Arrested on Live Television While Covering Minneapolis Protests." CNN, May 29, 2020. https://www.nytimes.com/2020/05/29/business/media/cnn-reporter-arrested-omar-jimenez.html.

Haines, Don C. "With Her Eyes Wide Open." HistoryNet.com. https://www.historynet.com/eyes-wide-open.htm.

Hanna, Jason, and Amir Vera. "CNN crew released from police custody after they were arrested live on air in Minneapolis." CNN, May 29, 2020. https://www.cnn.com/2020/05/29/us/minneapolis-cnn-crew-arrested/index.html.

Harmon, Amy. "The number of people with the virus who died in the U.S. passes 300,000." *New York Times*, December 14, 2020. https://www.nytimes.com/live/2020/12/14/world/covid-19-coronavirus/the-number-of-people-with-the-virus-who-died-in-the-us-passes-300000?campaign_id=60&emc=edit_na_20201214&instance_id=0&nl=breaking-news&ref=headline&regi_id=141056041&segment_id=46904&user_id=4e6bd6ade8282ab70299356d05856e39.

Harrington, Jerry. Crusading Iowa Journalist Verne Marshall: Exposing Graft and the 1936 Pulitzer Prize. Charleston, S.C.: The History Press, 2017.

Harris, Karcin. "'It just hurts my heart'—How COVID dissent pushed some Latter-day Saints away from their church." *The Salt Lake Tribune*, May 2, 2021. https://www.sltrib.com/religion/2021/05/02/it-just-hurts-my-heart/.

Harris, Shane. "Intelligence forecast sees a post-coronavirus world upended by climate change and splintering societies." *Washington Post*, April 8, 2021. https://www.washingtonpost.com/national-security/intelligence-globe-future-crises-/2021/04/08/303c350e-97df-11eb-962b-78c1d8228819_story.html.

Henderson, Cydney. "John Krasinski sells 'Some Good News' web series to CBS; some fans aren't happy." USA TODAY, May 22, 2020. https://www.usatoday.com/story/entertainment/celebrities/2020/05/22/john-krasinski-sells-some-good-news-cbs-fans-call-him-sellout/5247315002/.

Hensley, Tatiana. "Bolles: Cautious man, dedicated journalist." The *Arizona Republic*, May 28, 2006. http://archive.azcentral.com/specials/special01/0528bolles-profile.html.

Heredia, Christopher, Leslie Fulbright, and Marisa Lagos, "Hit man kills newspaper editor on Oakland street." *The San Francisco Chronicle*, August 2, 2007. https://www.sfgate.com/bayarea/article/Hit-man-kills-newspaper-editor-on-Oakland-street-2549667.php.

Holzer, Harold. *The Presidents vs. the Press: The Endless Battle Between the White House and the Media from the Founding Fathers to Fake News.* New York: Dutton, 2020.

Hsu, Tiffany, and Katie Robertson, "Covering Pro-Trump Mobs, the News Media Became a Target." *New York Times*, January 6, 2021. https://www.nytimes.com/2021/01/06/business/media/media-murder-capitol-building.html?fbclid=IwAR2Bb25N0UJ0ZtjMBf5bdPLU0zXaLz2uTk6N1jYyq0KaoQ2b8VH9VGlan10.

"I aimed for the public's heart, and … hit it in the stomach." *Chicago Tribune*, May 21, 2006. https://www.chicagotribune.com/news/ct-xpm-2006-05-21-0605210414-story.html.

"Image 3 of Thomas Jefferson to John Norvell, June 11, 1807." The Library of Congress. https://www.loc.gov/resource/mtjl.038_0592_0594/?sp=3&st=text.

"Indicators of news media distrust." Knight Foundation, September 11, 2018. https://knightfoundation.org/reports/indicators-of-news-media-trust/.

James Edwin Richards, Neighborhood News Killed in California, October 18, 2000. https://cpj.org/data/people/james-edwin-richards/.

Jensen, Elizabeth. "Looking To The Future: Restoring Public Trust In The Media."

National Public Radio, May 15, 2017. https://www.npr.org/sections/public editor/2017/05/15/528158488/looking-to-the-future-restoring-public-trust-in-the-media.

"Joe Morton: War Correspondent Executed by the Nazis," World War Two on Deadline. https://ww2ondeadline.com/2021/01/24/joe-morton-war-corresponde nt-ap-oss-ww2-dawes-mission/.

Jones, Tom. "President Trump thinks some journalists should be executed, according to John Bolton's upcoming book." Poynter, June 18, 2020. https://www.poynter.org/newsletters/2020/president-trump-thinks-some-journalists-should-be-executed-according-to-john-boltons-upcoming-book/.

"Joseph Morton, War Reporter, Slain by Germans," Associated Press, July 9, 1945. https://news.google.com/newspapers?ni d=950&dat=19450709&id=d8wLAAAAI BAJ&pg=3622,1546710.

"Journalism Sayings and Quotes," Wise Sayings. https://www.wiseoldsayings.com/journalism-quotes/#ixzz6dXFdtK6U.

"Journalist arrested amid protests in Lincoln, Nebraska." U.S. Press Freedom Tracker, May 31, 2020. https://press freedomtracker.us/all-incidents/journalist-arrested-amid-protests-lincoln-nebraska/.

Kelly, Laura. "House passes bill limiting arms sales to Saudi Arabia over Khashoggi killing." *The Hill*, April 21, 2021. https://thehill.com/policy/international/549617-house-passes-bill-limiting-arms-sales-to-saudi-arabia-over-khashoggi.

Keneally, Meghan. "From verbal taunts to shots fired: How journalists were attacked in 2018." ABC News, May 3, 2019. https://abcnews.go.com/U.S./verbal-taunts-shots-fired-journalists-attacked-us-2018/story?id=62778248.

"Killings of journalists rise as reprisal murders more than double in 2020." Committee to Protect Journalists, December 22, 2020. https://cpj.org/2020/12/killings-of-journalists-rise-as-reprisal-murders-more-than-double-in-2020/.

Kim, Jean. "Is Social Media Destroying Our Attention Spans?" *Psychology Today*, December 14, 2018. https://www.psychologytoday.com/us/blog/culture-shrink/201812/is-social-media-destroying-our-attention-spans.

King, Stephen. (@StephenKing), Twitter, June 17, 2021. https://twitter.com/Stephen King/status/1405480358011969536.

Knudson, Thomas J. "Trial Opens in Slaying of Radio Talk Show host." Special to New York Times, October 31, 1987. https://www.nytimes.com/1987/10/31/us/trial-opens-in-slaying-of-radio-talk-show-host.html.

Lancaster, Marc. "Ralph Barnes: First U.S. War Correspondent to Fall." World War II on Deadline, November 18, 2020. https://ww2ondeadline.com/2020/11/18/ralph-barnes-first-us-war-correspon dent-killed-wwii/.

"LAPD Announces Arrest of Suspect Who Murdered Community Activist." Los Angeles Police Department news release, March 11, 2002. https://www.lapdonline.org/march_2002/news_view/22295.

Lavoie, Denise. "Daunte Wright: Doting dad, ballplayer, slain by police." Associated Press, April 14, 2021. https://apnews.com/article/daunte-wright-shooting-minnesota-f70fb7fc4c205740507b7ec53 d7315f0.

Lawler, Kelly. "Morning TV anchors try to parse election results on Day 2: 'Big Dumps' and deep breaths," *USA Today*, November 4, 2020. https://www.usa today.com/story/entertainment/tv/2020 /11/04/how-tv-networks-covered-2020-election-day-2-no-winner/6158722002/.

Lee, Martin A., and Tiffany DeVitt, "Gulf War Coverage: Censorship Begins at Home." *Sage Journals*, January 1, 1991. https://journals.sagepub.com/doi/10.1177/073953299101200104.

Leger, Robert. "A Dangerous Job: Journalists, too, have a role in the fight for freedom, and sometimes the risks of reporting are great." Society of Professional Journalists. https://www.spj.org/dangerousjob.asp.

Levitz, Jennifer, and Jon Kamp, "In Fear and Violence, Slain U.S. Journalist Found Humanity." *Wall Street Journal*, August 20, 2014. https://www.wsj.com/articles/james-foley-u-s-journalist-killed-by-islamic-state-knew-risks-of-conflict-1408569500.

Logevall, Fredrik. "Bernard Fall: The Man Who Knew the War." *New York Times*, February 21, 2017. https://www.nytimes.com/2017/02/21/opinion/bernard-fall-the-man-who-knew-the-war.html.

Lopez, Robert J. "Journalist's Death Still Clouded by Questions: Friends say Ruben Salazar, whose stories often criticized police treatment of Mexican Americans, believed he was in danger. His 1970 slaying left a lasting wound." *Los Angeles Times*, August 26, 1995. https://www.latimes.com/archives/la-xpm-1995-08-26-mn-39122-story.html.

Lopez, Robert J. "No evidence Ruben Salazar was targeted in killing, report says." *Los Angeles Times*, February 19, 2011. https://www.latimes.com/archives/la-xpm-2011-feb-19-la-me-ruben-salazar-20110220-story.html.

Lopez, Robert J. "Ruben Salazar had clashed repeatedly with LAPD in months before slaying." *Los Angeles Times*, August 29, 2010. https://www.latimes.com/archives/la-xpm-2010-aug-29-la-me-salazar-20100829-story.html.

Lorenz, Taylor. "The News Is Making People Anxious. You'll Never Believe What They're Reading Instead." *New York Times*, April 14, 2020. https://www.nytimes.com/2020/04/14/style/good-news-coronavirus.html.

Mahoney, Barbara. "Ralph Barnes (1899–1940)." Oregon Encyclopedia, Oregon Historical Society. https://www.oregonencyclopedia.org/articles/barnes_ralph/#.YMfBQZNKiIs.

Mann, Alex, and Jessica Anderson. "Capital Gazette shooting: Maryland man pleads guilty to attack that killed five as chilling details emerge." *The Capital Gazette*, October 28, 2019. https://www.capitalgazette.com/news/crime/ac-cn-capital-shooting-hearing-1028-20191028-nkxc5ukn4nbzjdwoltewbmqx6u-story.html.

Markway, Kristin. "All agree on public's right to know." University of Missouri, as seen at National Freedom of Information Coalition. https://www.nfoic.org/all-agree-publics-right-know.

Mendenhall, Erin (@slcmayor). Twitter, January 6, 2021. https://twitter.com/slcmayor/status/1346951864995041282.

Miller, Adam. "Kidnappers: 24 Hours More, Then He's Dead." *New York Post*, February 1, 2002. https://nypost.com/2002/02/01/kidnappers-24-hours-more-then-hes-dead/.

"Minnesota journalist attacked by Trump supporter at rally." Associated Press, October 1, 2020. https://apnews.com/article/election-2020-joe-biden-donald-trump-journalists-minnesota-546e102d48ef79cb460857115ddee695.

Montini, EJ. "Don Bolles: Decades later, speaking truth to power earns journalists scorn." The *Arizona Republic*, June 1, 2018. https://www.azcentral.com/story/news/local/don-bolles/2018/06/01/decades-after-arizona-republic-reporter-don-bolles-killed-reporters-scorned/656948002/. Retrieved October 23, 2020.

Moore, Tina, Amanda Woods and Lia Eustachewich. "Cops arrest man for alleged wooden board attack on Post reporter." *New York Post*, July 14, 2020. https://nypost.com/2020/07/14/cops-arrest-man-who-attacked-post-reporter-with-wooden-board/.

Morrison, Patt. "Slaying of Venice Activist Proves Danger of Truth-Telling." *Los Angeles Times*, October 20, 2000. https://www.latimes.com/archives/la-xpm-2000-oct-20-me-39300-story.html.

Nelson, Joe. "Murder charges in fentanyl deaths? Riverside County carves new path in Southern California." *The Orange County Register*, March 8, 2021. https://www.ocregister.com/2021/03/08/murder-charges-in-fentanyl-deaths-riverside-county-carves-new-path-in-southern-california/.

Neuharth, Jan. Open letter posted at Freedom Forum. https://www.freedomforum.org/2020/06/05/this-first-amendment-moment/.

"NEW YORK TIMES COMPANY, Petitioner v. UNITED STATES. UNITED STATES, Petitioner v. The WASHINGTON POST COMPANY et al.," located at the Legal Information Institute, Cornell Law School. https://www.law.cornell.edu/supremecourt/text/403/713. See also the original court case here: https://supreme.justia.com/cases/federal/us/403/713/.

Noer, Michael. "Read The Original Forbes Takedown Of Stephen Glass." *Forbes* magazine, November 12, 2014. https://www.forbes.com/sites/michaelnoer/2014/11/12/read-the-original-forbes-takedown-of-stephen-glass/?sh=42b8cb1a683a.

North, Don. Inappropriate Conduct: Mystery of a Disgraced War Correspondent. iUniverse, 2013. https://books.google.

com/books?id=2XnP3ypSH6MC&q=
Joe+Morton+joined+the+AP+in+
Lincoln,+Nebraska&pg=PT75#v=
snippet&q=Joe%20Morton%20joined
%20the%20AP%20in%20Lincoln%
2C%20Nebraska&f=false.

"Oakland councilwoman plans memorial
for slain journalist Chauncey Bailey."
Bay City Times, The Mercury News,
August 2, 2019, https://www.mercury
news.com/2019/08/02/oakland-council
woman-plans-memorial-for-slain-
journalist-chauncey-bailey/ Retrieved
June 20, 2020.

On Two Fronts: Latinos & Vietnam. PBS,
2015. https://www.pbs.org/video/stories-
service-two-fronts-latinos-vietnam-full-
episode/.

O'Neil, Mike. "The Think Tank revisits the
Don Bolles story." KTAR, December 6,
2019. https://ktar.com/story/2868171/
the-think-tank-revisits-the-don-bolles-
story/. Retrieved October 25, 2020.

Osborne, Linda Barrett. *Guardians of Liberty: Freedom of the Press and the Nature
of News.* New York: Abrams Books for
Young Readers, 2020.

Page, Clarence. "Trump's war against leakers
shows why we need a 'shield law.'" *Chicago Tribune,* June 12, 2018. https://www.
chicagotribune.com/columns/clarence-
page/ct-perspec-page-trump-sessions-
espionage-act-cpj-0613-20180612-story.
html.

"The parting shot." *The Irish Times,* December 22, 2001. https://www.irishtimes.
com/news/the-parting-shot-1.343336.

Paul, Christopher, and James J. Kim. *Reporters on the Battlefield: The Embedded
Press System in Historical Context,* RAND
Corp., 2004, p. 118. https://www.jstor.
org/stable/10.7249/mg200rc.14?seq=2#
metadata_info_tab_contents.

Peele, Thomas. "Death stalks some reporters working their beats in U.S." *The Plain
Dealer,* August 1, 2012; updated January 12, 2019. https://www.cleveland.
com/opinion/2012/08/death_stalks_
some_reporters_wo.html.

Peele, Thomas. "Devaughndre Broussard:
I want the families to know I am sorry."
East Bay Times, Bay Area News Group,
June 16, 2011; updated August 15, 2016.
https://www.eastbaytimes.com/2011/
06/16/devaughndre-broussard-i-want-
the-families-to-know-i-am-sorry/.

"Pentagon Papers." History, August 2, 2011;
updated August 21, 2018. https://www.
history.com/topics/vietnam-war/
pentagon-papers.

Piccalo, Gina, and Kurt Streeter, "Venice
Anti-Gang Activist Killed in His Driveway," *Los Angeles Times,* October 19,
2000. https://www.latimes.com/archives/
la-xpm-2000-oct-19-me-38801-story.
html.

"Police, Protesters, and the Press." Reporters Committee for Freedom of the Press,
updated June 2020. https://www.rcfp.
org/wp-content/uploads/2020/06/
Police-Protesters-Press-2020.pdf.

"Police shove, make AP journalists stop
covering protest." June 3, 2020. https://
apnews.com/article/us-news-new-
york-city-manhattan-ny-state-wire-
journalists-1d2d9e4afdd822b27bfcce570
e0cbdb5.

Pope, Kyle. "Here's to the return of the journalist as malcontent." CJR, November
9, 2016. https://www.cjr.org/criticism/
journalist_election_trump_failure.php.

"Press Rights at a Protest," p. 10. https://www.
rcfp.org/wp content/uploads/2018/12/
Police_Protesters_and_the_Press_
2018.pdf. See also, https://www.rcfp.org/
wp-content/uploads/imported/
20180614_100229_rcfp_protest_tip_
sheet_0618.pdf.

"'Publick Occurrences, Both Foreign and
Domestic,' the First Newspaper Published in North America, Suppressed
after a Single Issue," Jeremy Norman's
HistoryofInformation.com. https://www.
historyofinformation.com/detail.php?
id=400#:~:text=Massachusetts%2C%20
United%20States-,%22Publick%20
Occurrences%2C%20Both%20Foreign
%20and%20Domestic%2C%22%20
the%20First, Suppressed%20after%20
a%20Single%20Issue&text=This%20
was%20the%20first%20newspaper,
hand%20around%20with%20the%20
newspaper.

Pyle, Richard. "4 photojournalists find resting place at last." NBC News, April 1,
2008. https://www.nbcnews.com/id/
wbna23908336.

Pyle, Richard. "Jury Convicts Colombian
Teen in Slaying of Anti-Drug Journalist."
Associated Press, March 9, 1994. https://
apnews.com/article/e2066765b1851b57c9
2faa7171973a19.

Raskin, A.H. "Thug Hurls Acid on Labor Writer." *New York Times*, April 6, 1956. https://www.nytimes.com/1956/04/06/archives/thug-hurls-acid-on-labor-writer-sight-imperiled-victor-riesel.html.

"Remembering the Only Photojournalist Lost on 9/11." 9/11 Memorial Museum. https://www.911memorial.org/connect/blog/remembering-only-photojournalist-lost-911.

"Remembering Virginia TV reporter Alison Parker and cameraman Adam Ward." ABC7, August 26, 2015. https://abc7.com/allison-parker-adam-ward-journalists-killed-reporter/957809/.

"Reporter, colleague arrested while documenting Elizabeth City protests." U.S. Press Freedom Tracker, May 19, 2021. https://pressfreedomtracker.us/all-incidents/reporter-colleague-arrested-while-documenting-elizabeth-city-protests/.

"Reporters' probe of Arizona crime draws mixed reaction from press." *Washington Post*, March 15, 1977.

"Reporting the Revolutionary War," an interview with Todd Andrlik, author of Reporting the Revolutionary War. George Washington's Mount Vernon. https://www.mountvernon.org/george-washington/the-revolutionary-war/reporting-the-revolutionary-war-an-interview-with-todd-andrlik/#:~:text=Benjamin%20Rush%20wrote%20to%20General,that%20%E2%80%9Cin%20establishing%20American%20independence%2C.

Reyes, Raul A. "Prominent Latino journalist Ruben Salazar killed 50 years ago, tackled racism, identity." *USA Today* network, published on NBC News, August 28, 2020. https://www.nbcnews.com/news/latino/prominent-latino-journalist-ruben-salazar-killed-50-years-ago-tackled-n1238011.

Rezendes, Michael, Matt Carroll, Sacha Pfeiffer, and Walter V. Robinson. "Church allowed abuse by priest for years," part 1 of 2. The *Boston Globe*, January 6, 2002. https://www.bostonglobe.com/news/special-reports/2002/01/06/church-allowed-abuse-priest-for-years/cSHfGkTIrAT25qKGvBuDNM/story.html.

Rhoter, Larry. "In Miami's Little Haiti, Fears of Assassination." *New York Times*, March 20, 1994. https://www.nytimes.com/1994/03/20/us/in-miami-s-little-haiti-fears-of-assassination.html.

Richmond, Todd. "Journalists allege police harassment at Minnesota protests." Associated Press, April 17, 2021. https://apnews.com/article/death-of-daunte-wright-shootings-journalists-minnesota-minneapolis-2f567f3c306d99ed146a6acb43c587a2.

Roos, Meghan. "Louisville Protesters Throw Brick Into Car Windshield of Local Camera Crew." Newsweek, June 16, 2020. https://www.newsweek.com/louisville-protesters-throw-brick-car-windshield-local-camera-crew-1511207.

Roth, Samantha-Jo (@SamanthaJoRoth). Twitter, January 6, 2021. https://twitter.com/SamanthaJoRoth/status/1346984853149868033.

"The Ruben Salazar Files," *Los Angeles Times*. https://documents.latimes.com/ruben-salazar/.

Ruben Salazar Park, Los Angeles Conservancy. https://www.laconservancy.org/locations/ruben-salazar-park#:~:text=On%20September%2017%2C%201970%2C%20East,march%20on%20August%2029%2C%201970.

Ruelas, Richard. "40 years later, final words of murdered reporter Don Bolles still a mystery." *Arizona Republic*, December 20, 2016. https://www.azcentral.com/story/news/local/phoenix-best-reads/2016/06/02/republic-reporter-don-bolles-final-words-emprise-mafia/84793594/.

Ruiz, Albor. "The death of a journalist." Al Dia, March 18, 2020. https://aldianews.com/articles/politics/opinion/death-journalist/57927.

Ruiz, Albor. "Killed for Reporting the Truth." Al Dia, March 14, 2018. https://aldianews.com/articles/politics/op-ed-killed-reporting-truth/51996.

Safi, Michael. Jonathan Watts, Oliver Holmes, Kareem Shaheen and Shaun Walker. "'You can get killed': journalists living in fear as states crack down." *The Guardian*, November 29, 2017. https://www.theguardian.com/media/2017/nov/30/journalists-living-in-fear-states-crack-down-press-freedom.

Sahadi, Jeanne. "How common is workplace violence?" CNNMoney, August 26, 2015.

https://money.cnn.com/2015/08/26/news/workplace-violence-virginia-shooting/.

Salazar, Ruben. "25 Hours in a City Jail: I lived in a Chamber of Horrors," *El Paso Herald*, May 9, 1954, as quoted in Ruben Salazar: 25 Hours in City Jail, *El Paso Times*, August 26, 2020. https://www.elpasotimes.com/story/news/2020/08/26/ruben-salazar-25-hours-city-jail-lived-chamber-horrors-el-paso-article-herald-post/5638166002/.

"Salazar's Beginnings As A College Student Journalist," Ruben Salazar Project. https://rubensalazarproject.com/2013/08/27/salazars-beginnings-as-a-college-student-journalist/.

Scott, Cameron. "Mexico's Most Wanted Journalist." *Mother Jones*, May 1, 2007. https://www.motherjones.com/politics/2007/05/mexicos-most-wanted-journalist/.

Section 230 of the Communications Decency Act, 47 U.S.C. § 230, a Provision of the Communication Decency Act, as found at Electronic Frontier Foundation. https://www.eff.org/issues/cda230.

Seymour, Tom. "'The camera is not a shield': life and death as a war photographer." *The Guardian*, July 26, 2016. https://www.theguardian.com/tv-and-radio/2016/jul/26/life-and-death-as-a-war-photographer-netflix-series.

Shadley, Steve. "New Podcast Revisits Murder Case of Arizona Republic Reporter Don Bolles." NPR's Knau, Arizona Public Radio, November 25, 2019. https://www.knau.org/post/new-podcast-revisits-murder-case-arizona-republic-reporter-don-bolles.

Shafer, Jack. "Who Said It First? Journalism is the 'first rough draft of history.'" Slate, August 30, 2010. https://slate.com/news-and-politics/2010/08/on-the-trail-of-the-question-who-first-said-or-wrote-that-journalism-is-the-first-rough-draft-of-history.html.

Shear, Michael D, Richard Perez-Pena and Alan Blinder. "Ex-Broadcaster Kills 2 on Air in Virginia Shooting; Takes Own Life." *New York Times*, August 26, 2015. https://www.nytimes.com/2015/08/27/us/wdbj7-virginia-journalists-shot-during-live-broadcast.html.

Shearer, Elisa. "Two-thirds of U.S. adults say they've seen their own news sources report facts meant to favor one side." Pew Research Center, November 2, 2020. https://www.pewresearch.org/fact-tank/2020/11/02/two-thirds-of-u-s-adults-say-theyve-seen-their-own-news-sources-report-facts-meant-to-favor-one-side/.

Silberman, Hollie, and Andy Rose. "Minnesota governor expresses regret for mistreatment of journalists during Daunte Wright demonstrations." CNN, April 18, 2021. https://www.cnn.com/2021/04/18/us/daunte-wright-minnesota-shooting-sunday/index.html.

Silverman, Craig. *Regret the Error: How Media Mistakes Pollute the Press and Imperil Free Speech*. New York: Sterling Publishing Co., 2007.

Silverman, Hollie, Janet DiGiacomo and Darran Simon. "Five dead in shooting at Capital Gazette in Annapolis, Maryland." CNN, June 29, 2018. https://www.cnn.com/2018/06/28/us/annapolis-maryland-newsroom-shooting/index.html.

Simon, Joel. "Why Were So Many Journalists Murdered in 2018?" *The New Republic*, December 19, 2018. https://newrepublic.com/article/152676/many-journalists-murdered-2018.

60 Minutes (@60Minutes). Twitter, October 22, 2020. https://twitter.com/60Minutes/status/1319316652412919808.

Smith, Dave, and Paul Houston. "Deputy Says He Did Not Know Kind of Missile." *Los Angeles Times*, October 6, 1970.

Smith, Laura. "This brash Jewish radio host was murdered by white supremacists for denouncing anti–Semitism," Timeline, November 6, 2017. https://timeline.com/alan-berg-jewish-murder-denver-57f54b2989dd.

Smith, Terrance. "Trump has longstanding history of calling elections 'rigged' if he doesn't like the result." ABC News, November 11, 2020. https://abcnews.go.com/Politics/trump-longstanding-history-calling-elections-rigged-doesnt-results/story?id=74126926.

Society of Professional Journalists Code of Ethics, revised September 6, 2014. SPJ. https://www.spj.org/ethicscode.asp.

Spaeth, Emma. "Spaeth: The importance of transparency in modern journalism." *Daily Emerald*, April 7, 2019. https://www.dailyemerald.com/opinion/

spaeth-the-importance-of-transparency-in-modern-journalism/article_f5cc 9d70-5972-11e9-a208-e7046b777390.html.

"Special Series: The Anthrax Investigation. Timeline: How The Anthrax Terror Unfolded." NPR, February 15, 2011. https://www.npr.org/2011/02/15/93170200/timeline-how-the-anthrax-terror-unfolded.

Stelter, Brian. "Arresting reporters at a protest is an affront to the First Amendment." CNN Business, May 29, 2020. https://www.cnn.com/2020/05/29/media/reporters-arrest-minneapolis-first-amendment/index.html.

Stelter, Brian. "Trump calls journalists 'bad people' at rally a week after newsroom shooting." CNN, July 6, 2018. https://money.cnn.com/2018/07/06/media/trump-montana-rally-media-attacks/index.html.

Stephenson, Emily, and Alana Wise. "Trump charges U.S. election results being rigged 'at many polling places.'" Reuters, October 16, 2016. https://www.reuters.com/article/us-usa-election-trump-rigged/trump-charges-u-s-election-results-being-rigged-at-many-polling-places-idUSKBN12G0SU.

Stone, Shomari (@shomaristone). Twitter, January 6, 2021. https://twitter.com/shomaristone/status/134694171589525 0949?ref_src=twsrc%5Etfw%7Ctwcamp %5Etweetembed%7Ctwterm%5E134694 1715895250949%7Ctwgr%5E%7Ctw con%5Es1_&ref_url=https%3A%2F%2Fthehill.com%2Fhomenews%2Fnews%2F533022-videos-show-protesters-outside-capitol-destroying-journalists-equipment.

Stracqualursi, Veronica. "Alison Parker and Adam Ward, Slain Virginia Reporter and Cameraman, 'Did Great Work Every Day.'" ABC News, August 26, 2015. https://abcnews.go.com/U.S./alison-parker-adam-ward-slain-virginia-reporter-cameraman/story?id=33330993.

Sullivan, Margaret. "What's a journalist supposed to be now—an activist? A stenographer? You're asking the wrong question." *Washington Post*, June 6, 2020. https://www.washingtonpost.com/lifestyle/media/whats-a-journalist-supposed-to-be-now—an-activist-a-stenographer-youre-asking-the-wrong-question/2020/06/06/60fdfb86-a73b-11ea-b619-3f9133bbb482_story.html.

The Sunshine Project, *The Laconia Daily Sun*. https://www.laconiadailysun.com/news/local/the-sunshine-project---series/collection_c5fce562-f050-11e9-bdf7-07debb13e4ba.html.

Swenson, Ali. "Photo of newspaper was edited to add 'President Gore' headline." Associated Press, November 8, 2020. https://apnews.com/article/fact-checking-9702032985.

Symes, Steven. "The Don Bolles Car Controversy." Motorious, February 14, 2020. https://buy.motorious.com/articles/news/398800/don-bolles-car-controversy.

Tadayon, Ali. "Memorial for slain journalist delayed." Bay Area News Group, *East Bay Times*, October 18, 2019. https://www.eastbaytimes.com/2019/10/18/memorial-for-slain-oakland-journalist-delayed/.

Talton, Jon. "40 years later: Who murdered reporter Don Bolles." *Tucson Sentinel*, June 2, 2016. http://www.tucsonsentinel.com/local/report/060216_bolles_murdered/40-years-later-who-murdered-reporter-don-bolles/.

Tavernise, Sabrina, Amy Harmon and Maya Salam. "5 People Dead in Shooting at Maryland's Capital Gazette Newsroom." *New York Times*, June 28, 2018. https://www.nytimes.com/2018/06/28/us/capital-gazette-annapolis-shooting.html.

Telnaes, Ann. "Opinion: World Press Freedom Day," *Washington Post*, May 3, 2021. See https://www.washingtonpost.com/opinions/2021/05/03/world-press-freedom-day/.

"The 10 Most Censored Countries," CPJ, May 2, 2006. https://cpj.org/reports/2006/05/10-most-censored-countries/.

Testa, Karen. "Man Charged With Murder in Slaying of Pro-Democracy Broadcasters." Associated Press, November 18, 1994. https://apnews.com/article/fd2c59 84d5b9c4c76a060d5d71a4c9b6.

"These Are the 5 People Who Died in the Capitol Riot." *New York Times*, January 11, 2021. https://www.nytimes.com/2021/01/11/us/who-died-in-capitol-building-attack.html.

"This Day in History, April 18: War correspondent Ernie Pyle killed," History. https://www.history.com/this-day-in-history/journalist-ernie-pyle-killed.

"This Day in History: May 11. President Kennedy orders more troops to South Vietnam." History. https://www.history.com/this-day-in-history/president-kennedy-orders-more-troops-to-south-vietnam.

Thomas, Pat. "Virginia journalists Alison Parker and Adam Ward remembered." WDBJ, as posted on NBC12, August 26, 2020. https://www.nbc12.com/2020/08/26/virginia-journalists-alison-parker-adam-ward-remembered/.

Thorn, April. "Fifteen journalists die while covering war in Iraq." The News Media & The Law, Spring 2003. https://www.rcfp.org/journals/the-news-media-and-the-law-spring-2003/fifteen-journalists-die-whi/.

"Three-part Herald video documentary, 'On the border,' captures snapshot of life on the border in northwest Minnesota." Grand Forks Herald, December 23, 2020. https://www.grandforksherald.com/news/6807940-Three-part-Herald-video-documentary-On-the-border-captures-snapshot-of-life-on-the-border-in-northwest-Minnesota.

Tirado, Linda. "I came to the Minneapolis protests to cover police aggression. Then I became the victim of it." TINK, NBC News, June 1, 2020. https://www.nbcnews.com/think/opinion/i-came-cover-aggression-minneapolis-then-i-became-victim-it-ncna1221241.

Tobin, James. Ernie Pyle's War: America's Eyewitness to World War II. New York: Free Press, 1997.

Tran, Delbert. "The Fourth Estate As The Final Check." Media Freedom & Information Access Clinic, Yale Law School, November 22, 2016. https://law.yale.edu/mfia/case-disclosed/fourth-estate-final-check.

"Trump supporter attacks BBC cameraman at El Paso rally." BBC, February 12, 2019. https://www.bbc.com/news/world-us-canada-47208909.

"2 indicted in N.Y. journalist's killing, Drug cartel said to order slaying." Newsday in The Baltimore Sun, May 11, 1993. https://www.baltimoresun.com/news/bs-xpm-1993-05-11-1993131217-story.html.

"2 men found guilty in murder of Bay Area journalist." ABC7NY, June 9, 2011.

"U.S. Explorer Killed in New Guinea." The Sydney Morning Herald, October 23, 1942.

https://trove.nla.gov.au/newspaper/article/17824904.

Valdemoro, Tania. "Anthrax victim's widow breaks four-year silence." Palm Beach Post, as quoted in UCLA Department of Epidemiology, School of Public Health, November 5, 2005. http://www.ph.ucla.edu/epi/bioter/fouryearsilence.html.

Vick, Karl. "The Guardians and the War on Truth." Time, 2018. https://time.com/person-of-the-year-2018-the-guardians/.

"Vietnam War Casualties by Race, Ethnicity and Natl Origin." The Names of Vietnam War Personnel, 1945 to 1970, The American War Library. https://www.americanwarlibrary.com/vietnam/vwc10.htm.

Vinograd, Cassandra. "WDBJ7 Reporter Alison Parker, Photographer Adam Ward Killed on Live TV." NBC News, August 26, 2015. https://www.nbcnews.com/storyline/virginia-tv-shooting/wdbj7-reporter-alison-parker-photographer-adam-ward-killed-live-tv-n416221.

Walsh, Lynn. "POINT OF VIEW: Journalists seek the truth," The Palm Beach Post, December 29, 2016. https://www.palmbeachpost.com/news/opinion/point-view-journalists-seek-the-truth/aRZirirGzrwvNqRglaX6YI/.

Walz, Tim. (@GovTimWalz). Twitter, April 17, 2021. https://twitter.com/GovTimWalz/status/1383539678704390149.

Warren, James. "The real problem with fake news? Citizen stupidity." Poynter, December 2, 2016. http://www.poynter.org/2016/the-real-problem-with-fake-news-citizen-stupidity/441029/.

Warrick, Pamela. "What a long, strange trip it's been." Los Angeles Times, March 20, 1997. https://www.latimes.com/archives/la-xpm-1996-03-20-ls-49715-story.html.

"Was an LA Activist Shot for His Anti-Crime Efforts?" ABC News, January 7, 2006. https://abcnews.go.com/U.S./story?id=95310&page=1#.UFJybrJlRQQ.

Welsh, John, and Gordon S. Wood. "Benjamin Franklin: American author, scientist, and statesman." Britannica. https://www.britannica.com/biography/Benjamin-Franklin.

Wendling, Mike. "The (almost) complete history of 'fake news.'" BBC, January 22, 2018. https://www.bbc.com/news/blogs-trending-42724320.

Wenzel, Korrie. "On the border: Struggles, successes in northern Minnesota come to the forefront." *Grand Forks Herald*, December 18, 2020. https://www.grand forksherald.com/opinion/columns/6806731-On-the-border-Struggles-successes-in-northern-Minnesota-come-to-the-forefront.

"Widow, U.S. Reach Settlement Deal In Florida Anthrax Death." CBS Miami/Associated Press, October 30, 2011. https://miami.cbslocal.com/2011/10/30/widow-us-reach-settlement-deal-in-florida-anthrax-death/.

"A Woman with Balls and Pearl Earrings," Charter for Compassion. https://charter forcompassion.org/dickey-chapelle-controversial-war-photojournalist/a-woman-with-balls-and-pearl-earrings.

"Workplace violence in Healthcare: Understanding the Challenge." Occupational Safety Health Administration.

"World War Correspondent Killed at New Guinea," *The Michigan Alumnus*, p. 139. https://books.google.com/books?id=u_rhAAAAMAAJ&pg=PA139&dq=Byron+Darnton+adrian+mi&hl=en&sa=X&ei=EOQMU7yNGca2yAHlyYGACw&ved=0CCsQ6AEwAA#v=onepage&q=Byron%20Darnton%20adrian%20mi&f=false.

"Writing on the Wall: An Interview with Hunter S. Thompson." *The Atlantic Monthly*, August 26, 1997. https://www.theatlantic.com/past/docs/unbound/graffiti/hunter.htm.

Young, Perry Deane. Two of the Missing: Remembering Sean Flynn and Dana Stone, Press 53, 2009.

"Your Black Muslim Bakery head guilty." UPI, June 10, 2011.

"Your Muslim Bakery Leader Guilty of Journalist Slaying." CBS SF, June 9, 2011. https://sanfrancisco.cbslocal.com/2011/06/09/your-black-muslim-bakery-leader-guilty-of-journalist-slaying/. Retrieved June 20, 2020.

Zuckerman, Neal, Alannah Sheerin and Anna Green. "For U.S. Journalism, the Future Is Brighter Than You Think." BCG, September 26, 2019. https://www.bcg.com/publications/2019/united-states-journalism-future-is-brighter-than-you-think.

Zweifel, Dave. "Journalism matters because democracy matters." *Times-Republic*, October 11, 2019. https://www.times republican.com/opinion/columnists/2019/10/journalism-matters-because-democracy-matters/.

Index

www.ingramcontent.com/pod-product-compliance
Lightning Source LLC
Chambersburg PA
CBHW031131270326
41929CB00011B/1575